Praise for *The Christ...*

"What an interesting book this is ...
gious believers joining in a frank ...
marked by a no-holds-barred disc...
cal study of sacred texts they both ...... All religious persons
will find these exchanges fascinating, even if they may not accept
their ultimate conclusions. Ultimately, Dr. Kendall comes across
as a totally committed evangelical missionary and Rabbi Rosen
as an admirable Pharisee in the best sense of the word."

—Cardinal Theodore McCarrick,
Archbishop of Washington, D.C.

"No punches are pulled, no fundamental question of faith is
avoided—but with humor, kindness, respect, and love, fundamental issues of religion are discussed and probed. A timely and
amazing book."

—from the foreword by Lord George Carey,
former Archbishop of Canterbury

"This is absolutely brilliant. It will be one of the best books ever
on Jewish-Christian relations."

—Canon Andrew White, CEO of The Foundation for
Reconciliation in the Middle East

"Judaism and Christianity have for centuries been divided by the
same holy Scriptures. Anyone seeking to understand the chasm
and how to bridge it should start by reading this erudite, civi-
lized, and charming debate. The exchange of letters not only ex-
plains the common roots of two great religions in ancient
Palestine, but also illuminates today's conflict between Israelis
and Palestinians."

—Anton La Guardia, diplomatic editor, *Daily Telegraph*,
and author of *Holy Land, Unholy War: Israelis and Palestinians*

"This is absolute gold dust. I have never read anything like it. As
a Christian leader with a Jewish family background, and a great
love for Jewish people and Jewish roots, I shall treasure and promote widely this amazing volume."

—Rev. Dr. Mark Stibbe,
vicar of St. Andrew's Church, Chorleywood

"It is not unusual to hear a Reformed rabbi and a mainline Protestant minister converse in a Jewish-Christian dialogue. But it is a rare experience to hear an Orthodox rabbi and an evangelical minister exchange views. The letters between Rabbi David Rosen and the Reverend R. T. Kendall are the intimate discussions of two brothers who share a common Father but see Him through different faiths. These two learned men honor one another with the clarity of their differences and the depth of their mutual respect."

—The Very Reverend James A. Diamond,
dean, Christ Church Cathedral, Cincinnati

"A fascinating book of dialogue between a leading preacher and one of the most famous rabbis of our time."

—from the Foreword by Chief Rabbi René-Samuel Sirat,
Former Chief Rabbi of France

"After a couple of generations of interfaith dialogue between Christians and Jews that seemed to deal mostly with surface issues, here is a dynamic volume which comes closer to the heart of the issue than any public interface before it. Kendall and Rosen, with boldness, much grace, some restraint, and a lot of brilliance, confront the various distinctives between Orthodox Judaism and evangelical Christianity. Jews will get a sense of the roots of passion that fill the hearts of Christians and Christians will come to a new appreciation of our Jewish roots from this volume. Read it and reap!"

—Dr. O. S. Hawkins, former pastor,
First Baptist Church, Dallas

"Reverend R. T. Kendall and Rabbi David Rosen have produced a remarkable book based on their remarkable dialogue concerning their respective faiths of Christianity and Judaism. Christians, Jews, and people of other faiths, as well as people of no faith, will find this compelling book to be a fascinating and informing read. I have never encountered anything quite like it."

—Dr. Richard Land, president, The Southern Baptist
Convention's Ethics & Religious Liberty Commission

# THE CHRISTIAN AND THE PHARISEE

*Two Outspoken Religious Leaders
Debate the Road to Heaven*

Dr. R. T. KENDALL

Rabbi DAVID ROSEN

NEW YORK   BOSTON   NASHVILLE

Unless otherwise noted, Scriptures are taken from the HOLY BIBLE: NEW INTERNATIONAL VERSION®. Copyright © 1973, 1978, 1984 by International Bible Society. Used by permission of Zondervan Publishing House. All rights reserved.
Scriptures noted kjv are from the King James Version of the Bible.

FaithWords
Hachette Book Group USA
1271 Avenue of the Americas
New York, NY 10017

Visit our Web site at www.faithwords.com.

Printed in the United States of America

Originally published in Great Britain by Hodder

First U.S. Edition: January 2007
10 9 8 7 6 5 4 3 2

FaithWords is a division of Hachette Book Group USA, Inc.
The FaithWords name and logo is a trademark of Hachette Book Group USA, Inc.

Library of Congress Cataloging-in-Publication Data
Kendall, R. T.
    The Christian and the Pharisee : two outspoken religious leaders debate
the road to heaven / R. T. Kendall, David Rosen.
        p. cm.  ·
    Sumary: "Letters between two prominent religious thinkers form a bridge
of understanding upon which Christians and Jews can meet and work together"
—Provided by the publisher.
    ISBN-13: 978-0-446-69734-7
    ISBN-10: 0-446-69734-6
    1. Christianity and other religions—Judaism. 2. Judaism—Relations—Christianity.
3. Bible—Criticism, interpretation, etc. 4. Kendall, R. T.—Correspondence. 5.
Church of the Nazarene—Clergy—Correspondence. 6. Rosen, David, 1951—
Correspondence. 7. Rabbis—Correspondence. I. Rosen, David, 1951– II. Title.
    BM535.K39 2007
    261.2'6—dc22                                                    2006016348

*Dedicated to all who seek*
*the peace of Jerusalem*

# Acknowledgments

We express our warm appreciation to our publisher, Rolf Zettersten, of FaithWords. We also thank the people there—Gary Terashita, Lori Quinn, Cara Highsmith—for their help, not to mention our gratitude to FaithWords for publishing our correspondence.

We particularly thank Lord George Carey for his kind foreword to our book.

R. T. would like to thank a number of friends who have read the correspondence, even if so many of their suggestions came too late. It was felt that we should publish our letters as they were originally written, even if we later saw things we might well have written differently. R. T. therefore thanks J. John, Michael McCrum, David Mitchell, Rob Parsons, Alan Bell, Lyndon Bowring, and his former secretary at Westminster Chapel, Beryl Grogan. Alan Bell and Lyndon Bowring accompanied Andrew White and R. T. on

viii · THE CHRISTIAN AND THE PHARISEE

their first trip into Ramallah—the event that actually led to an involvement with the Alexandria Peace Process. R. T. also thanks his wife, Louise, not only for her wisdom but for allowing him to be away from home and making no fewer than seven trips to Israel since their retirement.

David expresses his special appreciation to Sharon, his wife, partner, advisor, and invaluable critic and also to his administrative assistant, Avril Promislow, for her work and support as well as to Bernd Koschland for his review of the text.

# Contents

# Foreword
## by Lord George Carey

The relationship between Judaism and Christianity is arguably one of the longest in the history of interfaith and cultural associations. Sadly, it has been, on the whole, a history of bitter misunderstanding and deep conflict. From its earliest days, when Christianity, from within the bowels of Judaism, challenged the central tenets of that faith, the church has not always acted with kindness and grace towards its older sister. Whilst defenders of the church will also point out that Judaism must take its share of the blame, there can be no defense of the persecution of Jews through the medieval period up to modern times, resulting in Elie Wiesel's judgment in one of his many books: "All I know of Christianity," he writes, "was its hate for my people."

It is this background that stands for me the most extraordinary feature of this timely and amazing book. *The Christian and the Pharisee* emerges from a deep and very special friendship between an evangelical Christian and leader and a renowned Orthodox rabbi. Both of them I am delighted to call dear friends; indeed the three of us are actively engaged in resolving the deep divisions between world faiths that scar the religious landscape of our world. R. T. Kendall served with great distinction as pastor of the Westminster Chapel during my time as Archbishop of Canterbury and he graced that venerable pulpit with authoritative preaching and humility. Rabbi David Rosen is one of those remarkable rabbis whose attractive humanity, deep faith, and loving attention to people reveal the wonderful luminosity of Judaism.

So, in this book, two great men of faith meet as friends and yet on opposite sides of the divide between Christianity and Judaism. No punches are pulled in this book, no fundamental question of faith is avoided—but with humor, kindness, respect, and love, fundamental issues of religion are discussed and probed.

I have not the slightest doubt that this is a book for our times. We live in a polarized world in which people take sides too quickly and in which we are all sucked into old prejudices and rarely given a chance to think for ourselves. Here we are invited into a rich conversation that sets a model for interfaith cooperation and dialogue. This book is required reading for all believers and has the capacity to make a major contribution to healing some of the wounds of history.

*George Carey*
*Lord Carey of Clifton*
*Archbishop of Canterbury 1991–2002*

# Foreword
## by Chief Rabbi René-Samuel Sirat

*Then they who feared the Lord spoke to one another:*
*and the Lord listened and heard;*
*and a book of remembrance was written before Him*
*for those who fear the Lord and take heed of His Name.*
*And they shall be Mine, said the Lord of hosts*
*on the day when I pass Judgment*
*and I shall have compassion on them as a man has compassion*
*on his son who serves him.*

(Malachi 3:16–17)

This quotation from the prophet Malachi, last of the Hebrew biblical prophets, seems to me a fitting preliminary to this fascinating book of dialogue between a leading preacher, former minister of Westminster Chapel, and one of the most famous rabbis of our time, the former chief rabbi of Ireland and an indefatigable representative Jewish voice in interreligious dialogue.

I don't have the honor to know personally the Reverend R. T. Kendall. I hope to meet him in the near future during one of my trips or at an interreligious meeting, but the texts presented here greatly testify to his merit. I can also vouch for the excellence of the speeches, articles, books, and

debates through which Chief Rabbi Rosen reflects his remarkable intelligence and deep knowledge of as well as total
devotion to Judaism.

Since the Seelisberg Conference that took place in 1947
at which the foundations of the Jewish-Christian friendship
and cooperation were formulated; and especially since the
proclamation *Nostra Aetate* of the Second Vatican Council,
the interreligious dialogue has advanced considerably,
thanks to highly talented people like the two coauthors of
this book of such an extremely interesting exchange of
letters.

However, we must firstly realize that a fundamental
asymmetry exists here. Christianity sees its main task to
spread everywhere and at all times the idea that Christ
brought redemption to humanity. Its calling is therefore essentially to proselytize, whereas Pharisaic Judaism—
although it doesn't reject those who seek to convert to Judaism having fallen in love with the God of Israel—and why
should it reject them?—still refuses to engage in any kind of
proselytism whatsoever. When one approaches the Jewish-
Christian dialogue, one should be aware of this main difference between the two religions.

It is necessary to explain the reasons for this as formulated by the rabbis. Every man and woman has been created
in the divine image, and God in His supreme wisdom made
His creatures part of a particular people, church, or congregation, from birth. In order to obtain eternal salvation, he or
she who is not born within the Jewish people must observe
the laws that (Jewish tradition teaches) were communicated
to our common ancestor, Noah the patriarch. There are
seven such laws and commandments: 1) not to worship

idols, 2) not to blaspheme, 3) not to kill, 4) not to steal, 5) not to commit incest or adultery, 6) to submit to the jurisdiction of courts of law (otherwise, life in society would resemble a jungle), and 7) not to eat the flesh of a living animal (which is understood to mean not to cause suffering to animals).

Any non-Jew who observes those commandments—rather like the unconscious expression of Mr. Jourdain, in Molière's *Bourgeois Gentilhomme*—merits "the world to come." On the other hand, the salvation of a non-Jew who converts to Judaism is actually jeopardized if he or she continues to observe the seven Noahide laws but fails to keep the laws pertaining to the Sabbath, marital relations, the dietary laws, or the more detailed rules of Jewish ethics. What right would a rabbinic court have to encourage a conversion, unless it was absolutely convinced in all good conscience that the candidate was genuinely willing to become a fully observant Jew?

The greatest scholar of Jewish studies of the last generation—I refer to the famous Rabbi J. B. Soloveitchik, who resided in Boston—was in favor of interreligious cooperation, but at the same time he forbade his followers from taking part in any theological debate between Jews and Christians. This was at the very dawning of interreligious dialogue and he had good reason to be concerned about all possible mishaps. However, the situation is not the same today. The friendship between Jews and Christians has known a greater flourishing in the last fifty years than during the previous millennia.

This year we commemorated throughout the whole world and particularly at Troyes in France, his birthplace, the nine-hundredth anniversary of the death of Rashi (Rashi is the acronym of Rabbi Shlomo Yitzhaki: 1040–1105). I wish to conclude with the words of this brilliant commentator on the Bible and the Talmud, by quoting his exposition of the verse in Zephaniah (3:9) that appears in his commentary on the Babylonian Talmud treatise Avodah Zarah (24a).

The verse from Zephaniah reads: "For then I shall transform the speech of the nations into a purer speech, that they may all call on the name of the Lord to serve Him with one accord (literally: shoulder to shoulder)."

Rashi comments: "That means there will be no more differences between those who serve the Lord. The worship of Israel and the worship of the other nations will be identical and embrace all of God's commandments."

The dialogue, as represented in this book, brings us closer to this blessed time for which the authors deserve our great and warm thanks accordingly.

*Chief Rabbi René-Samuel Sirat*
*Former Chief Rabbi of France and*
*President of the Conference of European Rabbis*

# Preface

## *by R. T. Kendall and David Rosen*

*Pray for the peace of Jerusalem: "May those who love you be
secure. May there be peace within your walls and security
within your citadels."*

(Psalm 122:6–7)

This book is made up of letters we sent to each other during 2005. We first met because we were involved in the
Alexandria Peace Process, led by the former Archbishop of
Canterbury Lord George Carey and Canon Andrew White,
his envoy to the Middle East. This correspondence was
borne at a Shabbat dinner in Jerusalem. A friendly controversy emerged over a popular caricature of a Pharisee. The
Pharisee has not been very appreciated, especially by Christians. It may surprise some that Pharisees were not merely a
group that existed two thousand years ago but are alive and
well today. Part of the reason for our correspondence was to
state facts that are not entirely dependant on the way Pharisees are depicted in the New Testament.

But the correspondence became more than that. The
issue of salvation surfaced and the interchange focused
largely not on the road map to peace in the Holy Land but

the way to heaven. The debate inevitably touched on the issue of Messiah. One of us wasted no time in trying to convince the other why a Jew should acknowledge that Jesus of Nazareth was Israel's promised Messiah. The reply was firm, categorical, and consistent—and the reasons for this are clear: the letters speak for themselves.

Some of those who have read our letters have asked, "Are you still friends?" We can answer: Absolutely. More than ever. We hope that this dialogue will serve not only to enlighten the reader about our respective beliefs but will also promote a better understanding between Christians and Jews. There are many terms and names used in our correspondence which might be unfamiliar or confusing; therefore, we have included a glossary to assist readers in fully comprehending our message and intent.

We have in common a love for the Hebrew Bible, a conviction that what the Scriptures teach about Israel is true and relevant, and we maintain a strong desire to make peace in the Holy Land. We also have a deep love for Jerusalem. We not only lament the anti-Semitism that is rife in the world but especially condemn it when it has come from those who call themselves Christians.

We sincerely pray that our book will encourage and stimulate you. We dedicate it to all who seek for the peace of Jerusalem. "May the Lord bless you and protect you . . . and bestow upon you shalom" (Numbers 6:24, 26).

*David Rosen*                                    *R. T. Kendall*
www.rabbidavidrosen.net          www.rtkendallministries.com
*Jerusalem*                                  *Key Largo, Florida*
*September 2005*                            *September 2005*

# Introduction

## by R. T. Kendall

During my twenty-five years as the minister of Westminster Chapel, I prayed publicly every week for peace in the Middle East "and for the peace of Jerusalem." If ever there was a prayer one could be sure was absolutely right, this was surely it. Who would have thought that when King David urged people to "pray for the peace of Jerusalem" (Ps. 122:6) three thousand years ago that such a prayer would possibly be even more relevant today than it was then?

And yet I never dreamed that I myself would be the slightest bit involved in the peace process in the Middle East. But shortly after I retired and moved to America, and as a result of being a part of a tour of British Christians to the Holy Land in the summer of 2002, I was privileged to meet Canon Andrew White. For years he has been the Archbishop of Canterbury's envoy to the Middle East. In July 2002 Andrew took me into Ramallah to meet the late

Yasser Arafat. When Lord George Carey was Archbishop of Canterbury he also became the architect of the Alexandria Peace Process, a plan that was designed to bring the religious dimension into the efforts to make peace. Canon White thought that my being an American evangelical was relevant and hoped I might get on with the Palestinian leader. What would normally be a twenty-minute visit extended to an hour and forty-five minutes. A surprising friendship—entirely theological and spiritual, not political—developed between Yasser Arafat and me. I ended up visiting him five times and was with him only a month before he died in the autumn of 2004.

On the day I met with Arafat for the last time, I had breakfast at the Mount Zion Hotel in Jerusalem with Rabbi David Rosen, one of the original signers of the Alexandria Peace Process. At that breakfast David and I decided we should publish a book together, made up of our letters to each other. This book actually has its origin in an experience we had in Jerusalem in March 2004, and one for which I was not prepared. Rabbi and Mrs. Rosen hosted a Shabbat meal on a Friday evening for those of us who had flown to Israel in support of the Alexandria Peace Process, including Lord and Lady Carey, Canon Andrew White, Alan Bell, Dr. Richard Land, the Very Reverend James Diamond, Dr. Ravi Zacharias, and Christopher Long. It was a wonderful evening. That was the first time I met David. He is the Jerusalem-based international director of Interreligious Affairs of the American Jewish Committee. He was formerly the chief rabbi of Ireland and had been the rabbi of the largest Jewish congregation in South Africa. He endeared himself to all of us as he demonstrated with his wife and two children what their Sabbath evenings are like. It even brought us to tears. It was the high-water mark of a memorable week that was filled with meeting with various Jewish, Christian, and Islamic religious leaders of that part of the world.

But what startled me prior to my getting to know David was the complimentary way he referred to a Pharisee as he explained the meaning of the Shabbat meal. I was stunned at first because nearly all I have known about a Pharisee is not good, and calling one a Pharisee in the Christian community is no compliment. But Rabbi Rosen regards himself as a Pharisee in our day and wears the label as a badge of honor. If most Christians think that Pharisees are cold, I have to tell you that this man, who is truly a modern Pharisee, is very warm. To make sure I wasn't misunderstanding him, I asked him if indeed I rightly discerned that he regards himself as a Pharisee. Absolutely, he replied. Soon afterward he sent an informative e-mail on the matter. This was the beginning of our correspondence with each other. I had no idea that it would lead to this book.

But it was partly because I was in the process of finishing my book *Out of Your Comfort Zone: Is Your God Too Nice?* that a correspondence with Rabbi Rosen was so relevant. Readers of that book may recall that the final two chapters are about Pharisees—and they are not viewed in a very flattering way. I asked David if he would kindly read them, which he graciously did. His reaction and comments became the basis for the present book.

If you have not read *Out of Your Comfort Zone: Is Your God Too Nice?* you may wish to turn to the appendix at the end of this book and read "The Sin Jesus Hated Most," which is

xxii · THE CHRISTIAN AND THE PHARISEE

one of the two chapters David read. It refers to the self-righteousness exhibited by the Pharisees as depicted in the New Testament. Keep in mind that David also read the chapter called "Twenty-Six Reasons You Might Be a Pharisee," which is not included in the appendix. You need to know that Rabbi Rosen sees a very important distinction between those Pharisees Jesus is recorded as addressing and Pharisees as they are truly to be understood. He also believes that today's Pharisees' successors in Israel, of which he is one, bear no resemblance to those described in the New Testament. Not only that—he told me that he would feel much the same as I do toward those Pharisees Jesus is recorded as addressing. This is what precipitated the present book. A lively correspondence followed our initial interchange and what you now hold in your hands are those letters we have written to each other.

*Dr. R. T. Kendall*

*The Christian and the Pharisee*

# Letter 1

*Dear R. T.,*

I welcome the opportunity to respond to your writings for a number of reasons. Firstly, friendship requires that we speak our minds sincerely to one another and I know that we can do that in a manner that is sensitive and respectful to each other and our respective faiths. Secondly, as people of faith, we are seekers of truth and thus where we believe that the truth may be tarnished or misconstrued we have an obligation to say so.

However, I believe the most important reason for developing this dialogue is our very relationship. I don't mean just you and me, but that the relationship between Jews and Christians is something special—or at least should be. As the Jewish theologian Martin Buber put it, "We share a book and that's no small thing." I would even go so far as to say that there is a divine plan and purpose in our very differences, but perhaps it's too early for us to be talking about that. For starters, it is surely enough for us to acknowledge that we both see the Hebrew Bible—that you call the Old Testament—as the revealed Word of God. The very fact that we share such a bond with this text of divine revelation places us in a special relationship with one another and requires not only a level of communication, honesty, and love that tragically has been so lacking down the course of history but surely behooves us to work together for the values we share.

At the heart of these values are of course the Ten Commandments, one of which is the prohibition against bearing false testimony. Almost two thousand years of separation between Christians and Jews has tragically led to much pain and suffering. Thank God, most of this is behind us. Nevertheless some of the effects of the past still remain with us and even continue to lead people to unwittingly bear false witness against others. There is, of course, not just one culprit in this sin, but I greatly welcome the opportunity to tell you, your followers and readers, of how I see continued false testimony against my faith and people being maintained among many good Christians today. Let me reiterate that I do not suspect that this is generally intentional (otherwise I wouldn't call them *good* Christians)—and certainly not in your case, as I know your love for the Jewish people is sincere. The source of this false witness lies precisely in the historic break between the early Christians and the Jewish community from which they came and has been compounded in the course of time. The result is that not only do we know far too little about one another, we often have no idea how each one sees him- or herself even in contemporary terms, let alone historical ones.

So the first thing that I think I need to do is to tell you how I see myself and where I come from.

I see myself as part of the people descended from Abraham, Isaac, and Jacob (also known as Israel), with whom God made a covenant that was ratified at Mount Sinai with their descendants, the children of Israel. This covenant is an expression of God's everlasting commitment to the children of Israel to be an instrument of His purpose, testifying to His presence in the life and history of humanity. This testimony may take different forms, but ideally it should be through living a way of life as "a kingdom of priests and a holy nation" (Exod. 19:6). To this end the children of Israel were given a "road map" at Mount Sinai that we call the Torah. Indeed, as important as it was to find their way to the promised land, it was far more important to follow the course of religioethical living that was revealed to them at Mount Sinai. Ideally they would live this way of life in the promised land. In fact they were told at Sinai that their ability to live securely in the land was precisely contingent upon following this "road map" of life and that if we failed we would be exiled from it. Nevertheless we were reassured that God would always bring us back again (Lev. 26:44-45).

Jewish tradition maintains that all the teachings in the Torah—that is, the five books of Moses also known as the Pentateuch—were revealed at Mount Sinai, not just the Ten Commandments. Most Orthodox Jews like me accept this tradition. Others see the Sinai revelation as having contained an essence from which the other precepts flowed.

However, as anyone who is familiar with the Pentateuch

knows, it contains hundreds of commandments. According to Jewish tradition, 613 to be precise. Of course a large proportion of these relate to the temple: its construction, the offerings that took place within it, its maintenance, and matters of ritual purity connected with its function. In addition many of the commandments are conditional—even being dependent upon failure to fulfill others. For example the commandment allowing divorce (Deut. 24:1) is of course conditional on the failure of a marriage. Or more dramatically, the commandment to lighten the load of your enemy's donkey (Exod. 23:5) implies that one has already desecrated another commandment, for if one loved one's neighbor as oneself (Lev. 19:18), one wouldn't have an enemy in the first place—and one could go on and on. In other words, a far smaller number of commandments are practically relevant to the average person's daily life.

Nevertheless for the believing Jew, following these divine directions means living according to God's will and way. These precepts were revealed to us not only for our good, for our life (Deut. 30:15–16), but through following them we come close to God, to know and love Him (Deut. 6:5–6, 10:12–13, 11:22).

However many of them are communicated in shorthand. For example, we are told to "remember the Sabbath day to keep it holy" (Exod. 20:8). What does "holy" actually mean? How do we go about achieving that goal? According to Jewish tradition, when the Almighty revealed His written Word to Moses for the children of Israel, the meaning was explained. The explanations and clarifications of the Written Torah are known in Jewish tradition as the Oral Torah. And indeed the ongoing process of clarifying their application in changing times and conditions is part of its eternal vitality. Religious Jews have traditionally understood that the practice and study of the Written and Oral Torah are the way of life that God requires of them; that this is the source of the joy and beauty in their lives and is the secret of their survival.

Now, R. T., I am about to enter the historic context that is the focus of your faith: the Second Temple period two thousand years ago in the land of Abraham, Isaac, and Jacob.

Already by then much had happened to the children of Israel. The ten tribes of Israel in the northern part of the land had been conquered by the Assyrians and were lost to the southern tribes who were known by the name of the dominant tribe Judah (from which of course come the names *Judea* and *Jew*). Then Judea was conquered by the Babylonians, Solomon's temple was destroyed, but the Jews survived the cataclysm. The Persians let us return, the temple was rebuilt, but then we were subsequently subjugated by the Greeks and then the Romans. The result of all these comings and goings and various cultural influences was that by the time Rome ruled in the Middle East, the Jewish people was more diverse than ever.

Our main historic source for that period of time is Josephus, who describes four primary groups of Jews who were active at the time: Sadducees, Pharisees, Essenes, and Zealots.

The Essenes and the Zealots represented different reactions to the effects of oppressive Roman rule. The first of these chose to withdraw from general society, which was seen as corrupt and degenerate, and to prepare themselves for the end of the society that God would destroy and replace with one in their image. The Zealots believed that what God wanted was for them to take up arms to defeat the pagan Romans notwithstanding the latter's physical might.

However, the two mainstream groups among the Jewish people were the Sadducees and the Pharisees.

The purpose of all the historical retrospective that I have given is to explain to you now how generations of Jews over almost two millennia have viewed these two groups.

As Josephus records, the politically dominant group that was the usual address for the Roman authorities and often served as their surrogate was the Sadducees. They were made up of dominant priestly families who controlled the temple and wealthy segments of society, who felt themselves to be part and parcel of Roman culture as well.

Now there are scholars who view the Pharisees as having been a separatist group, but our traditional view has been that these were the teachers of Jewish tradition, our rabbis and their followers. We have seen them as the heirs of the prophets of Israel and as those who maintained the devotion not only to the Written but also to the Oral Torah. Indeed the historic evidence makes it clear that one of the main distinctions between the Pharisees and Sadducees was the attitude toward the Oral Tradition. The Sadducees saw this as unnecessary expansion of the Written Torah, which they took much more literally.

But there were many other distinctions, not least of all the overwhelming focus of the Sadducees on the temple service as the key to God's favor. While the temple was of course an important institution for the Pharisees, they taught—in keeping with the prophets of Israel—that what is most important is one's personal relationship with God and one's relationship with one's neighbor, wherever one may be. As a result, after the rebellion against Rome by the Zealots, the Roman destruction of the temple and Jerusalem, and the Roman exile of large segments of the Jewish population, the Sadducees, just as the Essenes and the Zealots, all disappeared. The only group amongst those to which Josephus refers that could survive political failure, the destruction of the temple, and exile was the group that nurtured the knowledge and practice of the Written and Oral Tradition as the divine purpose of Jewish existence wherever we lived.

The bottom line is that Jewish tradition for most of the last two thousand years viewed the Pharisees as the rabbis of our heritage, heirs of the prophets and biblical tradition, the teachers of authentic Judaism as enshrined in the Talmud— the religion of the Jews as it has been practiced and known until modern times.

Therefore, in the perception of most religious Jews today, to denigrate the Pharisees is in fact to denigrate Judaism.

We now approach the big question regarding Jesus' recorded comments regarding the Pharisees.

The question is even larger because of the overwhelming parallels between Jesus' teaching and that of the Pharisees— the rabbis of the Mishnaic period (the Mishnah is the first written version of the Oral Tradition) contemporaneous with Jesus. They emphasized the paramount principles of love of God and neighbor; the importance of the individual's personal relationship with God; the values of modesty, charity, and repentance; the significance of the afterlife; that as holy as the Sabbath is, when it comes to the preservation of human life it must be transgressed. One could go on and on drawing the parallels between the teachings of the Pharisees and Jesus.

In fact, I recall that the German scholars Strack and Billerbeck documented hundreds of parallels in the Mishnah and Talmud to the sayings of Jesus in the book of Matthew alone! Virtually all the sins Jesus is recorded as having chastised the Pharisees for are condemned by the rabbis (whom we see as the Pharisees) themselves. In fact, the similarities are so great that I find it compelling to believe that Jesus himself was part and parcel of that community.

Some scholars would say that the term *Pharisee* was used in different ways at different times and that at Jesus' time it did apply only to a limited particularist group that later became popular and widespread.

Another interpretation raises the question as to why the Sadducees are hardly referred to in the Gospels, especially as they would have been far more likely to have been the object of Jesus' criticism—controlling the temple, power, access, and resources to the degree they did. The answer, they suggest, lies in the fact that the Gospels were written well after the Sadducees as an identifiable group ceased to function. The very survival of the Pharisees in the form of Rabbinic Judaism led to the use of their name to describe those whom Jesus was criticizing, when in fact he was berating other groups that were no longer around or no longer relevant to the religious social reality when the Gospels were written.

However, I would point out something else which appears to me to be more important in resolving this riddle.

When the prophets of Israel chastise the people and say things like "O Israel, why have you forsaken God?" or "O

Judah, how long will you continue to sin?" they were not for one minute suggesting that they, the prophets, were not part of Israel or Judah.

Because Christianity—especially after the conversion of Constantine—tragically, increasingly detached itself from its Jewish roots, Christians forgot that Jesus was a Jew talking overwhelmingly to Jews—good Jews and bad Jews (and most of them probably in between, like most of us!).

When Jesus criticized Pharisees, he was doing so as a rabbi addressing other rabbis, saying, "You rabbis are letting the side down! Precisely because you *are* rabbis, you should know better and your sin is worse."

From my traditional Jewish perspective that views the Pharisees as the teachers of Rabbinic Judaism, Jesus *could not* be criticizing *all* Pharisees—especially if he was, as I believe, part of that community. Indeed to claim that he was addressing *all* Pharisees would not only be incorrect in my opinion, it would also imply that Jesus was judging and stigmatizing a whole community, which would surely be in complete contradiction with the most sublime religious moral values that he preached. So I am convinced that Jesus was criticizing *some* Pharisees—not *all* Pharisees.

I consider it important for Christians to recognize this, not only because I believe that it cannot be true that Jesus stigmatized a whole community for the sins of some of them, but also because I want Christians to be aware of how we Jews today see ourselves as the continuation of the Pharisaic tradition, of normative Judaism. That is why I am offended by the pejorative use of the word *Pharisee*, as I would be if someone used the phrase "to Jew somebody" to mean to swindle someone.

As I have said, the sins and hypocrisy that Jesus exposes in *those* Pharisees are precisely exposed by other Pharisees in our rabbinic literature. One of the criticisms is of a dry legalism that is divorced from the spirit of God's commandments. That, however, does not mean we think that we can disregard them or even treat them lightly. On the contrary, we believe that our fulfillment of these observances and their study is precisely the way of life God wants us to pursue: the way of life that gives us joy, beauty, and meaning to our existence. But obviously we have to be in consonance with their spiritual goal and purpose of making us holy.

Leviticus 19 opens with the commandment, "You shall be holy because I the Lord am Holy," and this chapter makes it clear that holiness is not only the discipline that makes us conscious of God's presence but above all is expressed in the love of God and neighbor that leads us to live with care and compassion for our fellow human beings—all created in the image of God. Thus arrogance, self-righteousness, and disdain for others; jealousy, greed, or speaking ill of others, etc., are all considered sinful ways to behave—in fact considered most un-Pharisaic ways to behave.

So all I ask, R. T., is that you might consider referring in your writings and sermons to *those* Pharisees or *some* Pharisees whom Jesus criticized and not to tar us all with the brush of individual sinners by association. Because when all Pharisees are presented as sinners, you bear false witness against me.

*Yours,*
*David*

# Letter 2

*Dear David,*

Thank you for the way in which you opened the first chapter. Your kindness, graciousness, and wisdom are like the fruit of the Holy Spirit—the very Spirit Jesus implied was absent in those Pharisees he addressed in the Sermon on the Mount (Matt. 5–7). You have set a very high standard—in courage, content, and clarity—in what you have written to me. Your own example, moreover, is the best vindication of your claim that those Pharisees Jesus addressed were not what Pharisees are supposed to be like, then and now. In one sense you have already convinced me! Indeed, I can even envisage some readers thinking as they read the previous chapter, *He sounds like a Spirit-filled Christian*. I would have to add that, in the time I have gotten to know you, you certainly do not seem to me to mirror the kind of person that I have always thought a Pharisee was like. It was probably that factor alone that has brought us together to produce this book.

I fear that there are Christians who, when entering into dialogue with those they do not always see eye to eye with, do not show the loving spirit I sense in you. Let it be said that many Christians can learn from at least one Pharisee that I know!

As you early on shared how you see yourself and where you are coming from, it seemed appropriate that I do this as well.

I am a Gentile Christian of the reformed wing of the Protestant faith. As you helpfully gave a brief history of the various movements in ancient Judaism—Zealots, Essenes, Sadducees, and Pharisees—I thought I would do the same to let you know how I fit into our various streams. You will know that Martin Luther (1483–1546) caused a big upheaval in the Roman Catholic Church in the sixteenth century when his rediscovery of justification by faith alone led him to break with Rome. I am a great fan of Martin Luther, but perhaps more so of John Calvin (1509–1564), who came a generation later. Calvin, stressing the inner testimony of the Holy Spirit in the context of the sovereignty of God, made Luther's teaching even clearer. Those who generally follow Calvin would be regarded as Reformed, or evangelical (although some who are evangelical may not be happy with all the points of Reformed Theology).

Your explanation of the differences between Pharisees and Sadducees pretty much rules out the comparison that is sometimes made—that evangelicals are more like the ancient Pharisees and nonevangelicals (liberals) are like the Sadducees. Since I myself would want to be governed entirely by Scripture and not tradition, perhaps I am more of a Sadducee than I thought! But it is my understanding that Sadducees denied much of what is supernatural (e.g., angels, resurrection) which Pharisees affirmed; so in that sense I guess I am more akin to Pharisees.

It seems suitable in any case that you and I, given our backgrounds and views, engage in this correspondence. You probably already know that the term *evangelical* is often used generally to describe a conservative theological position, e.g., the infallibility of Scripture, the full deity and humanity of the person of Jesus Christ, the need for all to be saved by trusting only Jesus' death and resurrection, Jesus' second coming, and the final judgment of all people.

But evangelical theologians are divided on the issue of Israel. Some say that the church replaced Israel altogether and that God has no further plans for His ancient people—or the land. I do not agree with this position, usually called Replacement Theology. But some go to the other extreme and claim that Jews don't even need to be converted—that God will give them a second chance when Jesus comes—I do not agree with this position either.

I regard myself as an evangelical but also one who has experienced the immediate and direct witness of the Holy Spirit. I trusted Jesus as my Savior on an Easter Sunday morning—April 5, 1942—when I was six years old. I entered the preaching and pastoral ministry as a member of the Church of the Nazarene (a denomination that stresses holiness). On October 31, 1955, I experienced what I would call the *baptism of the Holy Spirit*. On that occasion the person of Jesus became very real to me, a full assurance of my salvation was put in my heart, and the knowledge of the

Holy Scriptures became paramount. My theology changed considerably. From that day on I sought to be theologically sound, along with keeping a warm heart.

I loved what you said about the Book we have in common. I agree with you that the Old Testament is the revealed Word of God. On this we will have no difference of opinion. Sadly there are scholars in the Christian church who question the infallibility of Scripture and particularly denigrate the Old Testament—or perhaps I should say, the God of the Old Testament. We even have those who say, "I can accept the God of the New Testament but not the God of the Old Testament." I disagree. I accept the God of the Old Testament as well as the God of the New Testament as being the same God. I take the view that the Old Testament is "God-breathed" (2 Tim. 3:16) and that those who wrote it "spoke from God as they were carried along by the Holy Spirit" (2 Pet. 1:21). I regard the New Testament as equally inspired.

By the way, is it appropriate if I refer to God in print as *Yahweh*? I say that because I know you, as an Orthodox rabbi, do not pronounce His name but use *Adonai* instead. I want to respect your wishes regarding this; please forgive me if I have erred already.

I was even more pleased that you brought up the Ten Commandments. It is only a matter of time before you and I will focus on them and the way Jesus interpreted them to those men He called Pharisees. I was glad you put your finger on the ninth commandment—about false testimony. This I see as a reminder that I must be utterly, totally, and transparently honest in the way I quote you, answer you, and the way I quote from the Bible.

I expect to learn a lot from you. You have taught me already. If our readers learn from our dialogue, this will be good, of course; but I myself am eager to learn from you and I will ask you not to let me sweep anything under the carpet when I fail to address an issue you raise. This does not mean, of course, that we are going to agree with each other, but I hope we will be open and frank and not let the other off the hook when it comes to points either of us regards as important.

I would like to comment on your statement "I know that your love for the Jewish people is sincere." I don't know what I may have said that led you to believe this, but you are exactly right. I had a head start in thinking along this line. My parents were strong Christians. My pastor in Ashland, Kentucky, where I was brought up, always maintained a holy reverence for Jews and for Israel. We were taught unequivocally that the land of Israel was sacred, that Jews were special, for they were God's chosen people. This way of thinking began flowing through my veins at a very early age. I walked to school every day with a girl whose name was Connie Goldberg. At times I envied her because she was Jewish and I wasn't. I never dreamed I would one day be part of a book coauthored by an esteemed Orthodox Jewish rabbi. I feel so honored, David. You may call this over-the-top, but it is almost as if I am on holy ground.

When I was working on my first degree at Trevecca Nazarene University in Nashville, Tennessee, I spent summers working in Washington, D.C. I became fairly well acquainted with Rabbi Abraham Kellner, a well-known Orthodox rabbi in that area. He gave me some of his books. I always wondered why he referred to God as G-d. He and his wife invited me into their home for a meal. I remember one thing they served: a ground-beef patty (I think it was that). It was my first kosher meal and I can't say I enjoyed it. Sensing this, Rabbi Kellner brought some ketchup, which I doused on my meat!

In the course of the evening, discussing Isaiah 53, he lovingly chided me, "You would like to convert me, wouldn't you?" I blushed and admitted to my wish. He was very good about it and we kept in touch. He wrote me a most kind letter that closed with words I can never forget: "May you ever ascend to the Mount of the Lord—to which you raise your eyes."

If you are right, and I suspect you are, that we know far too little about one another, I pray this book will help remedy that. It is my urgent prayer that this book will be read equally by both Christians and Jews and that it will be impossible to tell who derives the greater benefit!

It intrigued me that you referred to the Torah as a "road map." President George W. Bush has popularized this phrase as he hoped to bring peace to the Middle East with his own plan. As I write these lines, President Bush's plan has not worked. And I think I know why. For the land to which all this pertains is no ordinary land. It goes back to God's ancient covenant with Abraham. It is special and God still has a soft spot for it. To achieve peace in such a part of the world requires that one bring God into the picture—something I fear has not been done. For God has given his own Road Map for peace in the land of Israel.

You mention Leviticus 26:44–45, that God would "always" bring the people of Israel back again to their land. It is not clear to me whether you think there was a necessary condition implied. So let me ask what seems to me to be a most important question in our dialogue. David, is the promise God gave His ancient people regarding possession of the land unconditional or conditional? If it is unconditional, then the people of Israel will inevitably be brought back to their land regardless of their keeping the ancient covenant God made with them. If it is conditional, then His covenant people must keep their promise to obey the Torah before they can *expect* to be brought back. Please tell me if it is fair and appropriate to raise this.

Let me return to the issue of the Pharisees. You refer to the matter of divorce. You will know that it is recorded that some Pharisees asked Jesus, "Is it lawful for a man to divorce his wife for any and every reason?" (Matt. 19:3). I was taught in seminary that there were two schools of thought on this in the ancient rabbinic community: 1) the Hillel school position, that you could divorce your wife even if you didn't like the way she cooked your supper, the other being 2) the Shammai school, which held that divorce was granted only in the case of adultery. You said divorce was granted on the basis of "failure of a marriage." Does this put you somewhere between the two schools? Who or what determines if a marriage has failed? Jesus made it clear in any case that He was unhappy with divorce, that Moses granted it because of their hearts being "hard" (v. 8). Would you agree with Jesus on this?

I note your phrase "the believing Jew." I am interested as to what you mean by that. In what does belief consist? What if a Jew does not believe? How serious is it?

Could I also ask you to say more about the Written Torah vis à vis the Oral Torah? Are you absolutely sure that they do not contradict each other? You probably know that a watershed in church history was the Council of Trent (1545) when the Roman Catholic Church decided that tradition was equal with Scripture. This gave a lot of stuff canonical reliability—like the Virgin Mary ascending to heaven, the Eucharist becoming literally the body of Jesus and the blood of Jesus, or the popes having infallibility when they speak "ex cathedra." I therefore know for sure that tradition in church history often goes against Scripture.

I am wondering whether you have the same problem in your ancient history. I ask this because Jesus, when addressing a group of Pharisees, is recorded as saying they nullified the Word of God for the sake of their tradition (Matt. 15:6). He also would introduce a thought with the words, "You have heard that it was said" (Matt. 5:21, 27, 33, 38, 43), when in fact He sometimes refers to the Written Torah and sometimes to tradition. In these references He is recorded as addressing Pharisees—at least some of them.

I have no doubt that there were good and genuine Pharisees—unlike those Jesus is recorded as addressing. And some of them—of which sort I have no idea—eventually became believers in Jesus. So I agree with you that we Christians, certainly many of us including me, have erred, even stigmatizing you, by painting all of you with a brush that does not allow for a valid distinction among you. So I apologize. I am learning from you. So I take your point: there were those Pharisees Jesus is recorded as having criticized but not all of them were like the ones He spoke against.

But you have opened another subject: what is a sinner? Because you imply that Pharisees are not sinners. Really? David, I myself am a sinner. It does not necessarily mean that I have broken any of the first nine of the Ten Commandments. I don't think it is all that hard to keep the letter of the first nine commandments. But what about the Tenth Commandment: "You shall not covet"? That one convicts me! And it is my understanding of Jesus' teaching in the Sermon on the Mount, when He addressed certain Pharisees, that He always had the tenth commandment in mind, even when He quoted any of the other nine. That is why He interpreted the Law and unveiled sin as He did.

I would have little trouble believing the idea you put forward that Jesus Himself may have been a part—to say part and parcel calls for too much speculation—of the Pharisaical community in His day. If so, He obviously knew it backwards and forwards. But this may also have given Him a greater authority to speak as He did, as you indicated, when you referred to the prophets who criticized their own nation. Jesus certainly could have been doing this, especially if His association with them was well known by them and also His hearers. We all get away with criticizing far easier when we criticize ourselves as opposed to criticizing another community.

By the way, you said that Sadducees are hardly mentioned in the New Testament. That is not quite accurate. And it is speculative to imply a late date on that basis for the writing of the Gospels. Pharisees are mentioned one hundred times, Sadducees fourteen times. Sometimes, however, Jesus lumped them together (Matt. 16:6, 11).

I note your comment that if one loved one's neighbor as oneself, one wouldn't have an enemy in the first place. I know what you mean by that. I would only point out that Israel has more enemies than anybody—and has done nothing to cause it. People hate Israel and Jews not because of anything they have done, even if an anti-Semitic person brings up his or her rejection of Jesus as Messiah. The world hates Israel, in my opinion, because Jews are God's ancient chosen covenant people. Christians therefore should be at the head of the queue in esteeming Jews.

I would bring this part of my response to a conclusion by saying the issue at the end of the day is: what is sin? This is what Jesus was after. He interpreted the Law in a manner that made all of us see we have not kept the Law but are, indeed, sinners. Those Pharisees He is recorded as addressing apparently had no concept of inward sin but only of what is outward: murdering, committing adultery, or giving false testimony. If, however, you tell me that you have a conviction of sin as being inward—as your letter to me allowed for (you mention jealousy and greed)—then I am compelled to say you are not like the Pharisees Jesus addressed.

*Your true friend,*
*R. T.*

# Letter 3

Dear R. T.,

I am already enjoying our correspondence to the degree that I am setting aside other things I should be doing in order to respond as soon as possible.

Before addressing your more substantive points, let me respond to your more "technical" questions.

Judaism does indeed teach us to revere God's name (in keeping with the prohibition not to take it in vain, Exod. 20:7) and as a result, observant Jews do not articulate the Tetragrammaton—the name made up of the four Hebrew letters YHWH—even in the liturgical reading from the Torah (which takes place every Sabbath morning in an annual cycle. The first part of the forthcoming weekly Torah portion is also read at weekday morning prayers on Mondays and Thursdays and at Saturday afternoon services). In its place, as you correctly mentioned, we use the Hebrew word *Adonai*, which means "my Lord." Yet as this word itself has acquired a kind of sanctity, observant Jews do not use it in conversation and tend to use other designations, such as *HaShem* ("the Name"), *Hakadosh Baruch Hu* ("The Holy One Blessed Be He"), *Ribono shel Olam* ("Master of the Universe"), *Avinu Shebashamayim* ("Our Father in Heaven"), and many other terms.

In fact there are other names of God whose common use is frowned upon and which are specified in Maimonides' Code of Jewish Law (based on the Talmud, the compendium of the Oral Tradition based on the Written Tradition). But all of this applies to these names in Hebrew! The practice of writing G-d instead of God has become very commonplace among religious Jews, but it is in fact quite unnecessary and even a little ridiculous because where will it end? Alm-ghty instead of Almighty? F-ther instead of Father? Sav-r of the Un-vrs? Taking an important principle (of respect for God's name) to such unnecessary minutiae might have been precisely the sort of thing that Jesus disliked in those Pharisees he criticized. But as you see, I, who view myself an heir of the Pharisaic tradition, am myself dismissive of such a practice that takes an important principle to unnecessary extremes.

At any rate, R. T., you may refer to God as you please and I will not be offended, for I know that however you are referring to Him, your intention is to do so respectfully—and that is the essential thing!

I find it difficult to understand Christians (to whom you refer) who distinguish between "the God of the Old Testament" and "the God of the New Testament." It puzzles me first of all because there is surely only one God! If they were to say, "The way God is portrayed in the Old Testament" at least I could understand it, even if I would disagree with it. God is portrayed in many different ways in the Bible and all of them must be anthropomorphisms, as we mortals can never understand God's essence (that's how Maimonides understands the meaning of Exodus 33:20). As the sages of the Talmud declare, "The Torah uses language that ordinary human beings can understand."

However, it seems to me that those Christians who make the above-mentioned distinction are guilty in Christian terms of the heresy of Marcion (of the second century CE) of trying to separate the Hebrew Bible from the New Testament. It would appear that even though this approach was condemned by the church as a heresy, it is still alive, strong, and kicking.

Parallel to this, I am of course aware of the supercessionist teaching that the church had replaced the Jewish people in God's design (an idea that the Catholic Church formally rejected in 1965 with the promulgation of the document *Nostra Aetate*, which came out of the Second Vatican Ecumenical Council). I am surprised, however, to hear from you that there are evangelical Christians—whom I assume are well versed in Scripture—who would hold to such a view. Aside from the Hebrew Bible's affirmation of the eternity of the covenant (to which I referred in my first letter to you and refer to below), doesn't Paul confirm this in Romans 11?

This leads us on to the subject of chosenness and the nature of the covenant that you raise.

Let me state categorically that chosenness implies no inherent superiority—perhaps the contrary (see Deut. 7:7). The covenant in fact places special obligations, responsibilities, and consequences upon the children of Israel. These expectations are not easy to fulfill, and, precisely because the expectations are higher, the consequences of failure are greater. (See Lev. 18:25–26; Amos 3:2.) It is in this light (or rather, shadow) that we have traditionally understood the reason for the destruction of our two temples and our subsequent exiles. We continue to recite in our festival liturgy, "Because of our sins, we were exiled from our land." Naturally we know that the Babylonians and the Romans were militarily stronger than us and defeated us; but we believed that if we had been fully true to God's Word, way, and will, the outcome would have been different.

There is of course a recognition here of conditionality, but the consequences of this relate to the condition (excuse the pun) of the Jewish people. If they observe God's commandments, then they will live securely in the land; if they do not—they will be exiled. In this regard the covenant is conditional. However, inasmuch as the children of Israel have been chosen to testify to God's presence in the world (see Isa. 43:10), God's commitment to the covenant is unconditional and eternal and thus, even after exile, the people will always be given another chance (Lev. 26:44). Moreover our rabbis teach that even in their very history of exile, the people testify to God's presence through their survival against all odds, which is made possible only through God's unlimited love and compassion (TB Yoma 69a).

I naturally rejoice in the knowledge that there are many good Christians like yourself who, being profoundly rooted in the Bible, care deeply about the Jewish people—especially those living in the land that the Bible indicates was divinely ordained as the homeland for the children of Israel. I know of course that there are many evangelical Christians who support the State of Israel and the ingathering of Jews from around the world within its borders, because they see this as facilitating Jesus' second coming. It is not this belief that disturbs me, but rather some of the things this belief leads many of them to advocate and support. Often it leads to politically militant positions opposing any possibility of a territorial compromise with the Palestinians, condemning us to perpetual conflict (these Christians are willing to support a battle to the last Israeli!).

Moreover, the above-mentioned conditionality of the covenant precisely requires the children of Israel to behave with respect, care, and compassion for all human beings—all created in the image of God. Our failure to do so—our failure to live in accordance with the divine commandments—prevents us from being able to live securely in the land, no less than the hostility of our assailants. All this means that we have an obligation to find a solution to the conflict that also respects Palestinians' personal and collective dignity—as well as our own. Christians who love and care for us should feel the imperative to care for the well-being of Palestinians as well. Only when there will be security and dignity of both Israelis and Palestinians will we live in the land in peace. I sometimes have the feeling that the eschatological focus on the meaning of Israel blinds some evangelicals to the human realities and needs of the peoples living here!

However, I agree with you that peace in the Middle East will not be achieved if the religious dimension is not there. Precisely for that reason we worked on the Alexandria Summit and Declaration of Religious Leaders of the Holy Land from the three Abrahamic faiths. There is much more that I could say on this and generally on the situation in the Holy

Land, but I want to return to the theme of covenant and the questions you raised in relation to it.

Already at the time of the ratification of the covenant at Sinai and thereafter, there was much sinning among the children of Israel (whether out of ignorance or weakness). We have always had different kinds of Jews, from the best to the worst (a wit once said "Jews are like everyone else, except more so!"). However, the very fact that the covenant was made with the children of Israel as a whole in perpetuity (see Deut. 29:14, 15) means that it is something of a catch-22. Once a person is part of the people, he/she is stuck in it and we are stuck with him/her! Yes, an individual can apostatize, run away, avoid all contact with other Jews, but as the Talmud teaches (TB Sanhedrin 44a). "Even if a Jew is a sinner, he remains a Jew." The idea of unbelief is of course very much a modern, secular concept and there are Jews who do not believe, just as there are non-Jews who do not believe. However, their lack of belief does not mean that they are no longer part of the people of the covenant, nor that we are discharged from our brotherly responsibilities toward them.

An additional very important point to make here is that "belief" for Judaism is not what it is for Christianity. In fact there is a profound distinction here between us. There is no explicit commandment in the Torah to believe in God. Even though Maimonides understood this to be the first of the Ten Commandments, most of our rabbis have seen that first sentence to be simply a statement of fact. God is the reality behind and within the Creation and history. To deny that is as sensible as denying that grass is green, which will not stop it growing the same way, or cows from eating it the same way.

Of course belief is important in Judaism, because that will lead you to live the godly way of life revealed in the Torah. But there's the rub: the purpose, for Judaism, is the way you behave and conduct your life. The purpose is not belief in and of itself. The idea that there is some redeeming power in belief itself is foreign to normative Judaism. (I say "normative Judaism" because we have produced sects from time to time, like the Sabbateans in the seventeenth century, who did make claim to a redeeming belief.) In fact, if Judaism has to choose between someone believing but not doing and someone doing but not believing, it prefers the latter. The "sinners" for Judaism are above all those who do not live in accordance with God's commandments.

Now we come to another distinction between Judaism and Christianity. Judaism sees us as sinning because we have free will. Having the power to choose means that we inevitably will make wrong choices here or there, some more often than others. We might do so out of ignorance, weakness, peer pressure, etc., but we do not make the wrong choice (sin) because we are inherently sinful. In fact Judaism teaches that human beings are basically good and, although we may be weak and easily seduced—unless we are "damaged" in some way by traumatic experiences—all things being equal, we will prefer to choose good rather than evil. Moreover as Ecclesiastes puts it (7:20), "There is not a man who does only good and not sin" (we might better translate it, "There cannot be a man who does only good and never sins"). Judaism teaches that God has given the answer to this inevitable problem in the concept of *Teshuvah*, inadequately translated as "repentance." Actually the word comes from the Hebrew root *shuv*, meaning "to return"—to return to

God and His right path. All of us, Judaism teaches, have within us this capacity for spiritual return and rehabilitation. All we have to do is be sincerely contrite for our specific misdeeds and resolve never to repeat them, and God accepts our sincere contrition unconditionally out of His unlimited love and compassion.

Finally let me respond to your questions regarding the Oral Torah.

In addition to that which was revealed at Mount Sinai together with the Written Torah, the Oral Torah is also the ongoing exposition and application of the tradition in relation to changing circumstances. This process in which learned rabbis base themselves on earlier principles and rulings to provide direction on current issues (new subjects today would be things like artificial insemination, heart transplants, stem cell research, etc.), is perceived by Jewish tradition to be guided by the "Holy Spirit." Obviously the Oral Tradition would not seek to abolish any principle in the Written Torah. However, there are examples of where the Oral Tradition rendered certain biblical injunctions inapplicable. One obvious example would be slavery. It is clear that the Bible permits slavery even though it does appear to disapprove of it (Exod. 21:2–6). However, the Oral Tradition makes such demands upon slave owners that the Talmud declares that "he who has a slave has acquired a master over himself." The result was the *de facto* elimination of slavery.

Another example relates to capital punishment. The Oral Tradition extends the laws of evidence in capital cases so that not only are two witnesses required to corroborate direct visual testimony of a crime before the perpetrator can be convicted for capital punishment (see Deut. 19:15), but two witnesses are also required to confirm that the perpetrator was warned of the consequence of his actions before performing them. To all practical intents and purposes, these requirements overwhelmingly eliminated capital punishment (and required some form of imprisonment in its place). This was obviously motivated by a concern to avoid any miscarriage of justice and out of reverence for human life.

Another example was Hillel's "prosbul." The Torah declares that the Sabbatical year annuls all outstanding loans (Deut. 15:2). This injunction was given in an agrarian society where money was not a commodity. The purpose of a loan was to enable a farmer who had had a disastrous harvest to purchase new grain to sow for the following year. If he continued to experience difficulties, he would not be able to pay the loan back and could be caught in a poverty trap. Therefore the Sabbatical year was designed, *inter alia*, to deliver people from such circumstances. However, by the second century BCE, society had become commercial as well and loans were an integral part of economic life. But the cancellation of debts in the Sabbatical year meant that wealthier citizens were holding back on loans as the Sabbatical year approached in case they didn't get their money back, despite the biblical prohibition against doing so (Deut. 15:9). As a result an injunction that was designed to assist the weak and poor in a changed socioeconomic context was now working against those it sought to help. In order to maintain the spirit of the Law that was now being undermined by the letter of the Law, Hillel introduced a document (known as a "prosbul") that basically placed loans in the hands of the courts in order to avoid their cancellation in the Sabbatical year. *De facto*, Hillel abolished this law, although he did so in a manner that maintained the institution *de jure*—all in order to guarantee the implementation of the spirit and purpose of the Law as the higher goal.

I would see this as having much in common with Jesus' own approach. Accordingly I would explain a criticism of those who nullified the Word of God for the sake of their tradition to be a criticism of those who precisely insisted on maintaining the literal tradition in the text at the expense of the Word of God—meaning its spirit and purpose.

However, Jesus' words as quoted in Matthew to which you refer—"You have heard it said, love your neighbor and hate your enemy"—have always perplexed me, as there is no such phrase in the Written or Oral Torah. Perhaps the Sadducees said this or perhaps again the writers of the Gospels did not recall Jesus' words correctly. Judaism teaches that we should hate evil, not people—i.e., the evil within malfeasant people, but not their being—on the contrary.

In keeping with this, let me clarify that when I commented in my previous letter that if one observed God's commandments one should not have any enemies, I did not mean that the righteous could be guaranteed that no one would hate them. I meant that a righteous person should not regard another as an enemy. If someone hates us because of our ethnic character, color, etc., that is, of course, his or her moral problem. While we must do everything necessary to defend ourselves from such hostility, we have to always try to bear in mind that even one who hates us is still created in the image of God.

As far as divorce is concerned, the rabbis ruled—where there are differences of opinion among the rabbis, the majority holds sway—in accordance with Hillel, that one did not need an accusation of adultery in order to facilitate divorce. However, Jewish tradition has always frowned upon leniency in this regard and the rabbinic courts will always try to facilitate reconciliation and encourage the partners to try to mend the relationship. The process of writing the bill of divorce is complicated and is precisely designed—*inter alia*—to provide time for reconsideration. Certainly divorce reflects a failure and is something to weep over. However, again, because we are not perfect creatures and moreover because sometimes people who are joined together in marriage may not be successfully suited to one another and even begin to dislike one another, it is better for them and generally for their children as well that they go their separate ways rather than living in conflict under the same roof.

I would agree that any breakdown in human relationships, especially between husband and wife, reflects a hardness of heart somewhere. But we should refrain from pointing an accusing finger. Here we are surely in profound agreement. Jesus says, "Judge not that you not be judged," and Hillel the Pharisee, who lived in the century before him, taught (Ethics of the Fathers ch. 2 v. 4): "Never judge your fellow until you are in his place." And as no one can ever be exactly in another's place, our sages teach us to avoid all self-righteousness and always strive to view others in a generous and magnanimous spirit.

*Yours,*
*David*

# Letter 4

*Dear David,*

I was pleased to read that you are enjoying our correspondence. For you to say that you are setting aside other things you ought to be doing shows you are not only enjoying these interchanges but that they are important to you. Knowing how busy you are, I am amazed how quickly you answered my last letter. But I am reminded of something my father used to say to me: "If you want to get something done, ask a busy person to do it."

You have to be the most unusual Pharisee I ever expect to meet! Whether you are considered atypical by your peers, I, of course, don't know. I was also fascinated by your gracious spirit toward Palestinians. I realize we were introduced to each other by Canon Andrew White, the architect of the Alexandria Peace Process, the religious tract for peace in the

Middle East, so I should not have been surprised. But I suspect many evangelicals (perhaps I should call them fundamentalists, certainly in America) would not expect an Orthodox Jewish rabbi to say that we should feel the imperative to care for the well-being of Palestinians as well as Israeli Jews. I fear that you are right, owing to a narrow eschatological focus, that some of my fellow American Christians don't want Israel to give an inch—for any reason—to Palestinians. Isn't it sad when our theology blinds us to the obvious: our ethical and moral responsibility?

I am thinking I should have defined fundamentalists in my previous letter. Doing this is not easy since there are several kinds. But, generally speaking, fundamentalists are seen as rather narrow evangelicals, holding to a brittle theological perspective that embraces an entrenched eschatology: the second coming of Jesus before His one-thousand-year reign, the restoration of the land to Israel—including the ancient city of Jerusalem (some would throw in the rebuilding of the temple)—and the conversion of Jews *after* the Second Coming.

But they lead the way in America as being "friends of Israel"! But, and I think you might agree, they must be more interested in the vindication of their eschatology than they are easing in the pain of suffering people in the meantime. And yet, and I suspect you will agree on this as well, some fundamentalists remind me of those Pharisees described in Jesus' day who, rather than rejoice that a man was healed, could only lament that it was done on the Sabbath (John 9)! You put your finger on a sensitive but salient point.

You seem surprised that an evangelical could believe in Replacement Theology. I have to tell you, many if not most of the evangelicals I know accept the view that the church has replaced Israel in God's scheme. Some prefer a different term, Fulfillment Theology, by which they mean that the church has fulfilled the role Israel once had. And they base it on the very chapter you refer to: Romans 11. Largely because Paul said "And so all Israel will be saved" (v. 26), they assume he must have meant the entire church—the complete company of God's elect. Otherwise it would mean that every single Jew, without exception, will be inevitably and ultimately saved—a view, as I said, that some fundamentalists actually embrace.

Some of these fundamentalists do not believe it is necessary to evangelize the Jews because they will get a second chance in any case after the Second Coming. It is then when all Jews, who had not been converted to Jesus, will finally believe that Jesus is their Messiah. As to those Jews who were deceased, they, too, will be raised from the dead after the Second Coming and given a second chance to believe in Jesus—which they would certainly do under such circumstances.

But the evangelicals I know don't believe that at all. They believe, as I do, that Jews must receive Jesus Christ as their Messiah *before* the Second Coming—or they will perish just like anybody else. In other words, many evangelicals see Israel as the "called out" (cf. Greek *ekklesia*)—those who are effectually called by the Holy Spirit. That way all Israel, all the called out, God's elect, will be saved.

As for Romans 11, this has as much to do with you as it does with me. David, you were born to privilege, if I may put it that way; you are called the "natural olive tree" by the apostle Paul in Romans 11; I, being a Gentile, am called a "wild olive shoot" that has been grafted in (v. 17). So, thanks be to God, I am now privileged in the end! But I don't deserve this mercy. And Paul tells me never to forget it!

In the meantime, God has not abandoned or replaced the natural olive tree. Far from it; Jews are "loved on account of the patriarchs" (v. 28)—proof to me that Replacement Theology comes short of Paul's point in Romans 11. The patriarchs can only mean Abraham, Isaac, and Jacob. God still has, as He has always had, a special love for Israel. Paul claims that the Jews were not able to accept their Messiah because of a blindness (Greek *porsis*—"hardening")—at least in part—because not all Jews rejected Jesus (Paul being a proof of that). I will tell you also that it is my view that there will be a lifting of the blindness that is on Israel, speaking generally, and that they will come in massive numbers to see their true Messiah—Jesus Christ—*before* the Second Coming. As to "all" of Israel being saved, I admit this is a difficult verse. I simply take it that all the elect from within the natural olive tree will eventually come to embrace their Messiah. I say this because Paul earlier stated that "not all who are descended from Israel are Israel" (Rom. 9:6).

On the other hand, I note that you hold that "the people will always be given another chance," by which you mean another chance to be restored to the land. And although you certainly do not believe that Jesus is the true Messiah, you would presumably say that, if He really were the true Messiah, you will be given a second chance at some stage to acknowledge Him. Please correct me if I have put words in your mouth! I am not meaning to be unfair, I am only surmising that you—if necessary—would be attracted to the fundamentalists' view that God will let you have a second chance to believe in Jesus after the Second Coming.

One thing I have not understood is where Orthodox Jews
stand with regard to Zionism. I have been told that some Orthodox Jews are anti-Zionists, something I have never understood, unless it is because Zionism had a rather secular,
nonreligious beginning in the middle of the nineteenth century. So, David, are you a Zionist? If not, why not? Many
Christians believe that the return of so many Jews to their ancient land is a part of God's providence and eternal plan. As
you are cognizant of the Palestinians' plight, how far are you
willing to go with regard to the walled city of Jerusalem, including the Temple Mount? Do you envisage a day when the
temple will be rebuilt—on the Temple Mount? Incidentally,
when I was at seminary I wrote a monograph entitled "The
Messianic Hope of Modern Israel," so this subject really interests me and I look forward to knowing your own views.

I loved what you said about the matter of being chosen,
that it has nothing to do with how deserving one is. My favorite verse in this connection is Exodus 33:19: "I will have
mercy on whom I will have mercy, and I will have compassion on whom I will have compassion." We apparently have
in common a robust doctrine of election, that God makes the
choice. No intelligent reader of the Bible can deny that God
chose ancient Israel. But some good people disagree on
whether God chose individuals, including Gentiles, in His
eternal plan. I believe He did. And again, the choice is not
based on our being deserving. Indeed, Paul said that we have
been called "not because of anything we have done but because of his own purpose and grace," then adding that the
choice was made "before the beginning of time" (2 Tim. 1:9).

I am, however, puzzled by your comments regarding belief. You even say that on this that "there is a profound dis-

tinction between us." First, I would have thought that "Hear, O Israel: The LORD our God, the LORD is one" (Deut. 6:4) is a fairly strong affirmation of belief quite apart from the first commandment. Second, Abraham's belief in God's promise to him is what counted for righteousness (Gen. 15:6). Third, Habakkuk's statement that the righteous shall live by His [God's] faithfulness (Hab. 2:4) is surely based on one's belief in God. Fourth, what is "trust" (in the Psalms, *passim*) if not belief in, or reliance, on God? Surely, however important godly behavior and conduct are, you cannot put the cart before the horse; what you believe is what leads to what you do. If I have understood you correctly, you are quite right—there is indeed a profound distinction between us when you say that "redeeming power in belief itself is foreign to normative Judaism."

You also say that there are Jews who do not believe but their lack of belief does not mean that they are no longer part of the people of the covenant. But is there no penalty for such unbelief—even if the idea of unbelief is a modern secular concept? Do they not forfeit anything by not believing? Also, is this what you mean by the term "observant" Jews and "religious" Jews—as opposed to Jews who do not believe? If you say they are not discharged from their brotherly responsibility, what if they live as though there were no Law? Is this not antinomianism? Surely you are not saying that merely being a Jew makes everything all right. You will know that the New Testament assumes two Israels: ethnic Israel, by being born into a Jewish family and being circumcised, and true, or spiritual, Israel—those who have believed. This is what is meant by the verse I quoted, "Not all who are descended from Israel are Israel" (Rom. 9:6).

This leads me to ask, is Moses more important to you than Abraham? You know that Abraham came some four hundred years before Moses. And since the covenant with Abraham—which was ratified by his faith—was in operation when the Law was given, this means that belief is prior to behavior. David, please tell me where I am going wrong here.

As to the further distinction you make between Judaism and Christianity, the issue of sin and free will, are you saying that every person born into the world is essentially the same as Adam and Eve *before* their sin in the Garden of Eden? We know they were created with free will—of course. But were not their offspring affected by their sin? So, yes, I agree: this is quite a major distinction between us. Would I be right in summarizing our difference at this point: you say a person is a sinner because he sins; I say he sins because he was already a sinner. He is innately a sinner, in my opinion, because his heart was prone to sin from birth. Is this not a good translation from the Hebrew: "Surely I was sinful at birth, sinful from the time my mother conceived me" (Ps. 51:5)? The ancient prophet said that "the heart is deceitful above all things" and desperately (or incurably) wicked (Jer. 17:9). Please correct me here, too, if I have got it wrong.

Thank you for clarifying the matter of God being spelled G-d by some. You even say that some in your own circles go to unnecessary extremes in the way they avoid misusing the name of God and that such might have been precisely the sort of thing that Jesus disliked in those Pharisees He criticized. You amaze me by your honesty and candor. I have long suspected that many Christians have not grasped the meaning of Jesus' interpretation of the third commandment

(Matt. 5:33–37). Many of us can only think of this command as being a prohibition against cursing by using God's name when they are angry. Of course God is against that. But the truth is, Jesus spoke against using God's name for the purpose of promoting one's personal interest—for any reason. Whereas Jesus was not speaking against swearing an oath in a court of law (as some surmise), He warned against misusing God's name by swearing: if I were to say, for example, "I call heaven and earth to witness that God is on my side," or "If I swear to you in the name of God that He has told me my eschatology is infallible," I have abused His name. It is the worst kind of name-dropping. But most Christians have not grasped this; they think they are free of abusing the third commandment only as long as they don't say things like "Oh my God." That is only a small part of abusing His name.

So if I am understanding what you say about some of your people—who supposedly feel they are doing their duty in fulfilling the third commandment by the way they spell God—so, too, are there Christians who have their own way of feeling they are not violating the third commandment when in fact they are. I am wondering if you have given much thought to Jesus' way of applying the third commandment.

I, too, have wondered about Jesus' words when He said, "You have heard that it was said, 'Love your neighbor and hate your enemy'" (Matt. 5:43). However, even though this is not a quote from the Torah, could there not have been a consensus after hundreds of years—through an unofficial oral tradition—that led to people commonly saying that? So although there is no explicit command to love your neighbor and hate your enemy, this was the way a good number of ancient people must have thought. In the Sermon on the Mount, from which this statement arises, Jesus sometimes quotes from the Torah, but not always. He did not say He was quoting from the Torah at that point.

I want to close by apologizing if I have put you on the defensive by any of my questions. But I am counting on you to do the same with me. I am learning from you and I want to learn more. I feel so honored in having this privilege to dialogue with an erudite rabbi and an Israeli of your stature. If more of this sort of thing could take place, there would be an ever-increasing mutual understanding and respect between Jews and Christians—not to mention more love than ever.

Finally, if all Israeli Jews were like you, despite what the fundamentalists may wish for, hostilities would surely diminish in our beloved Holy Land—so precious to both of us—and it would be a safer place.

*Yours,*
*R. T.*

# Letter 5

*Dear R. T.,*

Please do not apologize for your straight talk—especially when it is done respectfully and graciously as you do. Moreover I do not feel put on the defensive and am happy to answer your questions and challenges, to the best of my ability.

However, you raise so much in your brief epistle that it's difficult to know where to start or finish. In fact I'm sure that some points will have to wait for later discussion.

Let me, first of all, address those subjects that we have already discussed and where I need to clarify my positions to you.

You are puzzled by my comments concerning belief. Part of the problem is our failure to clarify our definitions of terms. What do we mean by *belief*? Is it the same as *faith* or *trust*? In the Hebrew language (and the Hebrew biblical mind—if I may use such a term!), they are indeed much the same thing. The words imply a sense of confidence, usually with good reason (i.e., experience). But this is not the same thing as a *command* to believe or a *duty* to believe. The "ancient Hebrew mind" would not have comprehended such a concept. God is the ultimate Reality. His presence was a given—obvious, understood, and affirmed. Moreover if for some reason a person was blind to the obvious, telling him that he *has* to see would be meaningless! If any of the biblical phrases you have quoted cannot be understood in this light, please demand further clarification from me.

If I understand Christian faith correctly (obviously as an outside observer), belief is a very different thing from just having trust and confidence. It is of a transcendent quality that relates to the salvation of one's soul. Judaism does not teach such an idea. It does teach that God wants us to follow a way of life of holy and moral observance. Those who follow that way of life are indeed those to whom I refer as "observant" and "religious" (although I recognize that there are many spiritual Jews who may be called religious in that sense, who are not very observant; however, for Orthodox Jews, religiosity and observance are very much intertwined). Theoretically it is possible (albeit unlikely) for a Jew to doubt the existence of God and still observe the religious way of life of Judaism. Why would he want to? Perhaps because the way of life is the essence of his identity; or perhaps because he experiences it as so "good" that he appreciates its value. Of course, if one does perceive God's presence all around and within one, and one believes that the Jewish way of life is divinely revealed, one is likely to have a far more intense commitment to it, but the value of the pudding is precisely in the eating (if I may be so crass!).

You ask if there is a penalty for unbelief. Our sages of the Mishnah (the first written version of the Oral Law) declare that "the reward of the good deed is the good deed itself; and the punishment for transgression is in the transgression itself." In other words, if you love your neighbor as yourself, no one is the richer for it than you. If you steal from him, you have done yourself far more harm than the one you have stolen from. Moreover, as far as unbelief is concerned, it is questionable as to whether this can be described as a "transgression." I would call it a "mental block"—perhaps the result of secular conditioning. I might and do regret the fact, but I cannot imagine that God would want someone to be punished for an incapacity!

But let's leave the agnostic aside for a moment and consider the believer who is a sinner—a more offensive person to my mind (e.g., someone who claims to be religious but swindles or even just takes advantage of people's ignorance to pursue material gains). Even this sinner remains a Jew by virtue of being part of the people of the covenant. He is a bad Jew—but still a Jew. And none of us can declare him otherwise as much as we may wish to! Such a transgressor should be punished and indeed would be punished in a theocratic context (though according to Jewish jurisprudence, such a context has to reflect the volition of the majority).

In modern democratic societies it is difficult for voluntary associations to initiate sanctions against its members (and one may even question the desirability and effectiveness of such). However, in the past and in certain cases and places even today, social sanctions and even restrictions regarding participation in religious ceremonies have been employed against those guilty of serious offenses.

You are correct, R. T., in your summary of the distinction between us regarding sin and sinning. Moreover, our traditional understanding of the verse in Psalm 51 to which you refer is not that the sexual act is sinful, nor that the child inherits sin.

In keeping with Genesis, we see the human person as inherently good, and in keeping with Deuteronomy (24:16) affirm the principle of personal responsibility as opposed to vicarious guilt. However, our understanding of the phraseology that the psalmist uses in Psalm 51 is of a graphic portrayal of how this capacity to err is there (indeed by virtue of free will) at the beginning of the creation of the human being. The traditional Jewish view of Adam and Eve's sin is that while there were consequences of their actions, it did not change the inherent human condition of being essentially good. Thus we reject the concept of "original sin."

Of course, this is not unrelated to the Messiah question. You know that the Hebrew term *Messiah* means "one who is anointed for a particular task." In its biblical use in reference to a king or to the high priest, for example, it always relates to a (fallible) human being who has been appointed for a particular service or task. The Jewish expectation of the Messianic Age resulted from the condition of exile and thus expressed the anticipation of return to the land and a renewal of the rule of the Davidic royal household. Accordingly, the scion of that household who would be a wise leader at that time is referred to as "the Messiah." However, even as far as the political redemption of the Jewish people from exile and oppression is concerned, it is God who is the Redeemer, not the Messiah.

The Messiah therefore has a functional role for society.

From a Jewish perspective, the condition of one's personal soul has nothing to do with the identity of the Messiah but is a matter between the individual and God. So here we see another big difference between us and another example of where we share sources and terms that, however, we understand very differently (and as a result often have unrealistic expectations of each other and disappointments accordingly).

In fact, the identity of the Messiah is quite peripheral to the essence of my faith as a Jew, which is my understanding of how God wants me to live my life here and now. For me, not only does the identity of the Messiah have nothing to do with the state of my soul, it has nothing to do with the divine character. But for the Christian, if I am not mistaken, it does have to do with both of these as the identity of the Messiah is inextricably bound up with the divinity itself and is at the heart of your religious affirmation. Thus your "second chance" that you hold out for me seems to be predicated upon an erroneous assumption.

I often echo the words of the late brilliant Orthodox Jewish scholar David Flusser who declared that when the Messiah arrives (tomorrow, as we pray!), he will approach him with his Christian friends and say, "Excuse me, sir, have you been here before?" And if he responds affirmatively we will know that Christians were right all along! But the truth is that this cute comment avoids the full issue. The real issue is not just whether Jesus of Nazareth is the Messiah, but what that function means!

When the majority of Jews originally denied his messianic claim, they simply stated what they saw and understood as a result. The Messianic Age as envisaged by the prophets of Israel would mean an end of foreign oppression, the ingathering of the exiles, and an era of universal peace. They saw none of these, thus they did not see any reason to acknowledge that any Messiah had arrived.

If I understand correctly, the first Christians had a religious experience that convinced them not only that Jesus was indeed the messianic figure, but that the rest of the Jews did not really understand the deeper, truer meaning of the messianic role. As I understand it, not only did Christianity claim that the social and political expectations would be fulfilled in a second coming (which, as far as the majority of the Jews were concerned, was a completely new idea, as the prophets present the messianic advent as one fully successful era), but that in effect if one believed in Jesus as the Messiah, then one was indeed no longer in exile and was in a state of true peace! Now, to understand the messianic idea that way, you have to have that conviction—that faith! We who are not Christians do not have it. What good will it do me—from your perspective—if I were to acknowledge Jesus as the Messiah, when all it means to me is that he is a wise leader at a time of universal conflict resolution and political harmony!?

Because the Jewish messianic expectation is a political as well as social and moral one, there were and are many Jews who saw and see the establishment of the State of Israel as "the first flowering of our redemption," i.e., the beginning of a messianic process. These people are often described as Religious Zionists and I would say that this is the outlook of the majority of modern Orthodox Jews, and I would include myself among them. Zionism was, however, bitterly opposed by the ultra-Orthodox Jews (often incorrectly labeled "Hassidic"—we'll leave that one for another discussion!). Ultra-

Orthodoxy (referred to in Hebrew as *haredi*) was and is a re-actionary withdrawal from secular society (as opposed to modern Orthodoxy, which seeks to find a balance between being a religious observant Jew on the one hand and living in the modern world and being a part of a wider culture on the other). Because Zionism was led by people who were not re-ligiously observant (and often even hostile toward Jewish tra-ditionalism), the ultra-Orthodox saw it as just a Jewish form of the devil they wanted to have nothing to do with: namely, the secular world. Moreover, the idea that this return and establishment of Jewish sovereignty had any religious signif-icance, let alone messianic relevance, they saw/see as an impiety, if not a heresy. Most of them believe that the whole messianic fulfillment will come miraculously and be manifest only in a fully religiously observant society. Eventually after the *Shoah* (the Holocaust) and the establishment of the State of Israel, they came to pragmatic terms with Zionism, but they still did and do not see the political movement of estab-lishing Jewish sovereignty in the land as having any religious, let alone messianic, significance.

I was both brought up in and (as I indicated) consider myself to be part of the Religious Zionist camp. However, I believe that there are those (far too many) who have allowed this perception of the prophetic (messianic) significance of Israel to go to their heads and warp their good sense and even their moral values. I refer to many of the Religious Zionist settlers in the West Bank and Gaza Strip and their supporters who are so eschatologically convinced of the messianic significance of Israel that they ignore the political, economic, demographic, and moral consequences of their actions and ideology. I believe that not only is this very dangerous (and actually threatens Israel's very survival), but it is in complete conflict with biblical/Jewish teaching and in fact makes an important means—the land—into an end in itself. That, R. T., is to my mind, idolatry—no less! To transgress our moral values and teaching in order to preserve a Jewish polity is to me a contradiction in terms.

As I mentioned in my last letter, our relationship to the land is conditional on our behavior. As I say, I do believe Zionism to have messianic significance, but that doesn't mean that its success is guaranteed. It can still fail, God forbid, and unless we behave wisely as well as morally, it will do so. As I also mentioned to you, this means that we are duty-bound to seek a territorial compromise with those who are not Jews who also live in the land, both because we do have biblically mandated moral obligations toward all human beings—all created in the divine image—but also out of enlightened necessity. If we try to hold on to it all right now, we may, God forbid, lose it all again.

So how far am I prepared to go, you ask? As far as I am concerned, as far as we have to! I hope that we will not have to give up the Old City of Jerusalem, and I believe that we can still arrive at a political resolution that could enable Jerusalem to be both part and parcel of Israel and a Palestinian state at the same time. If, however, there is no alternative, then just as Israel managed to develop Jewish life in an independent state without the Old City of Jerusalem until 1967, we should be prepared to do so again, if this is the price of peace and guaranteeing our future.

If this tragic necessity actually happens, it will not stop my praying and longing once more for the day when we can live again in all of Jerusalem, in the same way as I continue

to pray—like all Orthodox Jews—for the eventual reconstruction of the temple and the restoration of its service. In
practice, however, the latter is not a simple matter.

You may have seen, R. T., the signs at the entrances to the
Temple Mount set up by the chief rabbinate of Israel (sic!)
telling Jews not to enter the precinct of the Temple Mount!
This is precisely because Judaism teaches that the area
where the temple stood is intrinsically holy (in fact, the only
place on this earth that is totally intrinsically holy!) and, as
when the temple stood, so today we may not tread upon the
ground there in a state of ritual impurity. The Bible in
Leviticus lays down the rites of ritual purification that require elements we no longer have (most specifically the
ashes of the pure red heifer). Moreover, we are not exactly
sure where the precise boundaries of the temple and the
Holy of Holies are; and as this knowledge is essential for any
legitimate reconstruction, all these factors make it practically impossible for us today to rebuild the temple—even if
the whole Muslim as well as Christian world were to beg us
to do so!!

As a result, the mainstream Jewish tradition over the last
millennium has been that the third temple would appear su-
pernaturally in a pillar of fire from heaven. Even after 1967,
when Israel acquired control of the Old City of Jerusalem,
the Temple Mount has remained in Muslim hands and Israel
passed a law that year guaranteeing the integrity and maintenance of the holy sites for their respective religions. This
has not only been out of Israel's political good sense, but also
precisely because of the aforementioned mainstream Orthodox Jewish teaching. I see the traditional restrictions in Judaism against going on to the Temple Mount as a blessing in

the present context of conflict between Palestinians and Israelis, and as providing the means for ensuring that no tradition should feel that its holy sites are threatened by the attachments of another tradition. Naturally this is until the Almighty deems the full messianic advent to have arrived. And then it will be in an era of universal peace anyway, so whatever happens there and then, will have happened peacefully and by agreement!

As I say, all Orthodox Jews pray for that day when the temple will be rebuilt and its service reintroduced. However, you may recall, R. T., that my family and I are vegetarians, and like Rabbi Abraham Isaac Kuk, the first Ashkenazi chief rabbi in the Holy Land, I believe that when that temple service is restored, it will be vegetarian in practice and no longer require animal offerings. But perhaps we should leave the subject of vegetarianism for a future exchange, as I think that I've already touched on quite a lot for the time being. As I expected, I have not managed to answer all your questions in this letter, so please press me on those you want to make sure that I do not avoid.

*Yours,*
*David*

# Letter 6

*Dear David,*

It was such a pleasure to be with you in Jerusalem since our last correspondence. Louise, our son T. R., and I enjoyed our Shabbat meal with you so very much. As the first time we met was over a Shabbat meal, I was so thrilled that my family could now have a taste of this. I could only wish that there were many Christian families that do the equivalent at least once a week. What an example you set for us, David and Sharon.

Before I respond to your last letter, I wanted to answer a question you put to me just as we began to partake of the Shabbat meal. You will recall that you introduced the meal by sanctifying the day with the blessing over the wine, celebrating God's creation. Then, after the ritual washing of the hands, you broke one of the two loaves of bread. You indicated that these represent the double portion of manna that came down on the eve of Sabbaths and festivals for the children of Israel during their wandering in the desert to keep them from working by collecting the manna on the holy days. You then gave thanks for divine providence and asked me a question I have given serious thought to since (which I will paraphrase): Did Jesus intend that the Lord's Supper should be continued by His disciples *in addition* to the Sabbath and festival rituals with their own original meaning, or did He want the Lord's Supper to *replace* such rituals?

Very good question. My answer is, Jesus intended that the Lord's Supper should replace the ancient rituals because He became our Passover Lamb. The Last Supper was not a Shabbat meal (although there may have been similarities) but Passover. When Jesus said, "This bread is My body and this wine is My blood," He was announcing that He Himself—God's Lamb without spot or blemish—fulfilled Passover. There would therefore be no need to keep up the observance of Passover, which was carried out not only in gratitude to God for the miraculous deliverance from Pharoah but which also *pointed to* its perfect fulfillment in Jesus dying on the cross for our sins. The sprinkled blood over the door and on each side at Passover would anticipate the day when blood flowed from Jesus' head and hands. We therefore keep Passover when we eat the bread and wine at the Lord's Supper in remembrance of Him.

However, it is not uncommon for messianic believers (Jews who have accepted Jesus Christ as Messiah and Lord) to practice many of the ancient rituals because it reminds them of their original meaning and fulfillment. I see this as a good thing for them to do. It seems to me that this is not only a way of teaching essential doctrine but, just maybe, it would be a testimony—even an evangelistic opportunity—for Jews generally to learn more about their theological roots, not to mention to Jews who already take the Old Testament seriously. Therefore, although Jesus intended that the Lord's Supper would replace the ancient Jewish rituals, there is no harm in observing them when one knows it is not a requirement.

When it comes to the Law—ceremonial (the way God's ancient people should worship), civil (how they should govern themselves), moral (the Ten Commandments)—and the way that Law is interpreted in the New Testament, the key word for us is *fulfillment*. If in purchasing real estate nowadays the issue, as they say, is "location, location, location," I would say that the relationship to the Law and the gospel, the Old Testament and the New Testament, is "fulfillment, fulfillment, fulfillment." This will almost certainly be a recurring theme in our correspondence, so I will now address issues your last letter raised.

A profound distinction between us, as you say, is the matter of faith, or belief. You contend that there is no command "to believe" in ancient Israel. Since you are obviously the expert on the nature of the ancient Hebrew mind, I will ask you please to forgive me if I don't grasp what you mean. My opinion would be based not on what I know about the Hebraic mind but upon Old Testament Scripture. For example, was it not *faith* that lay behind the ancient Israelites' keeping the Passover? They must have believed that God spoke to them through Moses. It was surely based entirely on *command*. They would not have obeyed this unprecedented command if they did not believe it. So their faith must have been preceded by a command to believe. "The Israelites did just what the LORD commanded Moses and Aaron" (Exod. 12:28).

You also stated that Judaism does not teach the idea that faith relates to the salvation of one's soul. But would not any Jew have been destroyed the night of Passover had he not honored Moses' command? It seems to me this indicates that there is a connection between faith and the salvation of one's soul.

I would therefore want to argue that not only would the Israelites not have kept the command had they not, first of all, believed, but that God even prepared them for faith. You will recall that Moses' initial anxiety about his own calling was precisely how he himself would be accepted, or believed, by the Israelites. This is why he asked the Lord, "What shall I tell them?" when they ask why they should believe Moses. God then said to him, 'I AM WHO I AM. This is what you are to say to the Israelites: 'I AM has sent me to you'" (Exod. 3:13–14). The Israelites understandably needed some convincing, but when they were eventually persuaded, it is written that "they *believed*. . . . They bowed down and worshiped" (Exod. 4:31, emphasis mine).

Not only that—later on when Joshua and Caleb were outnumbered by the Israelites (who were afraid to press on and enter the promised land), God was angry with Israel. This was because the people did not believe that God would be with them to overcome the inhabitants of Canaan. "We seemed like grasshoppers in our own eyes, and we looked the same to them" (Num. 13:33). God swore in His wrath, of that generation, "They shall never enter my rest" (Ps. 95:11). There was surely but one reason for this: they did not enter in because of their unbelief. Only Caleb and Joshua entered the promised land later on, the rest having died in the wilderness—as God swore would happen.

This, to me, shows an important difference between the state of the souls of those who died in the desert and the souls of Joshua and Caleb. This historic incident in ancient Israelite history, I would have thought, shows an essential connection between faith and the state of one's soul.

This issue is made equally clear by the premise of Habakkuk's prophecy, which was based on living by the faithfulness of God. The quotation of Habakkuk 2:4: "The righteous will live by his faith" (quoted three times from the LXX [Septuagint] in the New Testament as "the just shall live by faith"—Rom. 1:17; Gal. 3:11; Heb. 10:38) was couched in the promise that God would reveal Himself eventually but unmistakably. "For the revelation awaits an appointed time; it speaks of the end and will not prove false. Though it linger, wait for it; it will certainly come and will not delay" (Hab. 2:3). Then came that significant word, as you, David, know in Hebrew that says, "The righteous will live by his [God's] faith" (v. 4). Living by the faithfulness of God is *faith* and this became the foundation for the New Testament teaching of justification by faith. It was based entirely upon the Old Testament promises and the fulfillment of them through 1) the person and death of Jesus, and 2) our transferring their trust in good works to what Jesus accomplished for us.

I want to say therefore that faith, or the command to believe, as we Christians believe, is nothing new. It is not a New Testament innovation but the heart of Israel's reason for existence. They *believed* they were chosen; they *believed* they had a future and it was entirely because they believed God's Word to them through the Law and the prophets. It was surely the basis and impetus for living in every servant of God in ancient Israel. It is what motivated the great men and women of the Old Testament to do what they did; the absence of it incurred the wrath of *Yahweh* again and again.

I was therefore surprised to hear you say that there is no warning in Judaism against not recognizing Messiah. Did I grasp what you were saying? "The identity of the Messiah is quite peripheral to the essence of my faith as a Jew," you say. You preceded this by saying, "The condition of one's personal soul has nothing to do with the identity of the Messiah." Does this mean that God is saying that Israel can "take it or leave it" (as to the acceptance of Messiah) and all is still well in their relationship with Him? It is good if they recognize Him, but "not to worry" if they don't? Unless I have misinterpreted you (please correct me—this is important), it is no wonder that Jews would not be disturbed, then or now, whether or not Messiah came and they missed Him! They remain Jews either way and that is apparently the important thing.

Am I right to think, then, that the crux of our disagreement comes to this: any Jew is a saved Jew—even if he or she does not believe? It comes down to ethnicity, race, or culture. But not faith. Is there no further responsibility for a Jew insofar as the state of one's soul is concerned? And if there is life beyond the grave, the only qualification for bliss in the resurrection is that one was a Jew? Please do tell me, David, if I have got this wrong because it would not be very productive if we continue to correspond under such a major misunderstanding.

I need to ask you another question. I realize you do not want to be associated with the attitude and self-righteousness of those Pharisees the New Testament describes. But would you have in common with them the teaching of the resurrection of the dead and life beyond the grave? To put it another way, was Jesus being faithful to Pharisaical teaching, or was it His own contribution, when He said, "A time is coming when all who are in their graves will hear his voice and come out—those who have done well rise to live, and those who have done evil will rise to be condemned" (John 5:28–29)? This teaching was, as I understand it, an essential difference between Pharisees and Sadducees; the latter did not believe in life beyond the grave or in the resurrection of the body. But Pharisees did. So I am assuming you do too. Therefore, what determines the status of one's soul after death? Is it only being a Jew—whether one be a Pharisee, Sadducee, or atheist?

As for unbelief being a "mental block," I think I know what you mean by that. For that is precisely what has set in on Jews (speaking generally), according to Paul in Romans 11. Your view is that God would not be fair in judging a person because of his incapacity, by which I think you mean an incapacity, or inability, to believe. I understand what you mean. But on the other hand, is this not God's prerogative? He said to Moses, "I will have mercy on whom I will have mercy, and I will have compassion on whom I will have compassion" (Exod. 33:19). He also said that His ways are higher than our ways and His thoughts are higher than our thoughts (Isa. 55:8–9).

I would therefore argue, David, that God does sometimes command us to do what *seems* unfair or unreasonable. He

commanded Abraham to sacrifice Isaac (Gen. 22:2). He
commanded Moses, "Raise your staff and stretch out your
hand over the sea to divide the water" when Moses was
trapped with the Egyptians behind him (Exod. 14:15). Had
Moses kept crying out to God that he had a mental block,
God would not have been pleased. But Moses did what he
was required to do. It required faith. And God wonderfully
acted. According to Jesus and Paul, the Jews rejected the
One offered to them and, as a consequence, were inflicted
with a "spirit of stupor, eyes so that they could not see and
ears so that they could not hear" (Rom. 11:8, echoing Deut.
29:4 and Isa. 29:10). And yet, like it or not, all of us (whether
Jew or Gentile) are equally commanded to believe. Those
who turn to the Lord Jesus are given faith in that moment.

I therefore have in mind continually when I write to you,
David, that it is such a great privilege to speak to you like
this. You are an exceedingly rare person to engage in this
kind of candor. I know too that there is no amount of persuasion that I can muster, however airtight my logic or ir-
refutable my biblical interpretation, that can convince you.
"A man convinced against his will is of the same opinion
still." It is only by the grace of the Holy Spirit that your eyes,
or anybody else's, will be opened. It is by the sheer grace of
God that my own eyes were opened. But at the same time I
have a responsibility to speak to you with all the love and
persuasion I have. I want you to see what is clear to me. If I
cross over a line when I have misunderstood or misinterpreted you, or you feel I am pressing you too far, I thank you
with all my heart for telling me. But you have known from
the outset that I have a desire for you to know Jesus not according to the flesh but as revealed by the Holy Spirit.

You will smile when I tell you that, at first, I honestly wondered if you were a secret believer in Jesus! Your gracious and magnanimous spirit made me think you must be a Christian! I'm serious! I know too many Christians who should learn from your attitude and kindness. But as we continued with our correspondence I was forced to admit that you are not a believer in Jesus—quite the contrary. But your openness and courage blesses me no end nonetheless.

Speaking of courage, I am amazed at your position with regard to Jerusalem and the Temple Mount. I never dreamed I would hear an Orthodox Jewish rabbi be willing to concede the ancient city of Jerusalem, including the Temple Mount—if that is what would guarantee Israel's safety and existence. You say you hope that you do not have to give up the Old City, but you would do it (as was done before) "if this is the price of peace and guaranteeing our future." This to me shows an awful lot of honesty and courage. You must have come under a lot of criticism from your fellow Orthodox Jews, not to mention rabbis. I think you would also be criticized by a lot of Christians, especially in America, who think that the Temple Mount must be occupied (and the temple rebuilt) by Israelis before Jesus can come back! So if the concession of the Old City were to be adopted by the Israeli government, the Second Coming would be postponed for a long time—except for one thing: the Bible nowhere indicates that the temple must be rebuilt before the Second Coming.

By the way, it is this same type of Christian—not me—who teaches that Jews are to be given a "second chance." This is certainly not my own position. If it were left up to me, yes, David, I would want to give you and your family

and all Jews—and everybody in the world who ever lived—
a second chance (even though you hint that it is not of any
great concern to you). I raise this only because you wrote in
your last letter, "Thus your 'second chance' that you hold
out for me seems to be predicated upon an erroneous assumption." I am sorry I have not made my position clear.
The "second chance" some Christians offer Jews is without
any warrant whatever in Scripture. This notion is taking the
*specialness* of Jews too far; it is predicated upon a severe misunderstanding of God's special place for Israel.

It is absolutely true that God's ancient people are special.
I agree that *you* are special. No doubt about that. I envy you.
But neither you nor I are in the position of being granted a
"second chance" when Jesus comes again. There is not a
hint of this in the Bible. So I would not want you to think I
am with those who treat you in this fashion. Although such
people love Jews, as I do, we would do you no favor to per-
petrate this—if we really do love you. It is a risk of incalculable proportion to teach anything that could lead a Jew (or
anyone else) to say, "Oh well, if I do not accept Jesus as my
Messiah, I will get a second chance anyway." I wish it were
true!

What you seem to be saying in that part of your last letter is this. The Messiah you envisage (whom you are still
looking for) is not divine in the first place. The Messiah Israel awaits, if I interpret you correctly, never was envisaged
to be God in the flesh who would die on a cross and be
raised from the dead but rather a charismatic political and
military leader who would restore the glory to ancient Israel, rebuild the temple, and become to his people much like
what King David had been. In any case, you are talking

about a man, very human—certainly not deity. If I understand you, this is why a "second chance" does not matter to you. It is because the Messiah you will recognize would not punish you if you did not recognize him. This is the reason I believe you are saying the salvation of one's soul is not connected to the identity of Messiah.

Before I close this letter, let me summarize generally what I perceive to be three major differences between us so far. First, the matter of faith. Second, the nature of Messiah. Would I be right to think that you believe the Messiah we Christians accept—Jesus—never saw Himself as God, that the church in the following century created this understanding of Him? I note in your first letter that the late date of Matthew is important to you. But apart from dates, whether viewing the synoptic Gospels, the Gospel of John, or the writings of Paul, it is essential to our belief that the One who came was the One Isaiah saw hundreds of years in advance, who would be called "Wonderful Counselor, Mighty God, Everlasting Father, Prince of Peace" (Isa. 9:6). And that His death meant that the Lord laid on Him our iniquity (Isa. 53:6). This brings me to the third big difference between us, namely, the nature of sin. I will postpone further comments on this until I hear from you next. But if I have not given adequate attention to any matter you have raised, please tell me.

*Yours,*
*R. T.*

# Letter 7

*Dear R. T.,*

While there are things you write as a profession of your faith on which I would not presume to comment, let alone argue, I am truly grateful that you probe and challenge me the way you do—above all because it enables me to clarify my own positions to you and anyone who reads our exchange, to the best of my ability.

It is clear from your latest response that I did not do so very well in my last letter and I need to restate certain comments more clearly.

Of course faith is very important in Judaism! What I had indicated, however, is that to live God's revealed way of life (the commandments) as manifest to us in the Torah (the Pentateuch and the Oral Tradition) is the *most* important thing for Judaism. As I said, it is difficult to imagine why someone would want to commit him- or herself to living this way of life without faith in God, but it is theoretically possible. In other words, what I am saying that what Judaism precisely rejects as being of little or no value is a faith that does not lead to action. So you have indeed "got me wrong"!

I will discuss the word *saved* below. But let me initially use it as if we have a shared lexicon here. No, a Jew is not "saved" individually because of her or his ethnicity. A Jew is "saved" because he or she leads a way of life in keeping with God's commandments. In fact, in a way it is harder for a Jew to be "saved" because she or he is expected to observe more commandments. Judaism teaches that prior to the covenant with Abraham, Isaac, and Jacob and their descendants, God established a covenant with all humanity (reflecting divine love for all) with the children of Noah after the Flood. Covenant is a two-way process, and rabbinic understanding of human responsibilities in this regard is to observe the prohibitions against idolatry, murder, sexual misconduct, blasphemy, stealing, eating part of an animal alive, and the positive obligation to establish courts of justice and abide by them. Every Gentile who follows such a way of life, according to Rabbinic Judaism, is guaranteed his or her "portion in the world to come." That is all Judaism understands in the term *saved*. As I have noted, we do not see humans as originally evil or condemned but in fact as being intrinsically good. Sin is the inevitable consequence of freedom of choice and it is that which deforms (or "condemns") our souls. Sincere repentance is what redeems our soul from the consequence of sin and in that sense our souls may be said to be "saved" by repentance (as I think I have mentioned, the Hebrew word *teshuvah* literally means "a process of returning"—returning to

God and our naturally good proximate relationship to Him and His way).

Rabbinic Judaism as the heir of Pharisaic Judaism believes emphatically in the concept of the afterlife or continuity of the soul and the reward (i.e., the consequence of our good actions) that the soul enjoys accordingly. However, precisely as this is the direct result of how we have lived our lives in this world, the Jewish emphasis is upon the latter, albeit in the full knowledge that "this world is like a vestibule before the banqueting hall."

The Sinai Covenant with the children of Israel revealed a far more demanding way of life than the Noahide Covenant. By living this way of life, the children of Israel would both enjoy its spiritual benefits and also testify to the divine presence in their midst. However, taking on these responsibilities means in effect that it is actually more demanding for the Jew than the Gentile to guarantee his/her portion in the world to come. Judaism teaches that righteous Gentiles, as righteous Jews, have their portion (reward) in the world to come. Moreover, in keeping with Judaic teaching regarding infinite divine compassion, great Jewish thinkers like Maimonides have believed that it takes an inordinately evil individual to destroy any goodness in his or her divine soul and thus of any reward/continuity. I should mention here as a footnote that there have been various Jewish interpretations of concepts that in English we call *heaven*, *hell*, and *purgatory*, but all interpretations see them as the consequences of our behavior, not of declarations or manifestos.

Of course, more often than not there is and indeed there should be an inextricable link between what we declare and what we do. But you know, R. T., as well as I, that this is not always necessarily the case. Above all, what I'm saying in this regard is that Judaism does not consider a declaration of faith or even a sincere belief to have any redeeming value in itself.

As I mentioned in my previous letter, the Hebrew word "faith" is generally synonymous with trust and relates to experience. Thus, when after the crossing of the Red Sea it says "and the children of Israel believed in God and Moses his servant," it clearly indicates that their experience had convinced them of (made them believe in) God and Moses.

Yes, indeed, as I tried to clarify in my previous letter, most practicing Jews today, like the children of Israel then, observe the commandments out of conviction that their source is the God in whom they believe. Until modern times the very idea of nonbelief would have been unthinkable. However, my point again is that belief in itself is of little or no value unless it leads to action. This is normative Jewish teaching and it is indeed one of the fundamental points of variance with Christian teaching which, if I am not mistaken, sees faith in itself as being of redeeming value.

I trust you can now see all the biblical texts that you quote in this light as well. We interpret them according to our own religious worldview—e.g., the reason that the children of Israel who did not hearken to Joshua and Caleb did not enter the land was because they *demonstrated* their lack of commitment to God's promise. That indeed reflected an inadequate faith in God Himself. But even if they had not had full faith in God Himself but had still followed His charge, they would have then entered and possessed the land!!

Incidentally, our translation of Habakkuk 2:4 is "The righteous shall live by *his* [own] faith" (not by God's!) and we understand that to mean precisely that the righteous is only he who actually lives in practice the implications of his faith.

Probably part of the reason for your misunderstanding of what I wrote is my failure to emphasize the difference between the individual (Jew's) relationship with God, and the collective relationship of the children of Israel with God. As far as the latter is concerned, Judaism teaches that a Jew is always part of a covenanted collective whose eternity is guaranteed by God and for whom divine forgiveness and restoration are guaranteed. However, the individual is totally personally responsible for his or her actions; and depending upon how one has led one's life, the individual Jew merits to "enter the Garden of Eden" (heaven) or does not (*Gehinnom* or hell).

Similarly, Orthodox Judaism teaches the principle of the resurrection of the dead and it is one of Maimonides's Thirteen Principles of Faith that has come to be accepted as a virtual theological credo by Orthodox Jews (and appears in the daily prayer book as such). However, Maimonides elsewhere (as I have indicated) dwells extensively on the concept of the afterlife (the continuity of the soul) and doesn't mention this in the Thirteen Principles. Accordingly many commentators have assumed that for him, the two are one and the same, and *resurrection* refers to the spiritual ascent of the soul after the body dies. Others have precisely interpreted the concept (in keeping with Ezek. 36) to refer to the collective resurrection of the people. Certain Religious Zionist thinkers have interpreted this passage of Ezekiel as anticipating the national resurrection of the Jewish people in the land of Israel after it appeared that they were just a valley of dead, dry bones after the Holocaust. However, most Orthodox Jews still believe in a physical resurrection at the end of times, and in all these respects Jesus was affirming traditional Pharisaic teaching.

You have indeed correctly summarized my view (to be more precise, Jewish teaching) regarding the concept of the Messiah and its relation to the above. Let me reiterate that the overwhelming majority of Jews did not accept Jesus as the Messiah because the prophetic idea of the Messianic Age indicated an end to foreign oppression and exile and this did not happen. However, your suggestion that they didn't care about it one way or another because they would remain Jews is misleading precisely because one does not have anything to do with the other. The Jews then were *eagerly* awaiting a Messiah who would deliver them from Roman subjugation to be free to lead their religious and national life. It is quite possible (even probable) that Jesus did think that God was going to deliver them from that oppression at that time and perhaps he did expect to be the one who would be the wise leader of the nation—the Messiah. However, you are correct in assuming that I personally do not think for one minute that Jesus saw himself in terms of the theological construct that Christianity affirms.

Finally, I wish to pursue your kind answer to my question about whether or not Jesus wanted his disciples to continue to observe the commandments and rituals revealed in or based on the Hebrew Bible. Your answer in essence is no; as the New Testament has fulfilled the Old Testament, there is no need to do so, although you don't see anything wrong if there are those who wish to introduce such observances into their lives today (even though they are unnecessary). You even suggest that moral teachings are also fulfilled through faith in Jesus.

Does this mean that one can be immoral and still be "saved"—in Christian terms? If you distinguish between moral and ritual teachings in the Hebrew Bible, on what basis do you do so? For example, the fourth commandment in the Decalogue dealing with the Sabbath is surely replete with moral purpose and content. I am very puzzled by this and look forward to your further clarification.

I might add in relation to this question and my earlier comments that as a believing and practicing Jew, I understand ritual commandments as well as moral commandments to have a religious, ethical purpose. As our ancient sages declare, "The commandments were given in order to ennoble people." The term the Hebrew Bible uses to describe, for example, the purpose of the dietary laws (Deut. 14:3–21) or of the Sabbath observance (Exod. 20:8) is holiness. In fact *holiness* is stated in the Bible as the purpose of all the commandments (Num. 15:40). In modern parlance one might call *holiness* "God consciousness" (more of an awareness of reality than a suprarational "faith").

A fully believing, observant Jew is conscious of the divine presence not only when praying three times a day, not only when encountering his/her neighbor—each and every one created in the divine image—but also when he or she eats and drinks, works and rests, etc.

Our sages declare (in the concluding Midrash on the Pentateuch) that if one rises in the morning and does not bless God for the sunrise or retires at night without having blessed God for sunset, one is "like a dead person." To understand this cryptic comment one needs to know that in Jewish practice one makes a blessing before partaking of any pleasure, food, or drink. Thus before eating an apple, for example, an observant Jew recites a formula as follows: "Blessed are You, Sovereign of the universe, who creates fruit of the trees." In so doing, one is raising a basic activity, eating, to a higher level of consciousness. One does not just instinctively bite in to the apple but pauses to acknowledge divine providence and to give thanks for the sustenance and pleasure one is about to enjoy. Therefore our sages are saying in that Midrash that if one's life is without awareness of the divine presence in the beauty of the creation around one, and indeed in one's neighbor and oneself, then one is not really living. One's body might be functioning, but one's soul is not really alive!

Accordingly for believing, observant Jews, the commandments are not only no chore, but a source of joy and beauty ennobling our lives; and even when Jews have experienced darkness outside around them (unfortunately more often than not in the course of history), they have known the light and beauty of the observance of Torah that has sustained us throughout the ages. As King David declares, "If it were not for the delight of Your Torah, I would have perished in my affliction" (Ps. 119:92). For faithful, observant Jews, in the very observance of the commandments not only do we find life, beauty, and joy, but we also find divine testimony, love, and salvation.

*Yours,*
*David*

# Letter 8

*Dear David,*

It is interesting to me that the more we write each other, the more I understand the nature of the particular issues we are discussing. The issues appear much the same as I outlined in my previous letter: 1) the nature of faith, 2) the nature of the Messiah, and 3) the nature of sin. The nature of faith has broadened to include the way of salvation; the nature of the Messiah now touches on the messianic consciousness of Jesus; the matter of sin comes down to whether a person is a sinner *before* he or she sins or if actual sinning is the *only* thing that makes one a sinner.

I suppose I should not be surprised that we would be on opposite sides of some of these issues so soon, and yet it is illuminating to me nonetheless that these matters have surfaced almost naturally. All this has arisen because of the original question that led to our correspondence in the first place: "What is a Pharisee?" Perhaps more issues will emerge, but your latest installment confirms these three things all the more. I don't think I was prepared for how much I would learn from our exchanges, so I am exceedingly grateful to you for helping to clarify these things by the gracious and articulate way you have written.

You began your last installment by saying there are things regarding my profession of faith you would not presume to comment on, "let alone argue." But surely, David, you must! You will recall that when the idea for our correspondence was conceived at the Mount Zion Hotel in Jerusalem, it was agreed that you would show why you should *remain* an Orthodox Jew and not be a Christian and that I should write to show why you *should* embrace Jesus as your promised Messiah. So I hope you will comment, even argue if you like, or I will think you are being convinced by me!

And yet I hope you will comment on the aspects of my profession of faith for another reason. I know, David, that you looked carefully at the verses I quoted, so please forgive me for repeating some of them. I guess I might worry that you could easily and unwittingly gloss over what is vital to me, namely, the very reason I believe you must do what most Jews in history have not done: *honestly examine* these Scriptures and consequently accept Jesus—*Yeshua*—as your own Messiah. You may think that the fulfillment of my wish to see you look at Jesus in this way is out of the question. But I lovingly plead with you nonetheless to look carefully again at the very Scriptures I put to you. It should be *easy* for you—you are the natural olive tree (Rom. 11.24)! After all, moreover, you are, it seems to me, already extraordinary and unique among Orthodox Jews and rabbis. And yet I admit that, humanly speaking, what I am really after in engaging in these dialogues with you is about as feasible as trying to touch the moon!

I can almost hear you saying that you were required to look at passages like this many times—that is, to see them the way Christians interpret them—because of your training as a rabbi. I have been deeply impressed, too, by how well you know the New Testament. But dare I ask if you have read Old Testament passages with the view that, just maybe, they have been wrongly interpreted after all by the sages of the centuries? What about those Jews who *have* received Jesus as their promised Messiah? What made them do it?

My conversation with you is not the first attempt on my part to see a Jew receive Jesus as the promised Messiah. It has been a wish of my heart for many years. You will recall my attempts with Rabbi Abraham Kellner. But he wasn't the last. Many years ago I also had a dialogue, not in writing but in face-to-face conversations, with Nathan Darsky, a Russian Jew who came to America as a young man and became the founder of Pepsi-Cola. I used to visit him at his home in Miami Beach and he always liked it when I prayed with him. He became fond of me for some reason and would come to see Louise and me at our old home in Fort Lauderdale. On one occasion I remember praying for him virtually all day, anticipating his coming to our home that evening for a meal. I had aspirations of seeing him embrace Jesus as his Messiah. I was so sure that, upon reading Isaiah 53, which I read to him with some commentary, he would immediately admit that the most rational explanation and obvious fulfillment of that chapter was the way the prophet foresaw how Israel would reject its promised Messiah (vv. 1–3) who came to this world with the very purpose to die on a cross (vv. 4–7).

But my friend Mr. Darsky dismissed this interpretation in one stroke: "This chapter is describing the suffering of my people the Jews." He then elaborated on what is absolutely true, how the Jews have suffered in ancient history and recent history (he referred to the Holocaust). I might have asked him to look at Isaiah 49:6–7—clearly promising Messiah and which could not possibly refer to the suffering people of Israel. I might have pressed him to read Isaiah 52:14: "Just as there were many who were appalled at him—his appearance was so disfigured beyond that of any man and his form marred beyond human likeness." Or I could have read and reread to him Isaiah 53:5–7, 12: "He poured out his life unto death, and was numbered with the transgressors. For he bore the sin of many, and made intercession for the transgressors," which could be referring only to a suffering individual. But I did not push him any further; I could see that all I hoped for was not about to happen. Whether anybody had put these matters to him before, or since, I do not know. Our friendship continued on after that occasion. We moved away from Fort Lauderdale and he has died since. I have witnessed to Jews, including Israelis, a number of times over the years, but only one of them—a lady from Moscow (who told me later she was Jewish)—accepted Jesus as her Messiah.

All I am asking of you, David, is to *consider* certain aspects of my theology, for example, how Isaiah saw hundreds of years in advance that Israel's promised Messiah would be called the "Mighty God, Everlasting Father" (Isa. 9:6). Is this not a promise that the coming Messiah would be *God in the flesh*? Is it not true that Isaiah also saw long before the event that the people of Israel would by and large *completely reject* their Messiah? "Who has believed our message and to whom has the arm of the Lord been revealed?" (Isa. 53:1). Isaiah foresaw that the very One Israel had prayed for would indeed show up—but be completely underestimated and, sadly, missed entirely by most Jews. This is because, far from being charismatic and obvious, Messiah would be like a "root out of dry ground," a lackluster figure without apparent attractiveness (Isa. 53:1–3). On top of that, He would be perceived by Jews as being severely but rightly judged by God (vv. 4–5) *and* that He would die as a substitutionary atoning sacrifice for our sins: "The LORD has laid on him the iniquity of us all" (v. 6). I will stop at that verse for now, only to point out that the Jews who *did* believe in Jesus as their Messiah two thousand years ago—and since—have found incalculable comfort and hope from Isaiah 53.

I was relieved to hear you say that a Jew is not saved because of ethnicity. I interpret you as saying also that a Jew could lose his or her soul in hell after one dies, even if that person has to be pretty awful to merit that state. But at the same time I am still amazed to think that anybody could be saved by keeping the works of the Law! If one were judged by good intentions, yes, there is hope for some of us. But if we are to be judged by whether we come up to the high standard required, namely, the fulfillment of 613 pieces of Mosaic legislation, I for one would not have a chance. You say that it is harder for a Jew since he has to answer to Sinai. Are you really saying it is easier for a Gentile because he will not be judged by the Law but rather by the covenant with Noah? I gather then you would say that I am exempt from the Law but not from the Noahide Covenant?

It is my opinion that when Jesus promised personally to fulfill the Law in Matthew 5:17, meaning not merely the Ten Commandments but—when you add them up in Exodus, Leviticus, Numbers, and Deuteronomy come not only to 613 but over two thousand pieces of Mosaic legislation—it was the most stupendous statement He made: "I have not come to abolish them [the Law or the Prophets] but to fulfill them." Nobody had done that, truly fulfilling the Mosaic Law in every jot and tittle. Nobody. Even James, who was a great defender of the Law in the earliest church, finally agreed with Peter that even their Jewish ancestors were not able to bear the yoke of the Law (Acts 15:10–21). But when Jesus said, "I will fulfill the Law," it was a major statement fairly early on in His ministry. So when He uttered the words on the cross "It is finished" (Greek *Tetelestai*—John 19:30), He was stating He had accomplished what He promised to do—fulfill the Law—because *tetelestai* was a word also understood as "paid in full."

This brings us back to the nature of faith. You are right, David, in saying we regard faith in itself as being of "redeeming value"—with one proviso: that the object of that faith is in Jesus, whose substitutionary death atoned for our sins. We believe that Jesus was our *substitute*. He not only took our place by bearing the wrath of God we deserve (Matt. 27:46; 2 Cor. 5:21) but was also our substitute in having performed the righteous deeds of the Law *on our behalf* (1 Cor. 1:30). Therefore faith justifies when I *rely* on Jesus as a person and as my Redeemer.

You asked whether a person could be immoral and still be saved. One of my predecessors at Westminster Chapel in London, Dr. Martyn Lloyd-Jones, used to say that if a person, having heard the gospel, *does not ask that question*, it probably means he hasn't yet heard the gospel! Dr. Lloyd-Jones went so far as to say if our gospel does not suggest the possibility of antinomianism (lit. "without law") we probably have not preached the gospel. But at the same time he added that if one thinks that a Christian *can* be immoral, he still has not understood the gospel! The gospel inevitably engenders good works. The Christian is unequivocally called to be holy (1 Thess. 4:3). "For we are God's workmanship, created in Christ Jesus to do good works, which God prepared in advance for us to do" (Eph. 2:10). But those works are not what saves us; it is faith alone in *Yeshua* alone that saves anybody. Good works flow from the *gratitude* we owe to God for giving us a Messiah who fulfilled the Law by paying our debt to it.

I mentioned James. In his short epistle, James came out so strongly for *works* that Martin Luther regarded James's letter as "an epistle of straw." But that was not Luther's only mistake! All Christians deeply regret statements this man made about Jews. All we can do is hang our heads in shame. As for James, he was not stating how to be saved or even how to know one is saved but what kind of faith will make an impact on the "poor man" (Greek *Protochon*—accusative masculine singular) in James 2:6. So when James said in 2:14, "Can such faith save *him* (accus.masc.sing.)?" he was still referring to the same poor man who would be singularly unimpressed with a faith that did not validate itself by works. My point David is this: Judaism is strong on works, but so were followers of *Yeshua* in the earliest church. We agree on the importance of works; the issue is whether works in themselves justify, redeem, or save; or if they validate or vindicate the premise that faith is truly present. It is the latter I am wanting to stress to you.

In the same paragraph in which you discussed your understanding of the word *saved* you state that all people are born "intrinsically good." David, are you saying that it is therefore theoretically possible for a person never to die? Then why *do* people die? Is it not because they sinned? Death would not have come into the world had Adam not sinned. But you are claiming that Cain and Abel were born intrinsically good. And yet it didn't take long before Cain's jealousy took over, did it (Gen. 4:5)? Where did this anger and jealousy come from? Surely it sprang from the fallen nature he inherited from his parents.

So I am curious to know, since you aver that people today are born as Adam and Eve were created *before* the Fall, why is it always the case—no exceptions—that people sin and die? Surely, David, if you are correct, somebody one day, among billions of people that have been born, would by now have proved your thesis that people are born intrinsically good. But all end up sinning, and all die. The one exception: *Yeshua* who died—because the Lord laid on Him all our iniquity—but was later raised to life for our justification (Rom. 4:25).

This is why the New Testament points to what came to be known as the doctrine of original sin, which you say you do not accept. You will know that Augustine put the position like this:

> *Posse pecare* (able to sin)—that is, Adam and Eve before the Fall
> *Non posse non pecare* (not able not to sin)—that is, people after the Fall

*Posse non pecare* (able not to sin)—that is, those who have
   faith in Christ

*Non posse pecare* (not able to sin)—that is, once we are in
   heaven

Even if you lay aside Augustine and the New Testament,
I would have thought that empirical evidence for people's
predictability—they *always* sin sooner or later—suggests
they must have been born with the propensity to sin. Where
did this proclivity come from? I therefore suggest that we
must go beyond the occasion they actually sin, when you say
(if I understand you correctly) they qualify to be "sinners." I
would have thought the most reasonable explanation for sin
in the world is what began in the Garden of Eden and then
handed down to their offspring. Cain is surely Exhibit A.

To put it another way, I would love to know if the sages
taught that Jesus departed from traditional Judaism when
He defined sin as being in one's thoughts. As you know (I
mentioned it in a previous letter), Jesus taught that lusting is
tantamount to committing adultery, hate is the equivalent to
committing murder (Matt. 5:21–30). This is why Christians
claim that all people are sinners and cannot keep the Law. If
keeping the Law were merely *external*, one could say it is
fairly possible to keep the first nine of the Ten Commandments. Saul of Tarsus felt comfortable in saying as much but
admitted that, when he was gripped by the tenth commandment ("Thou shalt not covet"), he was a goner (Rom.
7:9–11). The teaching, therefore, that we are sinners because of the fallen nature we were born with came from
Jesus before Paul taught it. So where did Jesus go wrong?

I note that you believe Jesus was sincere but misguided.

Your thoughts seem to parallel those of Albert Schweitzer. Schweitzer claimed that Jesus hoped until near the end of Matthew 11 that He would lead the nation from bondage to Rome but then gave up that goal and became willing to die. You even suggest that Jesus might have conceived Himself as the Messiah. But you do not think "for one minute" that Jesus saw Himself "in terms of the theological construct that Christianity affirms."

I suppose by that you mean Jesus did not consciously believe He was the Son of God or that He believed He was *born to die* on a cross; that it was what the writers of the Gospels conceived. I suspect this is why a late date for the Gospels is important to your own interpretation—it gives more time for the earliest stories to be embellished. I reply: nobody in the earliest church was clever enough to invent the resurrection of Jesus. Never—ever—would fishermen from Galilee have come up with the idea that Jesus died on the cross for our sins, that He was raised from the dead and ascended to heaven. It would have taken a thousand geniuses to create that idea!

The truth is, David, that the Twelve, or I should say, eleven, disciples to whom the resurrected Jesus appeared did not have a clue why He died or why He was raised from the dead until the Holy Spirit fell on them on the day of Pentecost. It was the Holy Spirit who enabled them to see for the first time what Jesus' coming was all about.

I remember Rabbi Kellner's sole reason for not accepting Jesus as the promised Messiah: "We still have wars, Messiah would bring peace." You are saying much the same thing when you state that the Messiah the Jews eagerly awaited was a Messiah who would deliver them from Roman subjugation. But I would gently ask you to consider that, all along, God had something different in mind for Israel at that time. When Isaiah was given privy to this divine information, he wrote those words as if he trembled; he knew that his people would not be very happy about the kind of Messiah that he was going to describe.

Finally, you suggest I might be distinguishing between moral and ritual teachings because I said that messianic believers' holding to some Jewish rituals was good but not required. My answer: first, the morality that was required for the ancient people of God is eternal and unchanging. It is at this point, David, you and I agree with each other wholeheartedly. The righteousness required by the Ten Commandments was regarded by the New Testament as the *minimum* standard of conduct for the believer in Jesus. But Jesus taught a righteousness of the *heart* that meant total forgiveness, no bitterness or hate, praying for enemies, and doing righteous deeds without drawing attention to them. It is still an extension of the same Law of Sinai you uphold, only that it goes beyond it, according to Jesus. This is why Jesus said that the kingdom of heaven required a righteousness that "surpasses" that of the Pharisees (Matt. 5:20). It was a righteousness that outclassed the letter of the Law.

Second, as for rituals, we believe that the Lord's Supper (sometimes called *Eucharist*—"giving of thanks") is a fulfillment of Passover. It is also an important means of ensuring and promoting holiness (1 Cor. 11:27–32), thus the moral and ritual teachings come together in this particular ritual. This also means we keep Passover when we observe the Lord's Supper.

As for the Sabbath, the issue is admittedly complicated. I blush to admit that we are generally divided on what is so clear to you. My relationship with you was born in the Shabbat meal you provided for us. The occasion was so moving it was almost enough to make me want to become an Orthodox Jew!

Some Christians have held that the Sabbath is still the seventh day (beginning at sundown Friday). But most Christians slowly dropped the seventh day for the first day, very possibly because of anti-Semitic persecution but also to commemorate the resurrection of Jesus. But whether it was to be kept legalistically has been variously interpreted by the best of our theologians. I would understand if you think we are vulnerable here. For my own peace of mind I am satisfied with the words of Paul: "One man considers one day more sacred than another; another man considers every day alike. Each one should be fully convinced in his own mind" (Rom. 14:5).

There is a reason, however, that Paul could say this. The fourth commandment is the *only* one of the Ten Commandments that is not quoted in the New Testament. This is because, as you say of the fourth commandment, which is replete with moral purpose and content, the Sabbath is ultimately fulfilled in the Sabbath-rest of the *heart* that the Holy Spirit gives the people of God (Heb. 4:1–10). It is fulfilled not by what one does or does not do on a particular day of the week but by the soul resting in God. It promotes the very holiness Jesus envisaged when He talked about the standard required for the kingdom of heaven. But I admit to you I would not go to the stake for what I believe about the Sabbath.

*Yours,*

R. T.

# Letter 9

*Dear R. T.,*

When I declare my reluctance to challenge you regarding your profession of faith, I am reflecting our fundamentally different attitudes toward one another. You see me as condemned because I do not share your faith, whereas I do not see you as condemned because you do not share mine. I believe that you will go to heaven if you lead a just and righteous life as God commands, whereas you do not believe that that will save me!

This fundamental difference in my approach to you leads me to acknowledge that I can never fully understand your faith conviction because I do not share/experience it. Therefore I cannot presume to empathize enough with it to properly question it. The idea that God is somehow exclusively incarnate in one human being is totally beyond my comprehension.

The idea of the Trinity leaves me baffled. The concept of vicarious atonement defies my moral comprehension—and I could go on.

But the fact that I cannot empathize with these concepts does not lead me to presume to judge them or those who believe in them. I accept and respect the fact that you hold them sincerely, but I see no point in challenging you on them. I am content in my belief that there are different paths to God (to salvation) and ours are parallel paths united by common origins but profoundly divided by their development.

These parallel developments mean that we look back on our shared Scripture (that you call the Old Testament) and interpret it differently.

For me, it is obvious that Isaiah 53 refers to the children of Israel. Indeed God's servant is referred to in various chapters of Isaiah categorically as "my servant Jacob," "Israel." Isaiah 41:8–9 declares, "And you O Israel are my servant; Jacob whom I have chosen; the seed of Abraham who loved me. . . . You whom I have taken hold of from the ends of the earth; and I have said to you, You are my servant: I have chosen you and not spurned you." Similarly, Chapter 42:1, 6 states, "Behold my Servant Jacob whom I uphold; my elect in whom I delight. . . . I have given you as a Covenanted people, as a light unto the nations." Chapter 43:10 affirms, "You are my witnesses saith the Lord and my Servant whom I have chosen"; and similarly, Chapter 44:1, 2, 21, 26, and 45:4. Chapter 49:3 starts out clearly referring to the same servant: "You are my servant, Israel in whom I will be glorified."

However, a fascinating process takes place in Chapter 49, where Isaiah interchanges Israel and himself as the servant personifying the former and with the responsibility to preach for the former's sake and for the sake of all nations. Otherwise, it seems to me to be most categorically clear that the servant is the people, Israel.

The basic message of the suffering of the servant in Chapters 52–53, however, is understood by Jewish tradition to have profound theological meaning.

In brief, our understanding of what Isaiah is saying is that if one is chosen by God (whether one is worthy of such or not) to testify to the godly and the goodly in the world, then all that is hostile to the godly and the goodly will be hostile to you!

You will bear their sins, not in the sense of vicarious atonement (which contradicts Deuteronomy 24:16) but because their sinfulness will be thrust upon you—it will target you and in that sense you bear (have to bear up with) their sins!

We have also interpreted our own failures to live up to the high standard of the Sinai Covenant as part and parcel of the reason for our historic suffering; and that in keeping with Amos (3:2), being covenanted means not only the responsibility to live up to higher standards, but also to have to face more serious consequences for failure to do so. Of course we knew that no matter how serious the consequences, divine love and promise would sustain us and eventually restore us to renew independent Jewish life in our ancestral homeland in keeping with Leviticus 26:44–45. Nevertheless our own failures did not seem to be adequate enough an explanation for the enormity of Jewish suffering.

Isaiah's brilliant interpretation enabled us to see the hostility we encountered as something that had to be endured as part of being "a light unto the nations" and as part of a process that would ultimately lead to the recognition on the part of evildoers of the perversion of their ways and inspire them and all humanity to walk along "the path of righteousness for His name's sake."

Accordingly Isaiah would not have been surprised by the fact that the might of the Nazi regime was so obsessed with the extermination of a small and weak people (even at the expense of Germany's own war effort!), because the Jewish people embody (through the eternal divine covenant) everything that was the antithesis of the pagan, ungodly, power-obsessed bestiality of the Nazi regime. The latter thus found the very existence of even a "Jewish embryo" to be intolerable!

To be God's servant is, of course, not just and not even primarily about suffering. It is, however, about standing and standing up for the godly and the goodly and this is our enormous honor, but also as a result all too often our burden to bear.

Concluding my words about the identity of God's servant referred to by Isaiah, one might also note that all references to him are in the past tense (hundreds of years before the birth of Jesus). It is interesting to note on this subject the words of the famous Christian Bible scholar O. C. Whitehouse, who comments on Isaiah 52–53 (Century Bible) as follows: "Christian exegetes should recognize that the path of Jewish exposition is in the main the right one and that the path of Christian interpreters down to the time of Rosenmuller have in the main been wrong."

However, R. T., I feel that Whitehouse has no right to say this to believing Christians (obviously he is entitled to his scholarly opinion), because what matters is the meaning people give to the text. If Christians like you want to read into it things that Jews like me do not believe are in the text, they have every right to do so. The text thus acquires a different character and meaning for them and non-Christians should respect the meaning that Christians attribute to it—for them!

But to ask me to recognize a meaning that flows out of a faith that I do not have is—if you will forgive me saying so—both rather presumptuous and totally futile.

About Isaiah 9:6: this is not just a matter of seeing different meaning in the text, but also literally reading it differently. The text refers to King Hezekiah, whose birth and ultimately his reign ushered in a new era for the Jewish people. The verse should be read "And he [Hezekiah] shall be called God the Mighty is Wonderful in Counsel, the Everlasting Father, Ruler of Peace." In other words, the description refers to God, and the child Hezekiah is given this additional name to recall the divine presence and promise fulfilled in his reign. Indeed the name *Hezekiah* itself means "God is my strength" (not that Hezekiah himself is the God of strength) and is similar to the meaning of the name of our second daughter, Gabriella. Calling people by names descriptive of divine actions and qualities is a most ancient Hebrew practice.

It seems to me to be precisely because we have such different theological perspectives (and perhaps also because I may not have explained myself adequately) that you are "amazed to think that anybody could be saved by keeping the Words of the Law!"

Let me reiterate, R. T., that from my perspective there is nothing to be "saved" from except from our own failures, which we can always rectify, because God in His unlimited mercy has given us the continuous capacity to reform ourselves and return to His path, His commandments.

Indeed as God has revealed a higher and more religioethically demanding way of life to the children of Israel in the

Sinai Covenant than that of the Noahide Covenant, I am indeed saying that paradoxically it is easier for a Gentile to meet divine expectations. Again the word *saved* might be misleading—I can understand it only in the sense of avoiding sin or reforming oneself from sinful ways. In these regards it is obviously easier to avoid transgressing barely more than half a dozen commandments than a few hundred.

The word *law* is often portrayed by Christians in a negative light (following what I presume to consider to be a mistaken interpretation of Paul—at least mistaken in terms of the extent to which it is applied) as opposed to *love*. In fact I might point out in passing that the concept of love of God appears far more in the Hebrew Bible than the concept of fear of God. Because I reject the idea that there is some kind of dichotomy between love and law, I prefer to avoid the latter term and thus its pejorative use. So translating your comment, let me say yes, R. T., you are exempt from those additional commandments in the Sinai Covenant but not from those of the Noahide Covenant!

In keeping with the above, the way I understand the comment by Jesus that he had come to fulfill the Torah (which is translated as "Law" but means the whole divine revelation at Sinai) is simply that he meant that he was a true and loyal Jew and had no intention of shirking his responsibility to live a life observing (fulfilling) the commandments of the Sinai Covenant—plain and simple!

In fact I presume to state that the normative Christian understanding of Jesus' use of the word "fulfill" seems strange to me. It seems obvious to me that to fulfill means to do everything one is expected to do, not to declare it unnecessary! Forgive me my impertinence, R. T., but it seems to me that the Christian interpretation of what Jesus said actually turns his words on their head and interprets them to mean the opposite of what he had intended!

Naturally I see no connection between his final words on the cross and the above.

Your question regarding death is similarly based upon an *a priori* perception of reality that is different from mine. You assume that sin means death—but I do not. Sin is failure—a stumbling for which yes, there are consequences, but not always death! Capital punishment is prescribed only for certain dire offenses (though Rabbinic Judaism *de facto* virtually eliminated the death penalty through its demands regarding testimony for capital cases).

People die for the same reasons animals and vegetative life die: there is a biological cycle that is the natural order of the physical creation. But because humans are not only animals but are created in the divine image, there is something eternal and imperishable within us that continues after our material being decomposes.

As far as the first narrative chapters of Genesis are concerned, I tend to share Maimonides' interpretation of them as allegorical with profound moral meaning. They are not, however, describing a biological reality. Certainly they warn us against disobedience against God. However, from the beginning of human existence, we have always been physically perishable products!

I do not share your premise that it is even theoretically possible for anybody to avoid all sin, precisely because we have free choice. The fact that every human being has at some stage in his or her life stumbled and fallen over does not prove that he cannot stand securely or run effectively!

Let me reiterate: choice means by definition that sometimes we make mistakes. That is the meaning of the words
in Ecclesiastes 3:20: "For there is not a man on earth who
does only good and never sins."

In response to your question, R. T., let me state that when
Jesus taught that sin is already to be found in one's thoughts,
he was indeed articulating Pharisaic teaching, which declares
much the same. Although the courts may not hold an individual culpable for such, our rabbis say that an individual *is*
culpable for such before the heavenly court! Nevertheless
they would have been unlikely to have gone quite as far as to
say that the thought of murder and adultery is actually the
same thing as performing such terrible deeds.

Finally, I fully agree with you and Jesus that we have to go
beyond the letter of the Law (in this case I'll allow myself to
use that term)—in fact, the sages of the Mishnah and Talmud
say that categorically. The medieval rabbinic authority Nach-
manides (thirteenth century) put it eloquently when he described those who keep the letter of the Law but desecrate its
spirit as "knaves who function within the Torah's boundaries."

But going beyond the letter of the Law does not mean to
neglect the letter of the Law, let alone to desecrate it, God
forbid. It means, for example, that it is not enough to avoid
bowing down to graven images, but that you must not be
subservient to money and greed, etc. That of course doesn't
mean that if you avoid the latter, it is all right to bow down
and worship an idol!

I believe that those Pharisees whom Jesus was criticizing
were those who were obsessed with the letter at the expense of
the spirit. Pharisaic rabbis of that time, and before and after,
condemned such behavior in no less harsh language if not

more so. They too required a higher righteousness, but not one that ignored the commandments; rather, they called for a higher righteousness that gives the practice of the commandments their full meaning and purpose, i.e., fulfills them!

Another example would be our sages' strong disapproval of prayer (a ritual of importance to both our traditions) that is not motivated by true consciousness of the divine presence and appropriate intention.

In fact, Jewish mysticism devoted much attention and many methods to increasing such consciousness and attention. However, any attempts to use this as an excuse for not observing the actual rituals was overwhelmingly derided and rejected.

I believe that it is a perennial human challenge to find the balance between form and substance, between structure and content. It is never an easy task. However, to reject form or structure because one has not found/experienced the appropriate substance and content is simply to throw out the baby with the dirty bathwater.

I believe that this is precisely the message that Jesus was bringing to "the lost sheep of Israel," but it appears to me that those who took up his charge gave it a totally different meaning from that which he intended.

I have been less diplomatic than my usual self and I ask your forgiveness, R. T., if anything I have said has in any way offended you.

With love and blessings from the land and the city that is dear and holy to us both.

*Yours,*
*David*

# Letter 10

*Dear David,*

I reckon we must be getting things about right when each of us is apologizing to the other for holding to staunch views and making statements with equal vigor. You, however, are truly a gentleman and a scholar and I doubt you are capable of being undiplomatic or ungracious.

I can understand your saying that my desire for you to recognize a meaning that flows out of a faith you do not have is "both rather presumptuous and totally futile." Presumptuous? Perhaps. Futile? I don't agree. All I am doing in these letters to you is what the Hebrew Scriptures call "casting [my] bread upon the waters" (Eccl. 11:1).

You know that the essential issue between us is whether Jesus of Nazareth was and is the true Messiah that was promised to Israel. If He was not, then He was a fraud and every church spire in the world is a sepulcher to a dead God. But if in fact Jesus was raised from the dead and is truly the one and only Son of God, you have (it seems to me) lost everything and will therefore know I am going to do my best to put the case to you and do so for basically two constraining reasons: 1) it is my mandate from Jesus Himself to urge you to become His disciple (Matt. 28:19), and 2) I want with all my heart to spend eternity in heaven with you and your family.

On the first point, yes, I do have a command from Jesus. The Christian faith is essentially evangelistic. Like it or not, the very assumption that Jesus is "the way and the truth and the life" and that no one comes to the Father apart from Him (John 14:6) compels us to tell everybody the truth about Him, especially our family and friends. It is not that we think we are a cut above others; we happen to take Jesus' words seriously and are required to tell all we meet that He is the Son of God, that His death on the cross was and is God's way of salvation, and that those who do not hear and believe this message have no promise of heaven.

On the second point, knowing as you do that I believe there are a heaven and a hell—and that only those "in Christ" are assured of heaven, what kind of friend would I be to you if I did not do all within my power to convince you! I am pleased to say that all my immediate family are "born again" (to use Jesus' phrase to Nicodemus—John 3:3) and I would be thrilled to no end to see this happen to you. When you say I see you as condemned if you do not share my faith, it did give me a slightly uneasy feeling that you suggest I am pointing the finger. But then I tell myself that you have the stature and magnanimity to know not to take

it personally since Jesus Himself said: "This is the verdict:
Light [meaning Himself] has come into the world, but men
loved darkness instead of light" (John 3:19). So please understand that I do not judge you in particular, David, because it was Jesus who said that he or she who does not
believe in Him is "condemned already" (John 3:18).

Speaking of Nicodemus, a leading rabbi in his day, you
will know that he was a secret believer in Jesus. Do you
think there are any rabbis in Israel today that might be secret believers in Jesus and believe in their hearts that He was
Israel's Messiah and raised from the dead?

I personally think that, as I get to know you, you are as
good as they come. I hope you discern that I really do mean
this. But being good is not what saves us. If so, do you think
a good Muslim could be in heaven without acknowledging
the true God? As for the Christian message of grace through
faith, Emil Brunner called it the "scandal" of the gospel that
we are saved by faith alone (apart from our demonstrating
good works) in Christ alone.

I would of course be thrilled to see a leading Orthodox
Jewish rabbi come to faith in Jesus as his Messiah. But what
Christian wouldn't be thrilled? And yet I am being totally
honest and blissfully candid when I tell you that I personally
have no doubt that the day is coming that the nation of Israel (and Jews generally) as a whole will affirm that Jesus of
Nazareth was and is God's promised Messiah after all—
*before* He returns the second time. If my interpretation of
Romans 11 is correct, this is guaranteed. How and when this
will happen is to indulge in unprofitable speculation, but it
is not unreasonable to assume that it could begin in earnest
by somebody like you leading the way. I would give my very

life for this to happen. So you should know that all I say as we write to each other is undergirded by the hope that God would use a dialogue like ours to ignite the flame that will blaze around the world.

What is my realistic hope that this might happen? It is because you are not only governed by integrity—a seeker and follower of truth wherever it leads—but also because you are as devoted to Holy Scripture as I am. You prove this by the way you defend your position *vis-à-vis* my own on passages like Isaiah 9:6 and Isaiah 53. You have taught me so much, not the least of which is how classic Judaism replies to the New Testament interpretation of the Torah and messianic prophecies (or what we believe to be messianic prophecies).

I would love to know whether you yourself believe that passages like Psalm 110, Isaiah 9:6, and Isaiah 53 *are* indeed messianic but some of which are still unfulfilled. You have kindly replied regarding the way the sages have understood the latter two, but I am interested whether there are still in some sense unfulfilled prophecies that *you* hold to as you await your Messiah.

For example, you will know that Jesus asked your ancient people the Pharisees how they understood Psalm 110:1 ("The LORD says to my Lord: 'Sit at my right hand until I make your enemies a footstool for your feet'") by asking, since David himself calls Him "Lord," how then can he be His son (Mark 12:36–37; Matt. 22:44–45)? Our Gospels indicate that they could not answer Jesus. My question is, how do you think they should have answered Him? And is there to be a priest "in the order of Melchizedek" (Ps. 110:4) down the road in your view? You will almost certainly know how our New Testament treats this in Hebrews 7, so I would hope to learn your way of handling this passage.

Thank you for bringing up the subject of the Trinity. I can understand your comment that the idea that "God is somehow exclusively incarnate in one human being" as being totally beyond your comprehension. I cannot grasp this either. Who can? Your namesake King David could not fully take in the matter of God creating and loving humankind: "What is man that you are mindful of him?" (Ps. 8:4) and felt much the same as he reflected on God's care and omniscience: "Such knowledge is too wonderful for me, too lofty for me to attain" (Ps. 139:6). Our greatest hymnwriter tried to put in words:

> *Let earth and heaven combine,*
> *Angels and men agree;*
> *To praise in songs divine*
> *The Incarnate Deity.*
> *Our God contracted to a span,*
> *Incomprehensibly made man.*

—Charles Wesley (1707–1788)

If we could fully comprehend such truths they would not be regarded as mysteries; neither would any of us need faith at all.

As for the Trinity, I am not about to tell you anything you don't know already, that we Christians do not remotely believe in three gods, for God is *one* (as in the *Sh'ma*): "Hear, O Israel: The LORD our God, the LORD is one" (Deut. 6:4). God is *one*, His name is the LORD (or *Yahweh*, known to you as *HaShem*). His Son, the Messiah, is the very image and reflection of God and He touches us and speaks to us by His

Spirit—the same Spirit who participated in creation (Gen. 1:2). The word *Trinity* is not in the New Testament, as you know. Tertullian (c. 200) coined the Latin word *trinitas* and was the first of our church fathers to refer to the Father, Son, and Spirit as *personae*. And yet I must tell you that one thing we are not willing to give up is the biblical teaching that God is one—it is not negotiable. Trinity is an *a posteriori* explanation of our church fathers how best to understand that God is manifest as Father, Son, and Holy Spirit.

So if you are baffled, David, so am I. But I would prefer to use the word *amazed*. To quote Charles Wesley again,

> *Amazing love, how can it be?*
> *That Thou, my God, should die for me?*

This reminds me of the first night we met—at your memorable Shabbat meal in Jerusalem, when we spontaneously sang together,

> *Amazing grace, how sweet the sound*
> *That saved a wretch like me!*
> *I once was lost, but now am found,*
> *Was blind but now I see.*

> —John Newton (1725–1807)

You no doubt believe that the Jews (in Israel and in the *diaspora*) who have accepted Jesus as their Messiah are deceived. But would you go so far as to say they have committed intellectual suicide? Some of the greatest minds in history, beginning with Saul of Tarsus, have crossed over from works to faith and did so with transparent integrity. Were you, David, to follow men like Nicodemus (John

3:1–10) and Joseph of Arimathea (John 19:38–42), you would *not* have to surrender your intellect or that brilliant mind the Lord gave you. For one thing you would not be baffled that God said, "Let *us* make man in *our* image, in *our* likeness" (Gen. 1:26, emphasis mine). The Hebrew Scriptures often use a plural noun (like *Elohim*) for God with a singular verb (like *bara*—"created"—Gen. 1:1). So after saying "Let us [plural] make man" come the words "So God created [singular]." The blueprint for what became known as the Trinity was imbedded in the very first chapter of Genesis. A person is in harmony with trinitarian beliefs and easily supports them once he crosses over the line from salvation by works to salvation by faith.

I was wondering why our belief in vicarious atonement defies your "moral" comprehension. Where do you think we got the idea in the first place? From you! From the Torah, from the whole sacrificial system from Passover to the Day of Atonement. The blood was always required. Always. Without the shedding of blood there is no remission. "For the life of a creature is in the blood, and I have given it to you to make atonement for yourselves on the altar; it is the blood that makes atonement for one's life" (Lev. 17:11). Works don't atone. Only blood. The word "scapegoat" is even used regarding the Day of Atonement to show that sins have been transferred to a vicarious substitute (Lev. 16:8–10).

The whole of the Epistle to the Hebrews is based upon the thesis that all that happened during the era of the sacrificial system (what we see as a thirteen-hundred-year parenthesis between the Law given through Moses at Sinai and Jesus' ascension to heaven) begged—indeed, cried out—for fulfillment. Good works were then given a noble motivation; they were to be carried out in *gratitude* as opposed to their earning our way—which is very humbling. Were you, David, to make the crossover to what I believe is the ultimate fulfillment of Passover, I think you better than anyone I have met could be the number-one apologist for these things.

And if you think that the Christian faith is devoid of the place for works simply because we believe we are saved by Jesus' vicarious atonement for us, you have not been talking to the right persons. Though we are saved by grace through faith and not by works, we are nonetheless commanded to demonstrate good works (Eph. 2:8–10). I am sure you know the book of James well. You might be amused to know that one of my books—an exposition of James 1–3—is called *Justification by Works*. That we are saved by a vicarious sacrifice does not mean we are not called to moral purity and holiness of life. The opposite is true! "By their fruit you will recognize" the true from the counterfeit, said Jesus (Matt. 7:20). As for my own definition of *being saved*, rather different from yours, I believe it refers in the main to being saved from the penalty of our sins, namely, eternal judgment.

Yes, we do differ as well on the result of the fall of Adam and Eve. You say that I say sin means death; what I meant to convey is, death is the consequence of sin. So you are saying that Adam and Eve would have died even if God had not warned them in the Garden of Eden—that they would have died even had they not sinned. The Orthodox Christian understanding is that their death came about *only because* they sinned.

Moving on to messianic prophecy, thank you for giving

your interpretation of Isaiah 9:6. I agree that you have provided a plausible interpretation. All I would want to add is, should you one day affirm Jesus as the true Messiah, you would not have to make a giant leap but a mere sidestep to embrace the most natural, logical, and grammatically sound translation of the verse—which I believe of course anticipates the Incarnation: "For to us a child is born, to us a son is given, and the government will be on his shoulders. And he will be called Wonderful Counselor, Mighty God, Everlasting Father, Prince of Peace."

As for your point that Isaiah has described what already happened ("a child has been born") and therefore does not refer to the future, I had thought that this manner of speaking was done quite often in the Old Testament. For example, did not God tell Joshua that the land promised was already his (Josh. 1)? Even Rahab said to the spies, "I know that the LORD has given this land to you" (Josh. 2:9). As for the destruction of Jericho, even before it was carried out, the Lord said to Joshua, "See, I have delivered Jericho into your hands, along with its king and its fighting men" (Josh. 6:2). In much the same way, God called Gideon a "mighty warrior" when he was a nobody, if not a coward (Judg. 6:12). God sees the end from the beginning (Isa. 46:10) and I would have thought that He can speak prophetically that something has already happened when in fact it is still future.

You make a good case, David, that the suffering servant of Isaiah is Israel. But is this the entire explanation? I would welcome you to sit down with me (so to speak, since we are some six thousand miles apart) and devote a future letter to Isaiah's messianic prophecies alone. I would be interested whether your point of view (that it is always a reference to a nation and not to a single man) will bear a scholarly scrutiny. I will go there if you will. Speaking personally, I would be willing for our entire dialogue to hinge on what Isaiah envisages, especially Chapter 53. I could start this journey right now but would prefer to hear you say, "Yes, R. T., I want to examine these passages with you."

As for your interpretation of the reasons Jews are persecuted, I was very moved—and persuaded. You state that "all that is hostile to the godly and the goodly will be hostile to you!" Yes. And the people of Israel, whether in the land or in Eastern Europe, have suffered too because they are, simply, chosen by God. The hatred that some people throughout the world feel toward Jews is largely traceable, in my opinion, to the very *fact* of God's word to Moses, "I will have mercy on whom I will have mercy" (Exod. 33:19), such people being the seed of Abraham, Isaac, and Jacob.

I happened to be in England last week on the sixtieth anniversary of the Holocaust. I wanted to fly to Poland. I don't know if I have told you, but I visited Auschwitz in June 1974. I will never forget it as long as I live. The word *horrible* doesn't even come close to how awful it was. I would have liked to be there last week, if only to do my part in apologizing to the Jewish people of this world for what was done— partly in the name of so-called Christianity.

Louise and I attended the play *Fiddler on the Roof* in New York a few months ago. I wept as it ended, tears rolled down our faces as we walked out, knowing not only how much Jewish people have suffered but that the persecution goes on and on. But seeing the play did, if anything, give me a greater love for Jewish people, and also their land.

I was just a little disquieted when you wrote in your last letter that all roads lead to God, or have I wrongly paraphrased your statement "There are different paths to God [to salvation]"? I had assumed that as an Orthodox Jewish rabbi, even if you offer the Noahide Covenant as a non-Jewish way of salvation, you would at least require that all people bend the knee to *Yahweh*—the God of the Bible. When you refer to the scholar who wrote in the Century Bible that a particular Jewish explanation for Isaiah 53 is the best one, you realize, don't you, that there are those within the circumference of the Christian community who do not believe at all that Jesus is the only way? Such people have departed from the Orthodox Christian faith just as some of your people have deserted the Torah. I thought this conviction—that *Yahweh* alone is the true God and has revealed Himself infallibly in the Torah—was partly what made an Orthodox Jew an Orthodox Jew! And yet you surely would not say that Jesus is an acceptable path to God—or would you?

Or perhaps there is in you, David, a liberal spirit that allows you to be very orthodox and very liberal at the same time? If this is the case (which I suspect), it is no doubt why you would enter into dialogue with me in the first place—and I am therefore so grateful. But on the other hand, my hope in seeing you come to affirm Jesus as your Messiah is mostly grounded in our common belief—in the full inspiration of the Hebrew Scriptures. This is why I am prepared to go into detail with you on Isaiah 53.

I think I am saying that my hope in these conversations with you, as I have candidly written from the first day, is based on our high view of Scripture. I have great confidence in seeing you make the crossover if we carefully examine Scripture, but I am less hopeful if you really do believe that all paths lead to salvation. But David, I will not give up on you, even if the latter turns out to be the case. Why? First, you are a man made in the image of God and I believe you need what I have, namely, a heart-to-heart relationship with your Messiah Jesus. Secondly, you are the *natural* olive tree that I have referred to before, and it will take little effort (if I may put it like that) by the Holy Spirit to bring you to the acceptance of the Messiah that I embrace.

I pray for you daily, admire you very much, and feel I am singularly honored to have this relationship with you. I doubt this happens to many people and I only want to do my very best to fulfill Jesus' command to me.

I wish most of all that you feel love from me. If you don't, I have utterly failed and let my Lord down. It is easy for an argument or proposition to take over and camouflage the love I really do feel for you. So if I have pressed you too hard again, thank you for forgiving me again! May I end this letter with the lovely benediction that closed your last one, with love and blessings *to you and to the land and the city that is dear and holy to us both*.

Yours,
R. T.

# Letter 11

Dear R. T.,

It seems that with all our mutual respect and affection, our conversation is now getting a little polemical and that probably is inevitable.

Let me begin my response to the main thrust of your last letter by telling you a personal story.

I came to interfaith relations as a result of my religious commitment to social justice. When I was rabbi of the largest Jewish congregation in South Africa more than twenty-five years ago, I sought to do something to counteract the iniquitous governing system of racial separation known as apartheid. One of the few ways one could bring people together across racial lines without automatically antagonizing the government and getting oneself thrown into jail or out of the country was through religious meetings. So

I founded an Inter-Faith Forum—a council of Christians, Jews, and Muslims—in order to enable communities to become better acquainted with one another first of all by bringing religious leaders together.

I hawked my wares around with the same opening gambit: "You know, Reverend [Father, Imam, Sheikh, Rabbi], the things that should bring us together are more important than the things that keep us apart," and they all concurred and agreed to be part of this initiative. However, in the South African context I knew that if I did not involve the Dutch Reform Church in South Africa, the enterprise was of limited value. The ruling party at that time was the Afrikaner Nationalist Party and the Dutch Reform Church was often referred to as the "Nationalist Party at prayer"!

In the demonology of the South African Dutch Reform Church, there were two famous perceived threats: one was "the black threat" and the other was the "Catholic threat."

I learned that a dominee—a Dutch Reform minister—in downtown Cape Town was involved in dialogue with Catholics. So I thought, *Well if he talks to Catholics, maybe he'll talk to Jews as well!* I arranged to meet him and after exchanging pleasantries I repeated my opening gambit, which had worked so well until then. "You know, Dominee," I said, "the things that join us together are more important than the things that keep us apart."

To my surprise he answered me, "To tell you the truth, Rabbi, I cannot agree with you. The most important thing in my life keeps us apart. That is my belief in Jesus as my personal savior. You do not share that, Rabbi, and I have to tell you the truth: that you will go to hell because you do not share that faith! And it is my duty to try to save you from going to hell. So the only reason for me to meet with you is to save you from that fate!"

Naturally I was a bit taken aback, but I said something that I don't know if I fully believed then but do now believe very much. I said, "Well, thank you for your honesty, Dominee. I still would like you to come along to our meetings and you will have your opportunity to try and convert me. But I think it is important anyway that I learn to understand you better and that you learn to understand me better." And indeed he did come to our meetings and became less doctrinaire and I believe more understanding of others' beliefs. He also brought other Dutch Reform ministers to our gatherings.

This was an important lesson for me. Firstly, not to react negatively to missionary claims or proselytizing initiatives (as opposed to most of my co-religionists—an attitude I will try to explain below) but above all to always encourage the human encounter that can enrich and broaden one's own outlook and that of others.

I often refer to Bishop Krister Stendahl (former presiding bishop of Sweden), who articulated three ground rules for interfaith dialog: 1) always try to understand others as they understand themselves, 2) try to view other faith communities by the best that are within them (and not the worst), and 3) leave room for "holy envy." It's nice when we can say, "That's just like what we do, have, or believe," but one should not feel the need to be reticent about admiring something in another faith that does not belong to one's own tradition. There is nothing disloyal to one's own heritage in viewing something with admiration in another tradition.

Getting back to the point, however. My reaction to being seen as an object for proselytization is not typical. The overwhelming majority of Jews find this to be highly offensive. To begin with, it is seen as disrespectful to our own Jewish integrity because it implies that our Jewish heritage—the faith of the patriarchs and the prophets of the Hebrew Bible—is deficient and flawed. However, it also conjures up for the Jew the whole tragic history of the "teaching of contempt" of Christendom toward Jews and Judaism that produced a theology not only of supercessionism but also of condemnation and persecution of the Jew. It is important, R. T., that you, and all Christians who share your worldview, should know how distressing and offensive most Jews find any attempt to proselytize them.

I personally am fully aware of the fact that not only do you feel duty-bound to try to do this, but that you actually feel that it would be wrong to desist from doing so. I cannot argue with you over this. I can only try to make you aware of how painful this is to most Jews and to suggest that in the shadow of all the terrible things that have been done to the Jewish people down the course of history, ostensibly in the name of Christianity, you might actually owe it to your own faith to rehabilitate its tragically negative image in the minds and hearts of so many of the nation into which Jesus was born.

Forgive me for making the point even more brutally. It must surely be a scandal for you that the very name of Jesus, who saw himself as a loyal son of Israel, still generates such negative reactions amongst the Jewish people. This, as you have acknowledged, is the result of the tragic experience of Jews at the hands of so-called Christians throughout the centuries. However, if sincere Christians today want Jews to react to the name of Jesus with respect and admiration, then Jews need to feel that Christians respect *them* for who and what they are. The overwhelming majority of Jews will never feel that that is the case as long as they perceive that they are being told they are deficient and condemned. To me, R. T., it seems that you are caught between what you see as your evangelical duty and your responsibility to honor the very name through which you pray!

You imply that it is completely compatible to be a believer in Jesus and still remain a Jew. I would say this depends upon who and what you believe Jesus is. For those who maintain that Jesus is the Messiah, as I have indicated previously, I fail to understand this claim in the face of the unfulfilled conditions of the Messianic Age as envisioned in the writings of the Hebrew prophets. However, I would not for a minute suggest that one cannot be a Jew and hold such a belief. As I may have mentioned, there is a Hassidic sect today that believes that its rabbi, who died a few years ago, is the Messiah and will reveal himself as such when the time is ready. No one (or hardly anyone) suggests that they cannot be considered faithful Jews as a result.

Indeed, a century after Jesus' death, arguably the greatest rabbi of all, Rabbi Akiva, believed that Simon Bar Coziba (known as *Bar Cochba*—"son of a star") was the Messiah; that he would throw off the yoke of Rome (which he actually did for a few years!), ingather the exiles, establish a rule of justice and righteousness, and usher in an era of universal peace. However, Bar Cochba did not succeed in bringing about the Messianic Age that the Jews so yearned for—on the contrary. His defeat led to even more Jewish suffering as the Romans intensified their persecution, executing large numbers including the religious leaders of the Jewish people—Rabbi Akiva among them.

In all probability, Nicodemus and other Jews who believed that Jesus was the Messiah had similar expectations. When these were not realized, they either gave up on the idea or reinterpreted it as did Christianity. I, R. T., am personally more generous than you appear to expect non-Christians to be regarding their perception of Christianity. I respect Christianity's reinterpretation of the messianic idea according to its own conviction, and I myself would not claim that Jesus or his followers who reinterpreted this idea were frauds. Rather, I view them as the progenitor and adherents of a new religion that was and is something quite different from the Judaism from which it sprang.

Accordingly, if Jews believe in the fundamental Christian concepts of the incarnation, the salvific sacrifice of the crucifixion, and the Trinity—if they are truthful—they will acknowledge that these ideas are incompatible with normative Jewish teaching. If Jews believe in these concepts, they should at least honestly identify themselves as Christians.

As we have noted before, we Jews and Christians interpret our shared Bible differently. I am not concerned here with biblical criticism but with explaining how Rabbinic Judaism interprets biblical texts. From a traditional Jewish viewpoint, sacrificial rites could not atone for sins in themselves unless they reflected sincere contrition in the heart of the sinner, which would be articulated accordingly. Thus the prophet Hosea says (14:1–2), "Return, O Israel, unto the Lord your God, for you have stumbled in your transgression. Take with you *words* and return unto the Lord your God. Say unto Him, take away all iniquity and accept us graciously; so *we will render as bullocks the offerings of our lips*" (emphasis mine). Similarly the prophet Joel declares (2:13), "Rend your heart and not your garments and turn unto the Lord your God; for He is gracious and full of compassion, slow to anger and plenteous in mercy and forgives iniquity." Our ancient sages affirm that "there is no atonement without repentance" (Mishna Yoma, 8, 8), that "sincere repentance and works of lovingkindness (charity) are the real intercessors before God's throne" (TB Shabbat 32a) and that "sincere repentance is the equivalent to the rebuilding of the Temple, the restoration of the altar and the offering of *all* the sacrifices" (TB Sanhedrin, 43b, emphasis mine). In terms of Jewish understanding of the sacrificial rites in the temple, while the blood of the sacrifice did indeed represent life, it was seen precisely in a representational role symbolizing "the complete yielding up of the worshipper's life to God" (Hertz, *Pentateuch and Haftorahs*, 487, Soncino Press, 1986).

Indeed, following on from the sages' affirmation that temple offerings were only of value as an outward manifestation of an internal condition, the medieval Jewish scholars Maimonides and Don Isaac Abrabanel (the latter basing himself on an ancient Midrash [rabbinic homily] on Lev. 17:7) viewed the whole sacrificial order as only a concession to the form of worship that was common and expected at the time of the Sinai revelation. They taught that the biblical sanction of this form of religious service was precisely designed to wean the people away from the prevailing primitive methods of idolatrous worship at the time. In keeping with our sages' teaching on the power of sincere repentance and prayer, these scholars believed that after the destruction of the temple, the sacrificial rites had been replaced by a higher form of divine worship, that of prayer.

Bottom line, R. T., Rabbinic Judaism does not accept the

idea of vicarious sacrifice. We can only atone for our own sins and are responsible for our own actions.

Regarding your questions about Psalm 110, it is actually not clear to me from the passages in Matthew and Mark as to exactly what the point was that Jesus was making. Simply read, it would appear to me that he is saying that the Messiah cannot be the son of David, but must be David himself! That seems to me to be a very interesting interpretation of the text and I can quite understand how Jesus' brethren may have felt that he had made a convincing argument.

I, however, would point out that the English translation of the verse in Psalm 110 is a little misleading. The same word "Lord" appears twice for two different words in the Hebrew version. They are the Tetragrammaton—the four-lettered name of God, *YHWH* and *Adoni*—which simply means "sire"! Now it is true that this latter word can be used in the highest reference to God Himself, but it is also used all the way down the human social scale as a courteous address to a stranger. My understanding (and the traditional Jewish understanding) of the psalm is that it is portraying God's special love and "respect" for David (in whose name the psalm is written). In this light, it would be perfectly logical to understand the word *Adoni* as simply indicating this special divine regard and endearment for David.

Indeed Psalm 110 *was* given messianic allusion by some, precisely in relation to David and his lineage. Personally, though, I'm not convinced that this was its original meaning and am more inclined to accept the view that the original intent of the text was to confirm the special place of the Davidic household.

To be sure, there are psalms and many passages in Isaiah

that are of messianic portent, though I do not consider Isaiah 9:6 and Isaiah 53 to be such. I do not accept your claim that the language in the latter can be compared to the references you give from Joshua, which, in fact, are expressions of imminent anticipation of events that are then subsequently described.

As far as your desire, R. T., to enter into these texts in greater depth, I am perfectly willing to do so. However, I have my doubts as to the value of this. I think it is already pretty clear how and why we will give our different interpretations.

You are probably correct in your suggestion that my religious pluralist outlook is not typical of most Orthodox rabbis. I should point out that the word *Orthodox* was not a word that observant religious Jews chose to describe themselves. It was actually borrowed from Christianity by Reform Jews to describe those Jews who remained doggedly attached to traditional Jewish practice. A more appropriate word to describe what is called *Orthodoxy* (meaning "correct belief") is *Orthopraxis* (meaning "correct behavior"). Judaism has always been able to tolerate a variety and differences of opinion on matters of belief (although obviously within certain limits). Where it has demanded consensus has been with regards to the observance of the commandments—the practice of the Jewish way of life.

As far as my own theological outlook is concerned, of course I believe that there is only one God, Creator, and Guide of the universe. But it seems obvious to me that just as He has created us and relates to us in all our diversity, so there are diverse ways of recognizing and relating to Him. Indeed I do *not* deny the Christian's choice of Jesus as his or her path to God. In fact I believe, in keeping with many of our greatest medieval sages (notwithstanding their suffering at the hands of so-called Christians), that the mystery of the Christian faith has enabled the truths of biblical revelation to be extended to a vast portion of humanity, thereby sanctifying the name of the one God.

I do not, however, believe that any one religious tradition can encapsulate the totality of the divine. Indeed I consider such a claim to be something of an impiety. I realize, R. T., that you do not share this view and that you feel an obligation to convince me that what you believe is the exclusive truth. As I have said, I am both confident enough in my own faith and pluralist theology not to feel threatened by this. Moreover I am fortunate that I myself do not consciously bear the scars, let alone open wounds, of Jewish history (even very recent history) that make others of my co-religionists react differently.

However, I continue this dialogue with you not out of any illusion that either of us will change in our commitments (for which, as I say, I have no desire, on the contrary), but out of the conviction that the more we understand one another, the better it is for us, our communities, and our world—and the more we are likely to fulfill the will and purpose of our Father in heaven whose name we seek to hallow.

I pray that we may each be worthy of this charge and that this goal may be achieved through respect for every person and each community's integrity.

*With every good wish and blessing,*
*Yours,*
*David*

# Letter 12

Dear David,

If our dialogue has become "a little polemical," I hope this is not necessarily a bad thing. You kindly say this was probably inevitable, but I fear that I am chiefly responsible for this. But your expression did give me pause. At some point in our exchanges I think I began "playing hardball," as we say over here, rather than softball—a safer, slightly slower sport I enjoyed as a boy in Kentucky. I prefer watching hardball (baseball, the American pastime) but I always preferred playing softball. I wasn't cut out for hardball. But I do thank you that you responded exactly as you did.

However, I am now wondering, David, for my own part, if I should play softball from now on. I do not intend to hurl a fastball or a curve, and I never intend to put you on the spot. If it should seem that way I can assure you I am trying to learn from you as well to write in a manner that is consistent with the agreed purpose of our correspondence—not to mention my obedience to Jesus' command.

You write with a compassionate heart for your people and express the hope that I might be aware of how painful it is to most Jews to be the "object for proselytization." To be honest, I don't think I was aware of this at all—until your last letter. I don't think I realized how highly offensive some of us, including me, have been. Not that I myself have had this kind of interchange with Jewish people all that often. I told you earlier about my conversations with Rabbi Abraham Kellner and Nathan Darsky. As far as I can recall, only one Jewish person—a lady named Luba from Moscow—accepted Jesus (as a consequence of my street ministry), and I did not know for several years that she was in fact Jewish. You therefore lovingly challenge me "to rehabilitate" the negative image in the minds and hearts of so many Jewish people that has been put there in the name of so-called Christianity. I want to do that as best as I can.

I hope you already know this, but let me say it emphatically: I do have a warm love and respect for the Jewish people, and I am thoroughly ashamed of what has been perpetrated on them by the so-called Christian church over the centuries. How can you forgive us? Israel, both the land and God's special people, has a unique place in God's heart and also His purposes, particularly in these end times. (Yes, I really do believe we are in the end times.) And many—and rapidly increasing numbers of—believers in Jesus are experiencing a heartfelt love for Israel and the Jewish people. I sincerely apologize for having allowed my own zeal to have too much rein.

I should add that our mandate from Jesus to "go into all the world" and preach the gospel to every human being (Mark 16:15) does not imply that any one group of people is any more deficient or flawed than another, and certainly not God's historic covenant people. "The LORD looks down from heaven on the sons of men to see if there are any who understand, any who seek God. All have turned aside, they have together become corrupt; there is no one who does good, not even one," as King David said three thousand years ago (Ps. 14:2–3). Again, "No one living is righteous before you" (Ps. 143:2). And yet surely the *least* flawed or *least* deficient (using your words) *should* be Jewish people because of their heritage and "head start" in knowing God's Word and God's ways. Therefore any attempt on my part in talking to someone like you about receiving Jesus as your Messiah does not for one second imply that I see you—or any Jewish person—as particularly deficient or flawed as human beings. I just regret—and apologize—that so many of us have failed in making this clear.

On the other hand, I must say with greatest respect, I believe your *belief system* is flawed. Otherwise the people of Israel generally two thousand years ago would have embraced their Messiah. And I should add that *all* people—not just Jewish people—are offended by efforts of the church to evangelize. I did it every Saturday morning right in front of Westminster Chapel in Buckingham Gate for twenty years. I talked with thousands and thousands and gave away countless pieces of literature in possibly fifty languages. *Nobody* cheered at first when we offered him a pamphlet or asked questions about his assurance of going to heaven if he was to die that day.

By the way, thank you for making it clear that you your-self are not offended by people talking to *you* about these things. I think this is brilliant. But when I first read your last letter, having just returned from London and in a bit of jet lag, I hastily thought you were saying, "Leave us alone," in-cluding yourself. And I thought, *Oh dear, what have I done and what do I do now?* I certainly felt better when I reread your letter the next day. And I can *truly* understand if you really do hope in your heart that Christians will leave Jew-ish people alone. Such Christians are not likely to do so, even if our correspondence is read by them around the world, but I do pray that I myself will apply your timely cau-tion in a manner that will be appropriate and dignifying to the name I hold dear.

I know you absolutely did not mean for me to feel un-comfortable or feel the slightest sting when you referred to the Dutch dominee. And yet the way you quoted him could be a paraphrase or summary of what I happen to believe about the need for anyone to accept Jesus. "Comparisons are odious," as Shakespeare said, and I do not believe you were comparing me to the dominee. But as Jewish people are sensitive about Christians trying to convert them, I too am sensitive—no doubt, too sensitive—in this matter of sometimes being lumped with empty-headed Bible Belt people, a number of them being racists, who believe the Scriptures "from Genesis in the front to maps in back," as some put it. Although never judged like this by you, David, I am at times in the awkward position of being lambasted and compared to fundamentalist Muslims and even ultra-Orthodox Jews. Some go as far as to say the root cause of evil in the world is religious people like this.

I am a strong evangelical. I do indeed believe that all people, whoever they are, need to be saved. I am fully convinced of the infallibility of the Scriptures and of my Reformed theology. But I *too* believe in social justice. And I have always sought friends and fellowship in and outside the Christian church with those who have different theological and political views from my own. Moreover, I led our church in Fort Lauderdale to have combined worship with a black church nearby—and that was in the 1960s.

As for South Africa, you would be delighted to know that my teaching on James 2:14 (the need for faith to be accompanied by works if that faith is to make an impact) had such an effect on Dr. Michael Eaton, who was pastor of a church on the edge of Soweto, that he opened his church to black people and claims that my ministry changed his life and direction from then on. I might add that my wife, Louise, began praying daily for Nelson Mandela during the last twelve years he was in prison. And she has continued praying for him every day since.

You and I really do have a lot in common. As you are not a typical Orthodox Jewish rabbi—and probably get not a little criticism from your fellow rabbis—so I know what it is to be isolated and warned against by Reformed ministers. But if I have tried a little bit too hard in our mutual exchanges, I ask for your forgiveness. My theology teaches that only God can save and that every person receiving Jesus is the result of the sovereign work of the Holy Spirit, but sometimes I still move ahead of the Lord and foolishly try to do His work for Him! Let me say again: know assuredly, David, that I see nothing flawed or deficient in you as a person. I have no doubt that you are as good as they come. But at the same time I believe that all men and women on the planet need the Savior who gave His life for the world two thousand years ago—then rose from the dead.

You will almost certainly know that the resurrection of Jesus from the dead is the linchpin of all I believe. He really did rise from the dead! Furthermore, His death vindicated all He *said*, all He *claimed* for Himself, and all He *did* when He died vicariously for our sins on the cross. He was the fulfillment of all that sacrificial system pointed to. Is it not interesting also that His death coincided perfectly with Passover? Had Jesus not been raised from the dead, all I believe is worthless. But since He did indeed come forth from the tomb on that first day of the week two thousand years ago, I must take seriously all that is said about Him in the New Testament—including His final words to His disciples before He ascended to heaven, namely, to make disciples of everybody we meet!

I still say that it is indeed completely compatible for you to be a believer in Jesus and remain a Jew. I have to add, a very good Jew indeed. I have no doubt whatever that you could do this without violating what is written in the Law, the prophets, and the writings. I detect a difference, however, between what was *written* in the Torah and what you believe was the *sitz im leben* ("life situation") at the time of Sinai that gave us the Torah. You did not comment on whether accepting Jesus would be committing intellectual suicide for you. But if you are convinced indeed that the sacrificial system was a big mistake, then yes, you would commit intellectual suicide by embracing vicarious atonement. But if you defended what is *written* in the Torah, you could accept Jesus with utter integrity and become one of the greatest apologists for the faith of Jesus in two thousand years. Would I be wrong, David, in surmising that embracing the Torah as it is *written* would be almost as great a leap for you as accepting Jesus Himself?

But what discourages me most, therefore, is not merely that you apparently do not believe in the concept of vicarious sacrifice; it is that you imply that the whole sacrificial system was ill-posed by Moses from the beginning. It was, you say, "a concession to the form of worship that was common and expected at the time of the Sinai revelation." This may be your conclusion but, in my opinion, it is the conclusion also of medieval Jewish scholars (whom you quote) who in my opinion lost heart about what Judaism once took for granted. I take the view that a disillusionment with the sacrificial system began to set in shortly after Jesus died, and most certainly after the temple was destroyed some forty years later.

As for Maimonides, did he not disagree with Rabbi Rashi in the eleventh century over the latter's departing from normative rabbinic thinking? Was not Rashi's interpretation of Isaiah 53 regarded as novel in 1050 when he claimed that the prophet was referring to the suffering of the nation of Israel because of the Gentiles? Is it not true that for centuries rabbis, virtually without exception, had seen Isaiah 53 as describing *not* the suffering of Israel but Messiah Himself? Rabbi Jonathan ben Izziel's Targum (first century) of Isaiah 52:13 ("My servant will act wisely; he will be raised and lifted up and highly exalted") implied this when he wrote "My Servant Messiah shall prosper."

I admit to skating on thin ice when I quote authorities like these men to *you*, David! It would be like you correcting my theological understanding by quoting John Calvin! But did not Maimonides write that *since the temple no longer exists*, and there is therefore no atonement altar, nothing is left but repentance; hence "repentance atones for all transgression"? In other words, since there is no altar or Most Holy Place, repentance alone would have to suffice.

I thought that the ancient prophets called on Israel to repent *and* offer the sacrifices from a true heart—not to repent *instead* of offering the sacrifices. But because of statements in Hosea 6:6 ["For I desire mercy, not sacrifice"], a verse Jesus was fond of quoting (Matt. 9:13, 12:7), were there not developing ideas which had been around since the Babylonian exile and the development of the synagogue and the home as an alternative to temple worship? It seems to me that this development ultimately came into its own once the medieval rabbis diverted from the way earlier rabbis had viewed Isaiah 53.

As for the prophets calling for observance of the sacrifices *with* a true heart, this is exactly what Paul meant in Romans 1:17 by the righteousness (or justice) of God being revealed "from faith to faith" (KJV). Had Paul not put it that way, one could infer that Karl Barth was right when he claimed that Jesus not only died for everybody without exception but even believed for us; that all were saved by the death and faith of Jesus whether they believed it (or even knew about it) or not. But faith being *joined* by faith meant that the faith of *Jesus*, which was saving, had to be *ratified* by *our* own faith in order for the atonement of the cross to be made effectual. I am trying to show, David, that vicarious atonement as taught in the New Testament is *not* effectual without our faith and repentance.

In my personal devotional reading this very morning, I read where Jesus told the Pharisees of His day, "You have let go of the commands of God and are holding on to the traditions of men" (Mark 7:8). (The issue at that moment was not the sacrificial system but the fifth commandment.) When you said that the "bottom line" is that Rabbinic Judaism does not believe in vicarious atonement, I was wondering, for whom are you speaking? All rabbis? All Orthodox rabbis today? All rabbis for the last two thousand years? Surely not the rabbis in the era that preceded the time of Jesus, or have I missed it here?

In other words, are you saying that Rabbinic Judaism has by universal consensus *changed* from what it used to be? Is this kind of reinterpretation of the Torah—or adding to it— not the very thing Jesus was concerned about with the Pharisees of His day? If so, is this an inherent characteristic or tenet of Pharisees to reinterpret as they go along? Is not the Law unchanging?

I take it that you don't like it very much when Jews who do accept Jesus refer to themselves as "messianic believers" rather than Christians. You want them to call themselves Christians—full stop. Surely the Jewish people who embrace Jesus are wanting to demonstrate that their belief is most certainly not a "new religion . . . quite different from the Judaism from which it sprang" but the fulfillment and ultimate reason for the Torah in the first place.

I agree with you that people like Nicodemus and other Jews who believed that Jesus was the Messiah had expectations of Rome being overthrown and the former glory of Israel being restored—not only Nicodemus but every single one of Jesus' disciples. Even *after* Jesus' death and *after* His resurrection (but before the Ascension), the disciples who were closest to Him still anticipated the very kind of Messianic Age you and most Jews still look for if the true Messiah does appear. Having asked Jesus, "Are you at this time going to restore the kingdom to Israel?" He replied, "It is not for you to know the times or dates the Father has set by his own authority" (Acts 1:6–7). He then promised the power that would come on them (which did indeed happen on the day of Pentecost). It was no doubt a major shift and radical adjustment as to what Messiah would be like and do that Jews then and now have to make when they accept Jesus as their Messiah. On this point we agree.

By the way, may I ask what kind of Messiah you really do envisage? Do you think he is going to appear soon? How would you and all the Jewish people recognize him?

Thank you for giving me your view of Psalm 110:1. That is very interesting. If I may give my opinion on the point Jesus was making regarding Psalm 110, I take the view that He was showing that immediately after Messiah's ascension into Heaven, when Jesus would take His place at the right hand of God, *Yahweh* (God the Father) would say to *Adonai* (the Son), "Sit at my right hand until I make your enemies a footstool for your feet." I would be delighted to elaborate on this if you like, but perhaps you feel this would have the equivalent value you envisage if we more fully explored Isaiah 53. I will not push either Isaiah or Psalm 110 on you. But even if you differ from the way Jesus interpreted Psalm 110:1, and although you vehemently disagree with it, will you not concede that Matthew's *redaction* was designed to prove that Jesus the Messiah was also the Son of God (Matt. 22:41–46)?

When I was at seminary over thirty years ago, I was introduced to the thinking of men like Rudolf Otto (*The Idea of the Holy*) and Adolf Harnack, who also saw a common denominator that was valid and authentic if not unifying in all the religions of the world. I suspect most of the students at the time (so it seemed) embraced this type of thinking with both arms. But I did not, for some reason. Had I done so, you and I, David, would not be having this challenging dialogue. Most of them became either universalists, annihilationists, existentialists, or all the above. Some of them left the ministry they had come to train for since they came to regard the Bible as a faulty and unreliable document and saw no reason to uphold the faith they once thought they believed. I was exposed to the same evidence they had examined, I read the same books they read and explored the same higher criticism of the biblical documents that so many of my friends took on board. I cannot tell you why I did not develop as they did. But here I am, now in my seventieth year, and I can look back with incalculable gratitude to God for preserving me from the heterodoxy that enthralled these old friends of mine.

I close by asking you once again: please forgive me for my zeal. Thank you, David, for teaching me so much, especially showing me that I must maintain a more tender spirit and empathetic understanding toward Jewish people and helping me to grasp your pain and theirs when people like me push the boat out too far.

*With warmest appreciation and respect,*
*Yours,*
*R. T.*

# Letter 13

*Dear R. T.,*

As you know, in the past a polemical debate had more negative connotations than it necessarily has today. Nevertheless I still feel that there is something futile in it—a kind of "he said/she said" quality. Indeed I myself relate to these kinds of discussions with a degree of what one might call tolerant resignation. But as I sought to make clear in my last letter, as far as the overwhelming majority of the Jewish people is concerned, the attitude of "Leave us alone" and "Get off my back" precisely reflects their feelings and attitudes towards missionary activity. With all the genuine love in the world, a proselytizing approach on the part of Christians will always mean tensions with the Jewish community and will never result in any kind of collective mutual respect.

Our personal relationship, R. T., is very much an exception to the rule and I reiterate that while I personally respect your beliefs, as opposed to you I am a pluralist (although not a relativist) and do not believe that there is one exclusive path to God (and again reiterate that I find that idea something of an impiety—implying in fact a "limitation" of the limitless reality of God's "character" and presence).

You question whether my comments about Jewish teaching really reflect the opinions of Orthodox rabbis today as well as those thousands of years ago and also whether or not the Law is unchanging. These questions make me realize that I need to provide a little more explanation of Judaism's understanding of the process of divine revelation.

If I'm not mistaken, I mentioned in an earlier letter that traditional Judaism teaches that not only were the five books of Moses revealed at Sinai (and not just the Ten Commandments) but also an Oral Tradition (the Oral Torah) that explained and elaborated upon the rather terse shorthand of the Written Torah. However, Judaism teaches that the revelation of God's Word does not end there. The very process of applying these teachings and principles to new situations and changing conditions is seen as the working of the Holy Spirit. Thus the ongoing work of rabbinic scholarship that continues today in providing response to contemporary questions and challenges is seen as part of this corpus itself.

This process is impacted upon by what may be called *revelation through history*. An example of this is the institution of slavery, which the Torah allows for but which became defunct both as a result of social conditions but above all through the growing awareness on the part of the rabbis of the undesirability of the institution (in light of key biblical values, e.g., the inalienable dignity of every human person) and their reading of this attitude in the text itself (although it is by no means explicit).

However, this process leads to differences of opinion. Indeed the Talmud is replete with disagreements between rabbis on matters of interpretation and decisions. The general resolution of these differences is through the process of scholars trying to convince one another on the basis of sacred text and tradition, eventually reaching a democratic majority opinion. Another factor, generally (but not always) determined by the former, is the position that the community of the faithful follows and which thus become normative practice.

Thus this democratic decision-making process among rabbinic scholars and the interaction with the community is itself also seen as the working of the holy spirit in the life of the covenanted community of Israel.

Most principles and teachings based on the sources are of course unanimously accepted. One of these is the principle that there is no atonement without *teshuvah* (repentance). On this all the rabbis are unanimous. Thus according to all rabbinic opinion, an atoning sacrifice that an individual offered in the temple was only of value as an external manifestation of an internal condition.

However, you are indeed correct in implying that the question of the restitution of the sacrificial order is a matter of debate among rabbis and scholars, with many of them believing, as you indicate, that when the temple is rebuilt there will be a need for both. (This is probably the view of most Orthodox Jews today. However, they still do not see the temple offerings as vicarious atonement, but simply as additional acts of devotion.)

You are correct that in quoting Maimonides and Abrabanel, I was selecting the opinions which I share (though please note that I also quoted Midrashic, Mishnaic, and prophetic sources in support as well).

Actually, your reference to Maimonides is interesting. In his Code (Yad HaChazakah) he refers extensively to the sacrificial order, but in his philosophical work *The Guide for the Perplexed*, he portrays it as a transitory step. This, however, is no contradiction, as in the Code, he summarizes all matters of Jewish practice including the order of service in the temple; whereas in his *Guide for the Perplexed*, he offered his own opinions.

You misunderstand me when you state that I imply that the sacrificial system was a mistake and certainly none of the rabbis I quote would have suggested that. Rather the idea is that it was appropriate for the time but not an ideal for the future. There are many aspects of legislation in the Torah that take into account human needs and failures (I mentioned slavery; divorce would be another example).

To take the Torah literally is indeed incompatible with normative Judaism. This was largely the orientation of the Sadducees and especially of the Karaites, who as a result cut themselves off from the Jewish mainstream. Judaism requires us to understand the written text through the prism of the Oral Tradition and exposition. Thus, for example, Judaism does not understand "an eye for an eye and a tooth for a tooth," etc. (Exod. 21:24) in a literal sense but to mean the affirmation of a principle of fair and commensurate compensation. Or another example is the prohibition against going out of one's place on the Sabbath (Exod. 16:29). Judaism does not understand this literally, but rather to mean that one should not travel away from one's home and community, etc.

So yes, you could say that I consider taking the Torah totally literally as incompatible with Judaism, as the theological postulates of Christianity are incompatible with Judaism. Your term "intellectual suicide" sounds strange to me. I would simply say that one cannot in integrity claim to be a religious Jew and a believing Christian at the same time.

Returning again to Isaiah 52–53, I do not deny that there are those Jewish scholars who saw and may even see the text as messianic. I personally, however, concur with the majority of rabbinic opinion, which does not see it as such. Of course seeing biblical texts as containing messianic allusions is for us quite unrelated to the claims of Christians that Jesus of Nazareth is the person being alluded to. As I believe I have also stated in the past, what is important for Judaism is what happens in the Messianic Age far more than the identity of the messianic personality. Indeed some of the prophets talk only of the Messianic Age and not at all of a messianic personality.

However, the predominant view is that when the Almighty ushers in the era of full redemption for Israel and universal peace for humankind, He will provide a wise leader from the royal house of David who will serve as a political and spiritual guide for the Jewish people and all humanity. For this, Orthodox Jews pray daily and the concluding statement of Maimonides's Thirteen Principles of Faith in most Jewish prayer books at the conclusion of the morning service declares, "I believe with perfect faith in the coming of the Messiah and even though he may tarry nevertheless I shall await his coming every day."

I have a sense, R. T., that the essence of our debate and discussion has now been substantially covered, although we could go on indefinitely on almost every point. I want therefore to conclude with some comments on how I would like us to view one another and how I believe Christianity might best be viewed from a religious Jewish perspective.

As I have indicated previously, for the majority of history most Jews have viewed Christianity and the church's behavior in a very negative light as a result of the disparaging and violent attitude that the Jewish community experienced in the name of Christianity and by people who called themselves Christians.

Nevertheless, there have been those who have been able to view Christianity as containing the moral values of biblical revelation and bringing these to humanity (e.g., Yehudah Halevi and Maimonides). Rabbi Menachem HaMeiri of Perpignan described Christians (and Muslims) as peoples bound by the ways of true religion—i.e., people who seek to live a religious, moral life. Scholars like Rabbi Moses Rivkes in the seventeenth century affirmed the unique relationship between Christianity and Judaism, long before modern Jewish philosophers like Franz Rosenzweig and Martin Buber. The latter's comment that "we share a book and a hope" were more than anticipated by Rivkes when he declared that Jews and Christians are bound together by the Hebrew Bible and its message of salvation, revelation, and full messianic expectation. But arguably the boldest of all these premodern, Orthodox rabbinic theologians was the great Rabbi Jacob Emden at the turn of the eighteenth century, who described Christianity with the Mishnaic designation as a "*knessiyah leshem shamayim shesofa lehitkayam*," i.e., "a gathering for the sake of heaven, of lasting validity." (Actually the Hebrew word *knessiyah* is a translation for "church"—so in fact Emden is referring to Christianity as a church for the sake of heaven that is part of divine purpose for humanity at large!)

These Jewish viewpoints see Christianity as the vehicle which through the person of Jesus of Nazareth brings God's revelation, revealed to the Jewish people through the Torah, in a more universal way to the world at large.

As a result we might be able to see ourselves as two parts of one message, each with its own integrity. One might speak of Judaism and Christianity as two different models. The one already defined community of the children of Abraham, Isaac, and Jacob infused with the divine presence in its life and history and called to live accordingly as a light unto the nations; and the other a model by which every individual outside the former community can encounter the truths and beauty within the Sinaitic revelation. Each has its own validity, power, and even complementarity for the other.

The far-reaching changes in Jewish-Christian relations during the last fifty years have led to new theological reflections in this regard. Such efforts at understanding our complementarity have included seeing Judaism and Christianity in a parallel role in which the Jewish focus on the communal covenant with God and the Christian focus on the individual relationship with God may serve to balance one another. Others have seen the complementary relationship in that Christians need the Jewish reminder that the kingdom of heaven has not yet fully arrived, while Jews need the Christian awareness that in some ways that kingdom has already rooted itself in the here and now. Another view of the mutual complementarity portrays Judaism as a constant admonition to Christianity regarding the dangers of triumphalism, while Christianity's universalistic character may serve an essential role for Judaism in warning against degeneration into insular isolationism.

As opposed to the underlying assumptions of the latter, there is a contention that it is actually Christianity's universalism that jars with a culturally pluralistic reality in the modern world. The communal autonomy that Judaism affirms, it is suggested, may serve more appropriately as a model for a multicultural society, while Christianity may provide a better response for individual alienation in the modern world.

These perspectives open up new ways in which Jews and Christians might be able to illumine one another while maintaining their own integrity and respect for one another.

In conclusion, I would like to reiterate the importance and great potential of shared text study (which of course in Judaism, is a sacred endeavor—even more than prayer!). While our respective different exegeses contain theological positions that are irreconcilable and make us the different faith traditions that we are, precisely because they are based upon the shared text of the Hebrew Bible, we are able, if we choose, not only to enjoy the illumination of the other's tradition, but also to plumb the unlimited richness of the Hebrew Scriptures themselves, out of a shared religious commitment to them.

In this regard let me quote in full the statement of Martin Buber to which I referred earlier in passing:

> We have in common a book and an expectation. To you the book is a forecourt; to us it is the sanctuary. But in

this place we can dwell together and together listen to the voice that speaks here. That means that together we can strive to evoke the buried speech of that voice; together we can redeem the imprisoned living word.

I pray, R. T., that we may be worthy of this challenge and that it might be possible for our communities to work together in genuine mutual respect to bring about that day when "the earth will be full of the Knowledge of the Lord as the waters that cover the seas" (Isa. 11:9).

With thanks for the Almighty's unlimited love for us all and profound appreciation for your friendship.

*Yours,*
*David*

# Letter 14

*Dear David,*

In June 2002 I addressed a group of British Christians at the Dormitian Abbey in Jerusalem, which, as you know, is located on Mount Zion. Some 250 of us were there on a Pray for the Peace of Israel Tour. A number of people from the area, including some Jewish people, had come to the Abbey for the occasion—not to hear me but to listen to London's All Souls Orchestra and Choir led by Neil Tredinik. I was asked to address the people for twenty minutes toward the end of the concert.

I stated that in my opinion permanent peace will not ultimately come to Israel until the Jewish people acknowledge Jesus as their own Messiah. I predicted that lasting peace will be delayed until this happens. This is not to say we should not try every avenue available in the meantime—as you yourself have been doing for years, not to mention Canon Andrew White who has labored tirelessly and courageously, and I myself in a small way have sought to do—to achieve peace in Israel. But because 1) the land of Israel is different from any other on the planet, and 2) the people who reside there happen to be God's covenant people, the normal way of making peace in the world that may have worked with other nations will not work in Israel.

The God of Israel is the God of the universe and He directs the affairs of humankind. The nations to him are like "a drop in a bucket; they are regarded as dust on the scales; he weighs the islands as though they were fine dust" (Isa. 40:15), and "Unless the LORD builds the house, its builders labor in vain. Unless the LORD watches over the city, the watchmen stand guard in vain" (Ps. 127:1). The issue, as I see it, is not political but theological.

In my talk I also asked the question: "What if you had five minutes to address the people of Israel—what would you say?" I have thought a good deal about this, especially since meeting you, asking myself what I myself might choose to say if I had the opportunity to speak to every Jewish person, one at a time, or to address the whole nation at once. Having to make every second count, what would I say?

Having had this valuable correspondence with you, having learned so much, I will have to rethink what I might actually say if I were fortunate enough to have this privilege one day. But here are two things I said: 1) All Jews should *take another look* at *Isaiah 53 and Psalm 110* and the relevant verses that you and I have discussed in this debate together—and said what I thought such verses meant, and 2)

I emphasized that the *Jewish people must not forget their true identity*—that they were indeed special, the living remnant of God's ancient covenant people. I fear that most Jewish people have forgotten their true identity, that they don't seem to realize how blessed they are to be who they are! And I then asked, by the way, who are the real friends of Israel today—are they not evangelical, Bible-believing *Christians*?

Why would some people in Holland like the Corrie ten Booms and others of this world risk their lives in World War II as they did? Because they believed from the Scriptures that God's Jewish people should be protected!

I closed the address by hoping that the day will come, having based my remarks on Romans 11, and believing with all my heart that so many Israeli Jews will come to receive Jesus as their own Messiah, that they will one day say to Palestinians, "Is it the Temple Mount you want? Take it, you can have it. We have found the reason Jesus died on the cross two thousand years ago and why the veil of the temple was torn asunder from top to bottom." And I went on to say, even if it is a pipe dream, that Palestinians would in turn say to Jewish people, "We never thought we would hear you talk like that—we want what *you* have." And then, but only then, would there be true peace in Jerusalem.

I believe that, David, to this very day.

But I must apologize one more time in behalf of thoughtless Christians over the years who have been either insensitive or incognizant of how much you and your people have suffered. You are extraordinarily gracious, absolutely magnificent—and vulnerable—to have this dialogue with me. I personally doubt there is another like you.

And yet I know it is because your heart is for peace in Israel and you see this as one more way to try to make things better. And it is my fervent prayer that our debate will somehow make things better. I can assure you that Christians who read our correspondence will learn a lot, will be all the better for it, because they will now have hearts and minds illuminated with new insights and perspectives. Who knows, David, how God might use our friendship?

But when I think that so much anti-Semitism was perpetrated by certain people called Christians, I am horrified. So I am aware that we as a church have failed you, and I am so sorry. My heart aches. If I could take a page from Nehemiah, who confessed the sins of his own generation as well as generations before him, and offer you and your people once again our apologies and sorrow over the way the church that bears the name of Jesus has hurt you, I do so now, David.

The problem is, notwithstanding Jewish attitudes toward what you understandably call "a proselytizing approach," the ultimate issue at the end of the day is *truth*. We who want to be obedient to our Lord bear the stigma of the claim that Jesus is not only the way but even the *truth* (John 14:6). I don't blame anybody for saying "Get off my back"—I fully understand this. But our experience also shows that by lots of prayer and loving persistence, there have been those Jews who lived long enough to thank us for sharing the truth with them. You as a people suffer for just being *Jews*, but we who hold up the name of Jesus have suffered for the *offense of the Cross* at the hands of people of all ethnic backgrounds, and it was not our idea that God chose to send His one and only Son into the world to die for our sins. No human being would ever have conceived such an idea. Only the God of the Bible would have thought of this.

And had the Law not preceded Jesus' coming into the world, the Cross would not have made sense. But His followers, through the illumination of the Holy Spirit, saw for themselves that the Law and the sacrificial system were pointing to what happened on that historic Good Friday in Jerusalem. This is but one reason we are eternally indebted to our Jewish roots.

Our correspondence was borne in what I think was your wish to make Pharisees today look better to Christians and to those who read the New Testament. I can assure you, David, you have argued your case well. You have won that battle with ease. Christians everywhere will be deeply moved, as I have been, by your spirit, humility, and kindness. I was touched by you when we first met, and I respect you more even now than I did then.

Moreover, you are *not* like those men depicted in the New Testament known as Pharisees—you are too self-effacing, for one thing! I have no idea what your own people will think of all this. No doubt some will criticize you, but I think that a great many will salute you. I know that Christians will, as I do.

There is in my opinion one thread that possibly links you to the ancient Pharisees described in the four Gospels. This I referred to in an earlier letter to you, namely, the place those Pharisees gave to tradition. I am surmising, David, that there was inherent in ancient Pharisaism an assumed right to let time and circumstances change the authority of the written word. You call it Oral Tradition. This is one of the things Jesus was critical of: that the Pharisees "nullified" the Word of God by their tradition (Matt. 15:6). It seems to me that Rabbinic Judaism has allowed Oral Tradition to have priority over the Torah itself. I do not know (if this is what you are saying) that Moses gave tacit approval to Oral Tradition, or an Oral Torah, but it is fairly obvious that such has not only been made equal to the Written Torah but has even superseded Scripture. I therefore fear that my quoting any Scripture, whether from Moses or the prophets, does not carry sufficient weight with you at the end of the day.

I would welcome a continuing debate to explore the application of "an eye for an eye" or the way slavery relates to the New Testament as well (Col. 3:22). I am resisting the temptation to discuss what you call an "impiety," namely that there could be one exclusive path to God in the light of the "limitless reality" of God's character, especially in an age of pluralism. I suspect that you feel this will not lead us very far. An even greater temptation for me is to pick up on what you say is the majority opinion of most Orthodox Jewish rabbis today, that the temple offerings would be seen not as vicarious atonement but as "additional acts of devotion." Most of all, I would have wanted to discuss what seems to be the case, that the messianic hope of modern Israel is largely anticipating an *age*, not a person—as used to be the case.

The truth is, is it not, David, that normative Judaism at some stage crossed over an epistemological line—from a robust doctrine of revelation to a different way of knowing? Therefore the application of the Hebrew Scriptures today becomes that which the majority—what you call "the working of the holy spirit"—decides to be true. If I have misunderstood you, I hope you will extend the correspondence since this is crucial in our mutual interchange. But if I have generally assessed things correctly, I acknowledge that I was not prepared for this when our correspondence commenced. It has not in the slightest changed my enthusiasm to dialogue with you. I am only saying that I have had to make a major adjustment in my perception of what I thought you believed as an Orthodox Jewish rabbi. But you, David, are being true to yourself, as Shakespeare said one must do, and I respect you for this.

I therefore concur that the essence of our debate and discussion has now been substantially covered, and I am prepared to bring the public part of our debate to a halt. I do hope you will allow me to correspond with you on and on and have more Shabbat meals together.

I feel I must say three things before I conclude. First, I want to leave you with my personal testimony. You may secretly wonder why I *really*, in my heart of hearts, hold to the vicarious atonement of Jesus for the sins of the world on Good Friday and His literal resurrection from the dead on the third day. It is because of two things apart from my belief in Holy Scripture: 1) the immediate witness of the Holy Spirit, and 2) the effect my faith has had on my personal life.

Many years ago as I drove in my car in Tennessee, I was carried up to what might be called "the third heaven" (2 Cor. 12:2). The person of Jesus was more real to me than anyone or anything around me. I saw Him. He was real—a real human being and interceding for me at the right hand of God. I was overjoyed. The peace that was given to me was the most wonderful experience of my life. I knew that Jesus was truly raised from the dead, that He was coming again, and that I myself was eternally saved. My own theology was utterly renovated.

This experience, David, is what held me when later on I faced the challenge of pluralism, neoorthodoxy, biblical criticism, Process Theology, and existentialism. I credit my faith to the sheer grace of God and to His kindness in granting me the gift of the Holy Spirit that made all I believe so real that I would stake my life on it even if I had to stand utterly alone against the world.

It is my view that the gift of the Holy Spirit was one of the main reasons three thousand Jews asked for baptism on the day of Pentecost (Acts 2:41). It is not that they questioned the content of Peter's sermon, for they obviously believed every word of it. But what gripped them was *what had actually just happened* to those 120 souls on whom the Holy Spirit fell: their speaking in unknown languages, hearing what was said in one's own language, the phenomena of the wind and the fire, and possibly most of all, the conduct of the 120 that made people think they were drunk on new wine (Acts 2:4–13)! I doubt people would have mocked these 120 men and women over the supernatural phenomena that they witnessed, but I reckon that the 120 were so filled with joy and laughter that they gave observers reason to think they must be drunk! Whatever it was, it was what three thousand wanted for themselves because Peter had to say to them that they too could receive the gift of the Spirit if they repented and were baptized (Acts 2:38).

I have given a lot of thought (and speculation) as to what might lift or remove the main obstacles that make it difficult for Jews to recognize Jesus—*Yeshua*—as their Messiah. I wonder if the biggest obstacle may have been the church and the attitudes and demeanor of Christians. I fear that we do not manifest this same joy as I just described but are so guilty of pointing the finger all the time at those who disagree with us. If this assessment is correct, it is shameful. But on the other hand I have wondered if the conversion of Palestinians could make a difference. One of my reasons for doing all I could to convince the late Yasir Arafat to accept Jesus was precisely this. It was partly based on Romans 11. Since the conversion of Gentiles was seen as possibly provoking Israel to "envy" (Rom. 11:11, 14), it crossed my mind more than once that his coming to faith in Jesus could make a difference among Israeli Jews.

Or I wonder if what would make it easy for Jewish people to accept Jesus as their Messiah could be the restoration of signs and wonders to the church, something I personally pray for every day. I am sure, in any case, it will not bypass God's ordained means, namely, the proclamation of the Word (1 Cor. 1:21). It will have to be a sovereign work of the Holy Spirit. But I think too the fulfillment of Romans 11:24 ("How much more readily will these, the natural branches, be grafted into their own olive tree!") may be when we Christians show such a change in our lives that we will make people *want* what we have. We see too little of this. David, I am guilty as anyone, and I cannot defend it. I am just sorry.

That brings me to the second thing, the change my faith has made in my own life. When I came across the teaching of total forgiveness (the title of one of my books), it literally saved my life and ministry. I went through such trials, both in my church and in my marriage, that had I not discovered firsthand the joy of the Holy Spirit that comes from *totally forgiving* everybody in the world, living or dead, who had hurt me or carried out some injustice, I would not have survived. The teaching of total forgiveness comes right out of the life of Joseph (the way he forgave his brothers—Genesis 45) and became the heart of Jesus' teaching. Once I took this seriously, I was changed all over again as a person as much as the aforementioned experience changed me when driving in my car. Experiencing *total forgiveness* from God and toward others made me a better husband, a better father, and a better Christian. This is why I know that what I believe is true: it works.

And yet I too often forget this in my witnessing for the Lord and resort to cerebral arguments as if such will make the world come running to Jesus. I am reminded of a poem my wife Louise brought to my attention:

*'Twas not the truth you taught, to you so clear, to me so dim;*
*But when you came to me, you brought a sense of Him.*
*Yes, from your eyes He beckoned me, from your heart His love was shed*
*And I lost sight of you and saw the Christ instead.*

(Author unknown)

The third and final word as I bring my last letter to you to a close is to quote my friend Joni Eareckson Tada, a legendary woman in America whose accident when swimming as a teenager left her quadriplegic: "I am a Christian not because of what Christianity does for me but because it's true." This is all that ultimately matters. It is a *fact* that Jesus was crucified outside the city of Jerusalem two thousand years ago, and those who believed in His resurrection from the dead did so because it was a *fact*, not something they made up.

Thank you for providing a theological framework for continuing dialogue between Christians and Jews. I can see this has been carefully thought out and I see further why you are so wonderfully used in this area all over the world. I would love to know whether you envisage that one with my own views (you know me pretty well by now!) could fit in with this. I will do all within my power to keep doors open to Jews, Muslims, and all Christians with whom I might have some disagreement, for I am no isolationist. I suppose I just need to know from you that a person with my views is welcome in any peace or reconciliation process.

So, David, I appeal to your graciousness one more time and ask you and all Jewish people to forgive us Christians for entering so often where angels fear to tread without the love and joy of the Holy Spirit. Thank you for the inestimable privilege of having this correspondence with you. I have enjoyed every minute of it. Please know that I thank God with all my heart for your friendship.

> The LORD bless you and keep you; the LORD make his face shine upon you and be gracious to you; the LORD turn his face toward you and give you peace. (Numbers 6:24–26)

*Yours,*
*R. T.*

# Conclusion

It is a reflection of the magnanimity of R. T. Kendall that he has graciously insisted that I have the last word in this book.

We have shared what evidently has been enjoyable discussion for us both, and when inquiring about each other's beliefs, practices, and interpretations of Scripture, I believe that it has been an edifying experience. I am sure that I speak for R. T. as well when I express the hope that the reader will also be able to both benefit from and enjoy this exchange.

However, at the heart of this debate there is an unbridgeable chasm, which is a Christian conviction not only that it is the possessor of absolute and exclusive truth but that its interpretation of Scripture is the only true understanding possible.

R. T. Kendall makes an interesting point (in fact an accusation) in his final letter that I cannot dismiss. While he has acknowledged my point that the Pharisees as a general group have received a "bad rep" (which does not mean that baskets of good fruit do not often contain rotten apples here and there), he suggests that there is "one thread that possibly links [me] to the ancient Pharisees described in the four Gospels" and that is "the place these Pharisees gave to tradition" to the degree that "not only [has it] been made equal to the Written Torah but has even superseded it."

Obviously Christians, like anyone else, may view Rabbinic Jewish emphasis upon the importance of the Oral Tradition as they choose. But it is essential for me to clarify that we do not see this emphasis as "nullifying" the Written Torah but rather as explaining it. As I mentioned in one of my letters, there is so much of the Pentateuch that simply *cannot* be understood without commentary. The example I gave was of the commandment to keep the Sabbath holy (Exod. 20:8; Deut. 5:12). What does that mean? How do you do that? Another example would be the commandment to dwell in booths on the Festival of Tabernacles (Lev. 23:42). What is a booth? How do you make one?

Furthermore, which is the fruit of a goodly tree, and what is a branch of the thick tree that one is meant to take with a palm frond and willows on that festival (Lev. 23:40)? Indeed, what does "take" mean and what is it for? One could go on and on. But what I wish to clarify here is that it is actually impossible to understand the whole Bible literally. As a result, Judaism does indeed give unique weight to the Oral Tradition, but precisely because it believes that the Written Tradition can only be *accessed* through the former. Moreover, because Judaism is a living tradition, it is continuously relating to changing conditions.

For those who believe that it is possible and correct to read the Bible literally, this must indeed be a perplexing if not an irritating thing.

However, I might repeat here a point I make in one of my letters, that this was actually the criticism of the Sadducees (who rejected the Oral Tradition) against the Pharisees. Ironically, the Sadducees were actually the religious and political Jewish establishment at the time of Jesus and who apparently handed him over to the Roman authorities with whom they collaborated. This literalist approach was also the attitude of the Karaites a number of centuries later. They were/are a group that broke away from Rabbinic Judaism and some Karaite communities still remain in different parts of the world, including Israel, albeit in tiny numbers (a few thousand) as a sect quite separate from Jewry.

R. T. Kendall suggests that "at the end of the day" the reason why his "quoting any Scriptures whether from Moses or the prophets does not carry sufficient weight with [me]" is because I don't take the text seriously enough. But I would claim the contrary and suggest that the reason I don't accept his claims is that without a Christian experience, there is absolutely no objective basis for Christian faith claims in the texts he quotes. In fact, Christianity itself makes an "oral tradition" the key to understanding Scripture. That "oral tradition" is the faith in Jesus and Christians' own experience of it, and it is accordingly that faith which is used to reinterpret the texts as referring to that which Christianity believes them to allude to.

The fact is that Rabbinic Judaism and Christianity are both interpretations of the Hebrew biblical text. We share that text but differ on our interpretations of it. I would like us to be able to recognize that and respect it. I would even like us to consider the possibility that there actually may be divine purpose and intention in the very existence of our different (but I would say, parallel) paths to the one truth. I believe that such perception could be mutually enriching and enlightening.

So, aside from my desire to educate non-Jews about Judaism and combat misrepresentations and possible prejudice, my interest in seeing this correspondence published is also a reflection of my commitment to Jewish-Christian dialogue.

While I would like the whole world to acknowledge the one Lord, Creator, and Guide of the universe (in keeping with the vision of Zechariah 14:9, "In that day He shall be One and the Name shall be One") and above all to observe His way (Gen. 18:19) of justice, righteousness, and lovingkindness, Judaism does not aspire to make everyone Jewish. While we are charged to accept those who wish to convert to Judaism with special love, Judaism insists that the "righteous of the nations have their portion in the world to come." There is no need to be Jewish in order to "get one's ticket through the pearly gates"! In other words, there is more than one path to heaven.

Moreover, I believe that the encounter with wisdom and insight from different traditions is an enriching and ennobling experience.

The relationship between Judaism and Christianity is unique, for we each see ourselves as rooted in the history of the divine message revealed in the Hebrew Bible. I quoted Martin Buber's comment that Christians and Jews "share a book and a hope." But the paradox is that the book that unites us often divides us, because we have come to interpret its meaning and terms in different ways.

This does not at all have to be an obstacle to mutual understanding, respect, and even enrichment. But it does require, if we are to dialogue honestly, to recognize this fact and to be informed about those differing interpretations and understandings.

Buber also refers to a "hope." Similarly, that messianic expectation that we share also divides us. But surely even if we are divided in its interpretation to a substantial degree, there is still much that we can and must do in practice to bring about the kingdom of heaven on earth. And surely, if there are moral, ethical, and social values that we do share, we have an obligation to them, as well as to their Source, to work together for their realization with all who affirm them!

The "book" also links us to the land of Israel. Of course the relationship of Christianity to the Holy Land is not the same as it is for Judaism, which sees it not just as a national homeland, but the place—as stated in the Bible—where the children of Israel should ideally live the way of life revealed to them at Sinai. Nevertheless by virtue of the special link of the Jewish people with the land, it became the birthplace of Christianity, contains venerable Christian communities within it, and is a place of pilgrimage for Christians from around the world.

All this surely places an additional common responsibility upon us to promote the well-being of all who live in this land—Jews, Christians, and Muslims.

Inevitably the conflict in the Middle East elicits very partisan views and there are Christians whose unqualified support for the State of Israel (often out of a belief that Israel is the vehicle by which the Second Coming, Armageddon, and the universal triumph of Christianity will occur) leads them to disregard the needs, well-being, and aspirations of Palestinians. There are other Christians whose identification with Palestinians, whether through their own links with Arab Christians or simply out of empathy for the Palestinian plight, lead them to insensitivity and even hostility toward Israel's needs and well-being.

Accordingly I am so grateful for the work of those Christians who genuinely care for all who live in this land and who through prayer or action or both seek to contribute to reconciliation and peace.

This was how I met R. T. Kendall, through my involvement with and his support of the Alexandria process. The Alexandria Summit initiated by Lord George Carey, then Archbishop of Canterbury, and directed by his emissary Canon Andrew White, brought leaders and representatives of the religious establishments in the Holy Land together for the first time ever in history. That fact is both pathetic and wonderful: pathetic that it had never happened before—and wonderful that it actually took place.

I presume to believe that the fact that this initiative was led by Christians was not coincidental. Indeed Christians have very much been the pioneers of interreligious dialogue in the Holy Land over recent decades, but this has generally been marginal and not impacted upon the religious institutions and their leadership. There is now a remarkable change in this regard, and I think that Christians of genuine goodwill to both peoples in the Holy Land can play a special role in promoting understanding, cooperation, and peace, if these efforts are done in a manner that respects the particular identities, faith affirmations, and attachments involved.

This is not an easy matter for those who believe that everyone should share his own faith affirmation. However, few things will undermine sincere Christian efforts to help bring peace in the Middle East more than the perception on the part of Jews and Muslims that the reason for such initiatives is simply to advance an exclusive Christian theological agenda. So those like R. T. who have the passionate, burning need to persuade others of their conviction, and who wish to be peacemakers at the same time, have to decide which of these roles will get the better of the other.

Another testimony of R. T.'s magnanimity was his declared desire that anyone reading our exchange would be impressed by both of our arguments. Nevertheless our hopes remain rather different. I hope that Christians reading this book will remain Christians, just as I hope Jews will remain Jews. However, I do also hope that readers will be impressed by the fact that notwithstanding our profound differences, it is possible to discuss even these respectfully without pulling any punches; that it is possible to say and hear tough things and still remain (indeed even grow as) loving friends. In that in itself, there is surely testimony to the divine presence, compassion, and love in our midst, and for this I express my thanks and affection to R. T. Kendall for having initiated this endeavor. May it be a source of blessing and enlightenment.

*Rabbi David Rosen*

# Appendix
## *The Sin Jesus Hated Most*

(from R. T. Kendall's book *Out of Your Comfort Zone: Is Your God Too Nice?*, Warner Faith, 2006)

In the four Gospels, the Pharisees are almost entirely portrayed as the bad guys. And yet I keep in mind that on at least one occasion Jesus accepted an invitation to have dinner with a Pharisee (Luke 11:37). The meal was paralleled by Jesus ruthlessly exposing the hearts of the Pharisees—whom He tended to put altogether in one lump—and called them "You foolish people" (v. 40). The Pharisee might have been a nice man, but Jesus was not very nice to him!

The Pharisees (a word which probably means the "separated ones") emerged in the second century BC. They were a strict sect made up mostly of ordinary Jews, unlike the Sadducees who were members of the families of priests.

Pharisees were far more numerous than Sadducees but not so prestigious. The Pharisees kept closely to the Mosaic Law and often embellished the Law with countless rules so that these rules were very hard to keep. They saw themselves as a cut above everybody else.

They counted work on the Sabbath as walking more than a kilometer from one's town, carrying any kind of load, or lighting a fire in the home. It led to people being concerned to keep the Law in every detail. The Pharisees believed that their rules built a "fence around the Law" so that by keeping these rules people would be in less danger of disobeying the actual Law of God.

One must not forget that many of them were, no doubt, pious men. Some scholars reckon that when Jesus described the Pharisee in the parable in Luke 18:9–14, some Pharisees really did do such things as he boasted of: fasting twice a week and giving a tenth of all they earn, not to mention the fact that they would never be guilty of wrongdoing such as robbing or committing adultery. They were regarded as the truly righteous people of their day. They were, without question, the backbone of their synagogues and would in some cases be like certain evangelicals today who carry their big black Bibles to church and would never smoke or touch a drop of alcohol or watch a movie that was anything but for the whole family.

But they tended to look down on those who did not keep their rules and called such people "sinners." Remember too that Nicodemus, who was a secret follower of Jesus, was a Pharisee. So was the apostle Paul before he was converted.

But given the fact that Pharisees were pious, faithful, and the stalwarts of the synagogues in ancient Judaism, why was

Jesus so hard on them? Should He not have congratulated them, as if to say, "You are greatly needed here in Jerusalem these days. I can't imagine what things would be like were it not for you"? No. He never congratulated them or gave the slightest hint they were either needed or appreciated. He was harsh and rugged with them.

What is most interesting to me is that Jesus was patient, loving, and gracious to the woman caught in the sin of adultery, unlike the Pharisees who were chuffed (but supposedly indignant) that they found this woman in the act of sin (John 8:1–11). Jesus did not ever appear to show tender feelings toward the Pharisees. He was not very nice to them, despite the fact that they upheld the infallibility of the Bible, believed in resurrected life beyond the grave (unlike the Sadducees), and adhered to a number of practices that Jesus also affirmed.

When I was a young Christian, I used to wonder why so much attention was given in the four Gospels to the Pharisees, since they do not exist today. Was this not a waste of space? Why should we have to read about irrelevant people? I have since learned of course that Pharisees do indeed exist today.

## The Pharisees' Comfort Zone

### THEIR TRADITIONS
Their extrabiblical rules became a tradition that you were required to keep or you did not love God or respect the Law. Some Pharisees came up to Galilee all the way from Jerusalem just to ask Jesus, "Why do your disciples break the

tradition of the elders? They don't wash their hands before they eat!" (Matt. 15:1–2). Imagine being so threatened by Jesus that one walks for three days just to see why He did not keep certain rules! This washing of hands was not merely a health matter, by the way, it was a ritualistic thing you did that showed you adhered to the "party line."

## How They Found Significance

One thing in particular was, according to Jesus, that they sought to achieve significance in being admired. "They loved to be greeted in the marketplaces and to have men call them 'Rabbi'" (Matt. 23:7). They "loved praise from men more than praise from God" (John 12:43). That was the essence of their comfort zone: being applauded, being complimented, being respected, and being openly referred to. Do that and you had no problem with them. Jesus didn't do that and had problems with them. These pious men were right in the middle of the conspiracy to have Jesus crucified (John 11:45–57).

They further sought significance like this: they compared themselves with others—always people they could safely label "sinners." That way they always came out on top. So in the aforementioned parable, the Pharisee boasted of his good works, then added: "God, I thank you that I am not like other men—robbers, evildoers, adulterers—or even like this tax collector" (Luke 18:11). We can all find someone who is less righteous than we are to whom we can compare ourselves and we therefore come forth smelling like a rose. "Comparisons are odious," said Shakespeare, referring to comparing one person against another; but it is perhaps even more odious when we do this to make ourselves look good. "At least I'm not as bad as so-and-so."

They even got their sense of significance in the way they dressed. Jesus said, "Everything they do is done for men to see: They make their phylacteries wide and the tassels on their garments long" (Matt. 23:5). Dress is very important to a Pharisee; always has been, always will be. They will not be the slightest bit convicted over holding a grudge or speaking evil of fellow believers, but they go to pains to look good.

We are talking about the chief enemies of Jesus—who saw right through them—who found their significance in what people said positively about them, by comparing themselves with others and by their very appearance. I wonder how many preachers today need the good suit or clerical garb just to look successful in order to feel important and significant. If I am not careful, I will end up a Pharisee in judging them, but I only know so many give the impression, even if unintentionally, that their appearance is an essential ingredient to their sense of significance.

## MOTIVATION

How do you persuade a Pharisee to give to the poor? The answer is very simple: hire a couple of trumpeters—a band would be better—and get everyone's attention with the music. They announced their giving by the sound of trumpets in the synagogues and on the streets for one reason: "to be seen of men." And how do you suppose you get a Pharisee to pray? Jesus said, "They love to pray." If Jesus had said only that they love to pray, He would have complimented them. I love to pray. Do you love to pray? Nothing wrong with loving to pray. For that's good. But with the Pharisees, "They love to pray standing in the synagogues and on the street corners to be seen by men" (Matt. 6:5). The way you get them to stop praying is to walk away while they are doing it. For there is no motivation left if no one is noticing.

And since we know that Pharisees fasted twice a week, what do you suppose lay behind that worthy practice? They made sure you saw them. First, they looked somber (possibly not too hard for some Pharisees anyway). Second, they disfigured their faces: they put on a facial expression that told you they were carrying heavy-duty burdens; this was important stuff, mind you. They didn't even comb their hair (they were afraid you wouldn't otherwise notice) when they skipped a meal or two. Read it all in Matthew 5:1–18.

In a word: they were starving for recognition. As long as they got credit for giving, praying, or fasting, you could count on them every time. Take away the credit, the tax exemption, the plaque on the wall, the public knowledge of a generous donation, the thanks before all for doing the flowers in front of the pulpit or for washing up in the church kitchen, then there aren't many in the queue wanting to help.

The problem with Pharisees was they so often had no objectivity about themselves. This is because their main problem was that they had no sense of sin. None. Sin to them was always in what you do or don't do. Not what you think or feel. It was all outward appearance. They forgot that God looks on the heart (1 Sam. 16:7).

## Priorities
The theological assumptions and priorities of Pharisees can be quickly summed up: their theology was more important

than people. They really didn't care about people. It was all theology: Hold to the truth. Contend for the faith. Keep the party line. Above all, remember the Sabbath.

It is almost hilarious that Jesus again and again seemed to wait for the Sabbath before He healed people. Read Matthew 12:2; Mark 2:24; Luke 6:2, 6, and Luke 14:3 for a start. You get the picture that He sees a needy person but says to Himself, *It's only two more days until the Sabbath is here, and I will wait in order to heal this person then.* In other words, Jesus attacked the Pharisees, not for their upholding the Law but for putting their traditions and party line alongside Holy Scripture as if they were of the same authority. There isn't a single word in the Law that says a person should not be made well on the Sabbath.

This partly is why they hated all that Jesus preached and did. He did not hold to the party line. They never saw their own sin—ever, as far as we can tell. This is why Jesus said that it was the tax collector, so looked down on by the Pharisee, who was justified before God rather than the Pharisee. For the tax collector prayed, not even being able to look up to heaven "but beat his breast and said, 'God, have mercy on me, a sinner'" (Luke 18:13).

They further perpetuated their comfort zones by loopholes they somehow found that set them free from the kind of obedience they were uncomfortable with. The fences that they erected that supposedly protected the Law actually served in some cases to give a way out *not* to obey the Law strictly at all! Jesus nailed them to the wall in this area. The commandment to honor both father and mother was undeniable, this being the fifth commandment. But they had a way of keeping their parents from receiving money that ought to go to them by a rule that enabled them to divert it to the temple or synagogue instead.

> You [Pharisees] say that if a man says to his father or mother, "Whatever help you might otherwise have received from me is a gift devoted to God [the money should go to the Lord instead in this case]," he is not to "honor his father" with it. Thus you nullify the word of God for the sake of your tradition. (Matthew 15:5–6)

When Jesus said that one cannot enter the kingdom of heaven unless one's righteousness actually surpasses that of the Pharisees, nobody could believe their ears. For the ordinary Jew living at the time thought he was so far beneath a Pharisee, the thought of exceeding the righteousness of a Pharisee seemed over-the-top. But Jesus knew exactly what He was talking about: not only are we justified by faith in Jesus, who perfectly fulfilled the Law in our behalf, but our very righteousness, when we follow Jesus, far outdistances that of the Pharisee. For the Pharisee never felt any conscience about speaking evil of another, hurting his reputation, holding a grudge, or not forgiving an enemy.

We are getting closer to the answer to the question posed above: since Pharisees were vanguards for the Law and were moral and sound on many essential matters, why didn't Jesus congratulate them? Why was He so hard on them? Even if He saw through them, that they were phoney in their righteousness, why didn't He leave them alone and attack wicked tax collectors, harlots, and drunkards?

The answer is: they did so much harm. They converted people over to their party line and made those people "twice as much a son of hell as you are" (Matt. 23:15). People like this get more excited over changing a person's theology to suit their own than they do about leading a person to Christ. They will spend more time attacking an enemy who threatens them than going into the world to save the lost. It is like King Saul who was more worried about young David than he was the archenemy of Israel, the Philistines! This is how lopsided people can get and why Jesus knew the Pharisees were dangerous. They did harm to people.

One of the hardest things Jesus said to them was this: "You shut the kingdom of heaven in men's faces. You yourselves do not enter, nor will you let those enter who are trying to" (Matt. 23:14).

But Jesus also knew that Pharisees would be the ones who would lead the way to His own death. There was never a thought that such a conspiracy would be instigated by the notorious sinners of the day: drunkards, whoremongers, adulterers, or even murderers. Not that they were incapable of such. But, generally speaking, people like that don't tend to send an innocent man to the cross. But religious people do. Jesus therefore had their number and declared war on them from almost the first time He opened His mouth. "Do not think that I have come to abolish the Law," He said early on in the Sermon on the Mount (Matt. 5:17). Why say that? Why bring that subject up? It was because Jesus wanted to get to the heart of the matter as soon as possible. When He began to attack their interpretations of the Law, He knew He would be in a constant battle with them from then on. It worked. They led the way in getting Him crucified. But that is what He came to do! He came to die on the cross for our sins and, in the meantime, establish the kind of people who would be saved. "I have not come to call the righteous [by which He meant those who purport to be righteous], but sinners to repentance" (Luke 5:32).

"The common people heard him gladly" (Mark 12:37 KJV). On one occasion the Pharisees sent a temple guard to bring Jesus in so they could arrest Him. These guards came back shortly—but without Jesus. "Why didn't you bring him in?" they were asked.

The guards replied, "No one ever spoke the way this man does."

"You mean he has deceived you also?" the Pharisees responded. This sort of thing thrust Pharisees right out of their comfort zone. They resorted to their theology: "This mob [people following Jesus] . . . knows nothing of the law" (John 7:45–49). Their ultimate weapon against common Jews was the threat of putting anybody out of the synagogue who confessed faith in Jesus (John 12:42). The typical ploy of a Pharisee is to motivate by fear.

Their attack lay in the idea of guilt by association. This tactic was used by Pharisees then and continues to be used today. If people who are attracted to you, or people you spend time with, are unworthy, theologically inarticulate, not of good stock or of respectable credentials, all of you are in the same boat together and should be regarded as being cut out of the same cloth. You are all equally guilty. You prove your guilt by those you are friendly with.

The Pharisees' trump card therefore: the kind of people that Jesus allowed to be around Him, the quality of people affirming Him, and the backgrounds of those who were brought closest to Him. "This man welcomes sinners, and eats with them" (Luke 15:2). This, to the Pharisees, should be enough to indict Jesus as one to be shunned and should surely cause everybody to turn against Jesus! But it didn't work. Jesus even pleaded guilty to the charge and told several more parables (Luke 15–16) to show that the Father loves and welcomes sinners into His family.

Pharisees yesterday and today love to repudiate a person by the quality of the people they seek to reach or who admire them. Jesus surprised everybody by choosing a tax collector to be one of the twelve disciples. That was just not right! The Pharisees, on the other hand, quickly write off those who mix with those who do not adhere to their party line.

The worst thing of all, however, was this: the Pharisees' search for significance outside God and from the praise of people lay at the bottom of their inability to recognize God's Messiah when He stood before their very eyes. Have you wondered why ancient Israel missed out when Messiah came? Have you wondered why they still reject Him? I can tell you. It is because they chose the immediate gratification of receiving praise from people rather than to seek what it would have been like had they sought the honor that comes only from God. Seeking the honor, praise, and glory that comes from God alone means letting go of the applause of men and women. It also means a lot of patience, because you don't feel anything the first day you make this a lifelong pursuit. So it isn't easy. The Pharisees said that not only is it too hard but also they simply weren't going to go that route. Surely their reverence for the Law was good enough. The Law is God's product; the Law isn't God Himself. And those who give priority to the Law inevitably end up as Pharisees and miss out on God's next move, just as the Jews missed out on their own Messiah

Therefore Jesus was not surprised at their refusal to

believe in Him. He gave the explanation Himself and summed up their unbelief in a simple question He asked: "How can you [how could you possibly] believe if you accept praise from one another, yet make no effort to obtain the praise that comes from the only God?" (John 5:44). They made a choice: they preferred compliments, adoration, admiration, and glory from people. Jesus said they "make no effort" to see what it would have been like had they sought their significance in the sheer glory of God. But they opted for the glory of man. This felt better. Possibly, for a while. But at the end of the day one who makes this choice will pay for it dearly and suffer for it bitterly—forever—unless God mercifully steps down, as He did in the cases of Nicodemus and Saul of Tarsus. And me. And I hope you.

What breaks your heart is that the Pharisees were the ones who led to Jesus' weeping over the city of Jerusalem, in a lengthy denunciation of the Pharisees in Matthew 23. It culminated in Jesus crying out,

> O Jerusalem, Jerusalem, you who kill the prophets and stone those sent to you, how often I have longed to gather your children together, as a hen gathers her chicks under her wings, but you were not willing. Look, your house is left to you desolate. (Matthew 23:37–38)

## Author's Note

This is the way Chapter 7 was concluded in my book *Out of Your Comfort Zone: Is Your God Too Nice?* I will not repeat any of Chapter 8, partly written humorously, "Twenty-Six Reasons You May Be a Pharisee." Let me remind you that Rabbi

David Rosen read all of both chapters before. The first letter he wrote in response to my stuff is Chapter 1 of this
book. The rest speaks for itself.

It is our wish that the book will create an ever-increasing
love and understanding between Christians and Jews. I myself have learned so much. Keep also in mind that, whereas
the ancient Pharisees were preeminently concerned with
what people thought, Rabbi Rosen has come forward with
remarkable courage and risks his reputation by being associated with me and this book.

# Glossary

**Abrabanel (or Abarbanel):** Isaac the son of Judah, fif-teenth-century statesman, philosopher, and biblical commentator.

**Adonai:** Literally "my Lord," using the most respectful grammatical construct (i.e., plural). The word is used by Jews only to denote God.

**Aggadah:** The nonlegal or homiletical corpus of the TAL-MUD and MIDRASH.

**Akiva:** Arguably the greatest Jewish sage of the period of the MISHNAH. He systematized the structure and content of the Oral Tradition (see TORAH). He was tortured to death by the Romans for his promotion of the practice and study of Judaism after these had been outlawed subsequent to the failure of the BAR COCHBA rebellion in 135 CE.

**Annihilationism:** The denial of conscious eternal punishment, the belief that the entire person (body, soul, spirit, mind) is rendered nonexistent after death or final judgment, as though he or she had never been created.

**Antinomianism:** Literally "against law," this word was invented by MARTIN LUTHER to refer to a teaching that denied the role of the Law in the Christian life. Although many who have been called "antinomian" have been godly people, the word tends to be used to mean "licentiousness."

**Anti-Semitism:** The term used to denote prejudice and hostility against Jews.

**Ashkenazi(c):** Jews who live in/originate from Christian (European) lands. More specifically, those who follow particular German/Polish customs and order of prayers.

**Atonement:** The Jewish view: the process by which a person is purified from sin through repentance and good works. The Christian view: a sacrifice which has the effect of canceling the guilt of sin. This is achieved through Jesus' death when ratified by one's faith.

**Augustine (354–430):** Major Christian theologian born and raised in North Africa. Bishop of Hippo; considered a saint by the church.

**Bar Cochba (Bar Coziba):** Simon, the leader of the Jewish rebellion against Rome that was initially successful in the year 132 CE. Perceived as the anticipated Messiah by the people, he was given the name *Bar Cochba*, meaning "son of the star" (in keeping with Numbers 24:17). Ultimately, the rebellion was put down ruthlessly by the Romans in the year

135, leading to severe repression of the practice and study of Judaism as well as mass exile. Bar Cochba then became popularly referred to as *Bar Coziba*, meaning "the son of falsehood (false hopes)."

**BCE:** Before the Common (or Christian) era (see CE).

**Billerbeck, Paul:** Nineteenth-century German scholar of the New Testament and rabbinic literature.

**Buber, Martin (1878–1965):** Jewish philosopher/theologian, born in Vienna; immigrated to Palestine (later Israel) where he taught social philosophy at the Hebrew University of Jerusalem.

**Calvin, John:** Sixteenth-century French theologian who lived in Geneva. One of the fathers of Protestant Christianity. He was a proponent of the doctrine that salvation is obtained only by divine grace and that faith is an unconditional divine gift.

**CE:** The Christian Era (or the Common Era), a form of dating that many Jews prefer to AD, as the latter designates Jesus as Lord.

**Ceremonial Law:** Those aspects of religious practice that relate to ceremonies and rituals.

**Chief Rabbi:** One who is appointed to a position of Jewish communal religious authority, often involving the licensing and appointments of other rabbis as well as overseeing matters of religious personal status (marriage, divorce, etc.) within a specific Jewish community. Primarily, chief rabbinates were established to fulfill a representative role to the non-Jewish authorities.

**Christian:** A faithful follower of Jesus, who is acclaimed as the God-man and Christ (i.e., MESSIAH).

**Circumcised:** A male whose foreskin of the penis has been removed.

**Civil Law:** The secular law of the land.

**Codes:** Extensive guidebooks to Jewish practice and observance.

**Conservative Judaism:** One of the main streams of modern Judaism (Conservative and Reform Jews make up some 90 percent of the identifying Jewish community of the U.S.). It emerged out of what was known in the nineteenth century as Positive-Historical Judaism. The term "conservative" does not mean that the movement's adherents are politically conservative. Rather, the term denotes that Jews should "conserve" religious tradition rather than radically reform it, let alone abandon it. However, the Conservative movement teaches that Judaism has adapted to changing conditions throughout history. Accordingly, as opposed to predominant Orthodox Jewish attitudes, the Conservative view is that Judaism can and must adapt itself to modernity and modern needs. Conservative Judaism therefore occupies a middle position between Orthodox and Reform Judaism. The Conservative movement is now overwhelmingly egalitarian and in recent decades has introduced the ordination of women for the rabbinate.

**Constantine (the Great):** Born in the late third century, he was the son of a Roman officer and became emperor of Rome. After his conversion to Christianity, his empire became known as the Holy Roman Empire, in which Christianity was the state religion.

**Council of Trent:** The nineteenth ecumenical council of the Catholic Church, which took place in the mid-sixteenth century with the main objective of defining the doctrines of the church in answer to "heresies" of the PROTESTANTS. The council also sought to implement a thorough reform of the inner life of the church by removing numerous abuses that had developed within it.

**Covenant (including NOAHIDE COVENANT, ABRAHAMIC COVENANT, and SINAI COVENANT):** The Hebrew word *brit* indicates a binding commitment between parties and is used in the Hebrew Bible to designate God's undertaking and expectations accordingly.

*The Noahide Covenant* (i.e., covenant with Noah and his descendants) reflects God's commitment to care for all humanity and not destroy it (Gen. 9:9–11). In return He expects all humanity to lead a moral life (Gen. 9:4–6).

*The Abrahamic Covenant* contains the basic promise that Abraham will be given "seed" (descendants) and inherit the land of his sojourning. The Christian view is that the seed refers to Jesus and to those who believe in the promise; this became the foundation of Paul's teaching of JUSTIFICATION BY FAITH (Rom. 4).

*The Sinai Covenant* (Exod. 19) is the confirmation of God's everlasting commitment to the children of Israel (the children of Abraham, Isaac, and Jacob) and His expectation that they would live in accordance with the revelation at Mount

Sinai (which, according to Jewish tradition, means all the commandments in the Pentateuch). The Christian view is that Jesus fulfilled the Law by His sinless life and sacrificial death, and that His followers would, out of gratitude, uphold the righteousness of the Law.

**Day of Atonement:** The tenth day of the Hebrew month of Tishrei, when it is prohibited to eat or drink (for twenty-five hours). The day of fasting and prayer is devoted to seeking divine forgiveness for sins in keeping with Leviticus 23:27–32 (see also Lev. 16).

**Decalogue:** Literally "the ten sayings," commonly known as the Ten Commandments.

**Deity:** God.

**Divine Presence:** In Hebrew *Shekhinah*, indicating God's indwelling in a specific place or in the world at large.

**Elect:** Chosen.

**Eschatology:** The theology of the end of days.

**Essenes:** A semimonastic Jewish sect that functioned in the late Second Temple period and is generally associated with the Qumran community on the west shore of the Dead Sea.

**Evangelicals:** PROTESTANT Christians who uphold the divine inspiration of Scripture, the TRINITY, and the essential teachings of the NEW TESTAMENT, such as the need for all people to be saved through the vicarious ATONEMENT of Jesus Christ and His bodily resurrection. They also believe in his second coming and the final judgment.

**Existentialism:** The philosophical approach based on the idea that there is no difference between the external and internal world and that all existence is in the state of mind. Religious existentialism affirms that religious truth is to be found in religious experience itself.

**Faith:** The term has different meaning for Christians and Jews. The Hebrew word *emunah* denotes having confidence and trust in something or someone. This is the Jewish understanding of faith. The Christian understanding is that faith is reliance on the death of Jesus, not one's own good works, as well as trusting in God's promises as revealed in Scripture.

**Flusser, David:** Twentieth-century Jewish scholar of early Christianity and the New Testament, who taught at the Hebrew University of Jerusalem.

**Free Will:** The divinely given human capacity to make free choices for good or evil.

**Fundamentalism:** Originally this word was used to describe a literal approach to reading Scripture. Today it is loosely used to denote exclusivist religious belief systems, and sometimes it is used to refer to those who wish to impose their views on others.

**Garden of Eden:** The location in which Adam was placed by God (Gen. 2:15) and where the first human family was established. The term is also used in Judaism as a synonym for Paradise, the heavenly abode.

**Gentile:** "One of the nations." The term is used in the Bible to denote those who are not the children of Israel (i.e., the rest of the world).

**Gospels:** Accounts of the ministry, death, and resurrection of Jesus and commonly referred to as the first four books of the New Testament: Matthew, Mark, Luke, and John.

**Halachah:** The corpus of Jewish religious law and practice.

**Hassidism:** The Jewish religious revivalist movement that emerged in the late eighteenth century in Central and Eastern Europe, which appealed to the less-educated Jewish masses in particular. The movement was typified by ecstatic (mystical) devotion, personal spirituality, and charismatic leadership. Today the term is often used (imprecisely) as synonymous with Ultra-Orthodox.

**Hebrew Bible:** Also referred to by the Hebrew acronym TaNaKh—i.e., Torah (Pentateuch), Nevi'im (Prophets), Khetuvim (Writings)—that make up the body of literature that Christians know as the Old Testament. Jews prefer not to use the term *Old Testament* out of concern that this might reflect the ideas of Replacement Theology.

**Hillel (the Elder):** Jewish sage of the first century BCE, probably the greatest scholar of his time; Pharasaic leader known for his compassion and tolerance. He founded the School of Hillel—the center of learning that followed his orientation/teaching.

**Holiness:** God's essential nature (see Lev. 19:2), indicating that He is absolutely pure, clean, and devoid of evil; the opposite of profane. It is a requirement of His people that they too be holy (e.g., Lev. 11:44).

**Holocaust:** The attempted extermination of the Jewish people by the Nazis and their collaborators during the period of World War II. The Nazis succeeded in murdering 6 million Jews, including 1.5 million children.

**Holy of Holies:** The most sacred and innermost part of the temple into which no one entered other than the high priest on the holiest day of the year, the DAY OF ATONEMENT.

**Infallibility of Scripture:** The belief that all the books of the Bible were inspired by God and are absolutely true in all that they affirm.

**Islam:** The religion revealed to the prophet Mohammed at the beginning of the seventh century in the Arabian peninsula, written down in the Quran (Koran).

**Jerusalem:** Centrally located between the Dead Sea/River Jordan and the Mediterranean Sea and between the northern mountains of the Holy Land and the southern desert, it was a Jebusite stronghold until captured by David, who made it his capital, uniting the disparate tribes of Israel around it. Subsequently it was joined to a hill north of it on which the temple was built and from where the city expanded to the west.

**Jew:** Term used to identify the descendants of the children of Israel and thus synonymous with Israelites and Hebrews. However, its origins are from the name *Judah* (Jacob's fourth son) and the Roman form of the name, *Judea*. After the rule of Solomon, his kingdom split into two, the northern kingdom known as Israel and the southern as Judah (where the tribe of Judah was dominant). The tribes in the north were conquered and exiled by the Assyrians in the eighth century BCE and were assimilated into other populations (the ten lost tribes). Thus only the tribes of Judah remained, and the names Judah and Israelite became synonymous.

**Jewish Mysticism:** See KABBALAH.

**Josephus (Flavius):** First-century Jewish military leader during the war against Rome; historian and major source of data regarding Second Temple Judaism; one of the chief representatives of Jewish-Hellenistic literature.

**Judaism:** The religion of the Jews.

**Justification by Faith:** The Christian belief that one is declared righteous in God's sight by faith, not good works, the object of faith being Jesus Christ.

**Kabbalah:** Sometimes used interchangeably with the term JEWISH MYSTICISM. However, the mystical search for union with God has always been a part of Judaism. Kabbalah is the medieval esoteric system of knowledge that describes a mystical cosmology, i.e., explanation of how the world functions and is influenced.

**Karaites:** Jewish sect originating in the eighth century whose doctrine is chiefly characterized by its denial of Talmudic/Rabbinic tradition.

**Land of Israel (Holy Land, Promised Land, Land of Canaan, Palestine):** Name(s) to denote the territory that the Bible describes as the divinely mandated homeland of the descendants of Abraham, Isaac, and Jacob.

**Law:** An imprecise translation of the Hebrew word TORAH, which is more correctly translated as "instruction."

**Lord's Supper (also referred to as Holy Communion):** The partaking of bread and wine that Jesus instituted with His disciples (Matt. 26:26–30) and continued by His followers to commemorate and partake in the body and blood of Jesus.

**Luther, Martin:** Sixteenth-century PROTESTANT reformer who revived the teaching of JUSTIFICATION BY FAITH alone but sadly also known for his anti-Semitic views.

**LXX (Septuagint):** *Septuagint* is the Greek word for "seventy" and is used to refer to the Greek translation of the Hebrew Bible, traditionally attributed to seventy Jewish sages brought together for this purpose by Ptolemy in the third century BCE.

**Maimonides (1135–1204):** Moses Maimonides (i.e., the son of Maimon) was the greatest Jewish scholar, philosopher, and codifier of the Middle Ages. Born in Cordoba, Spain, he eventually settled in Cairo (Fostat), Egypt, where he served as physician to the Sultan.

**Marcion:** Second-century Roman Christian who propounded the heresy that all Christian connection with the Hebrew Bible (the Old Testament) should be severed.

**Messiah:** The Hebrew word for a person anointed with oil as a sign of special status/role. The term is used in the Hebrew Bible in reference to a priest or king, and especially in prophecies of the restoration of the royal house of David. Christianity identifies this role with the redeeming sacrifice of Jesus who is thus called Christ (*Kristos*, Greek for "anointed one").

**Messianic Age:** The biblical vision of an ideal religioethical society.

**Messianic Believers:** Usually used to denote Jews who believe that Jesus is the Messiah.

**Midrash:** The Jewish homiletical exposition of biblical texts. The classical period of Midrashic works is parallel to the period of the TALMUD.

**Mishnah:** The first written compendium of the legal sections of the ORAL TORAH written down c. 200 CE by Rabbi Judah the Prince.

**Mitzvah:** Commandment; also used to mean a good deed.

**Moral Law:** Those aspects of legislation that refer to morality, as opposed to those that refer to ritual or symbolism.

**New Testament:** The Christian succession to the Hebrew Bible (called the Old Testament by Christians); twenty-seven books beginning with the GOSPELS, containing the first history of the church (Acts) and twenty letters, thirteen of which were written by Paul the apostle.

**Noahide Covenant:** See COVENANT.

***Nostra Aetate:*** The document issued in 1965 by the Second Vatican Ecumenical Council, which rejected the idea of Jewish guilt for the death of Jesus, both at the time as well as thereafter; affirmed the eternity of the divine covenant with the Jewish people; and condemned anti-Semitism. This document revolutionized Catholic teaching regarding Jews and Judaism.

**Oral Torah (Oral Tradition):** See TORAH.

**Original Sin:** The Christian belief that the sin of Adam and Eve in the Garden of Eden was transmitted to the entire human race; consequently people are born with a sinful nature and a propensity to commit sin.

**Orthodox Judaism:** Jews who call themselves Orthodox mean by this that they are committed to the body of Jewish practice/law (in Hebrew, *halachah*), which they believe to have divine authority. Therefore, while *halachah* has rules and method of application to address changing situations, the structure of *halachah* should not be changed. Orthodox Jews are most obviously distinguished from their Reform and even Conservative counterparts by the degree of meticulous observance of Jewish ritual practice, e.g., the dietary laws, the Sabbath, and formal prayer three times a day. In Orthodox synagogues, men and women sit separately and there is no Orthodox ordination of women as rabbis.

**Palestine/Palestinians:** After the Jewish rebellions against Rome in the first and second centuries, the Romans exiled much of the population and sought to eliminate vestiges of particular Jewish attachment to the land. In addition to replacing the name *Jerusalem* with *Aelia Capitolina*, they replaced the name *Judea* with the name *Palestine* (taken from the name *Philistines*, the ancient tribes that populated the southwest coastal region). Until the establishment of the modern State of Israel, all residents of the Holy Land were referred to as Palestinians. After the establishment of the state of Israel, the word *Palestine* came to be used to denote only the Arab residents and in particular those in the West

Bank and Gaza who seek an independent state by that name.

**Passover:** The spring festival that celebrates the exodus of the children of Israel from Egypt (see Exod. 12:14–20); Christians believe that they continue the celebration of Passover through the LORD'S SUPPER.

**Pentateuch:** The five books of Moses (Genesis, Exodus, Leviticus, Numbers, Deuteronomy) also known as the WRITTEN TORAH, which traditional Judaism has taught were revealed by God to Moses at Mount Sinai after the children of Israel's exodus from Egypt. Thus all the commandments contained in the five books (which, according to Jewish tradition, come to 613) are viewed by the tradition as having been revealed/confirmed at Sinai (not just "the Ten Commandments").

**Pharisees:** Possibly first used to refer to a particular religiously devout sect but came to be used to denote those Jews who followed the teachings of the Oral Tradition (see TORAH) as well as the Written Tradition, believing both to be of divine authority. They placed special emphasis on the study of the tradition and established schools of learning for this purpose. Central to their theology were the doctrines of free will, reward, and punishment (heaven and hell), resurrection, and the importance of prayer—virtually all of which were not shared by the Sadducees.

**Pluralism:** The idea that there is no one exclusive claim on truth. The word is now widely used interchangeably with the idea of freedom of religious worship and practice.

**Prophets:** Persons chosen by God to bring His Word to the people.

**Protestant:** First used in 1529 at a meeting in Spier, Germany, the term is used to denote one who follows the form of Western Christianity that rejected (i.e., "protested against") the absolute authority of the Roman Catholic Church and some of its teachings and practices.

**Providence:** God's overruling grace in the affairs of people.

**Rabbi:** Literally "master." The word refers to one who has acquired advanced competency in Jewish learning and knowledge of the religious tradition. For most of the last two thousand years it has been used to denote one who has been examined and found proficient in the corpus of *halachah* (Jewish practice and custom) and competent to give religious rulings accordingly. Thus the role of a rabbi as a congregational leader in the Jewish community has always been an educational one and not a liturgical one. In modern times, especially in less-educated Jewish communities, rabbis have assumed more liturgical prominence. However, a rabbi is *not* a priest and has no intercessory standing. Judaism teaches that all people are able to enjoy "direct communication" with God.

**Rabbi Akiva:** See AKIVA.

**Reform Judaism:** Also known as Progressive Judaism, this is the modern stream of the Jewish religion that rejects the concept of divine origin and authority of the Written and Oral TORAH, believing that an individual's personal autonomy overrides traditional religious law (*halachah*). The

Reform movement made radical changes to Jewish liturgy and rejected ritual observances that were considered irrelevant and inappropriate for modern society. However, the principle of autonomy has led to a great diversity in this movement and in many cases a new return toward greater traditionalism may be observed. Reform Judaism was the first Jewish religious movement to ordain women for rabbinic leadership.

**Reformed Theology:** The main teachings of John Calvin regarding sin, faith, predestination, and the ATONEMENT of Jesus Christ.

**Replacement Theology:** The idea that the church has replaced the Jewish people as the recipient and beneficiary of divine biblical promise, i.e., the church is the New Israel in place of the Old Israel, the Jews.

**Righteousness:** One of God's essential attributes (see HOLINESS); also the standard of behavior required by God for all His people.

**Rosenzweig, Franz (1886–1929):** German Jewish theologian who founded the independent house of Jewish learning (*Lehrhaus*). Author of *Star of Redemption*.

**Sabbath:** The divinely ordained day of rest on the seventh day of the week, to be kept as a holy day in remembrance of creation and the Exodus (see Exod. 20:8–12 and Deut. 5:12–15).

**Sacrificial System:** The order of religious devotion in the temple involving the offering up of animal and/or vegetable donations.

**Sadducees:** The party among the Jewish people during the Second Temple period that was made up primarily of leading priestly and wealthy landowning families. The Sadducees rejected the extensive Oral Tradition (see TORAH) of the PHARISEES. They also rejected the latter's approach that religious leadership in the community should be based on knowledge and piety rather than status of birth.

**Salvation:** The Jewish use of this concept generally refers to the deliverance of the Jewish people from its enemies, the restoration of the exiles to the land (that would also be accompanied by the reconstruction of the temple and the reestablishment of the Davidic kingdom), and the ushering in of an era of universal peace (see MESSIANIC AGE). The Christian view is that one is saved from sin and its penalty through faith in Jesus Christ (see JUSTIFICATION BY FAITH).

**Saving Faith:** The Christian view that faith renders one righteous before God as opposed to a general faith in God without trust in Jesus.

**Second Coming:** The Christian teaching that the same Jesus who died and rose from the dead will come a second time—that the fulfillment of the messianic prophecies in the Hebrew Bible (and New Testament) concerning universal peace, etc., would then be ultimately achieved.

**Second Temple:** The temple in Jerusalem reconstructed on Mount Moriah on the site on which Solomon's temple, the first temple, stood before being destroyed by the Babylonians in the year 586 BCE. While the reconstruction of the second temple began at the end of the sixth century BCE, it only reached its full glory in the Hasmonean era (last two centuries BCE) and especially under the rule of Herod the Great.

**Second Temple Judaism:** A term used to describe the diverse expressions of Jewish life in the last centuries BCE and the majority of the first century CE, prior to the destruction of the second temple by the Romans in the year 70 CE.

**Sephardi(c):** The term is commonly used (though imprecisely) to describe Jews from Muslim lands, or more specifically those who follow specific customs and liturgical rites accepted in those lands. The word actually means "Spanish," reflecting the degree to which Jews from the Iberian peninsula settled in North Africa, Asia Minor, and the Middle East after their expulsion at the end of the fifteenth century. However, Sephardic communities also existed in Christian Europe both before and after the expulsion from Iberia.

**Septuagint:** See LXX.

**Sermon on the Mount:** Jesus' best-known sermon (Matt. 5–7) in which He unveiled His view of the Torah (especially the Decalogue) and contrasted it with the narrower interpretation of other Jewish authorities of his time.

**Shabbat:** See SABBATH.

**Shabbat Meal:** On Friday night and Saturday during the day, festive meals celebrate the Sabbath with food, drink, study, and song, giving thanks to the Creator and Guide of the universe.

**Shammai:** Jewish scholar who lived in the first century BCE, usually referred to in the context of debate with his contemporary, HILLEL. Generally Shammai takes a stricter line/interpretation than Hillel. Similarly to the latter, he established a school (the School of Shammai) that followed his approach.

**Simon Bar Coziba:** See BAR COCHBA.

**Sin:** Failure to do the right thing/live the right way in accordance with God's commandments or will.

**Sinai Covenant:** See COVENANT.

**Stendahl, Bishop Krister:** Former presiding bishop of the Church of Sweden and former dean of the Harvard Divinity School.

**Strack, Hermann:** Nineteenth-century German scholar of New Testament and rabbinic literature.

**Supercessionism:** See REPLACEMENT THEOLOGY.

**Tabernacle:** While the term is used in reference to the sanctuary that housed the ark of the covenant, it is also used to describe the booth that Jews construct for the Harvest Ingathering Festival (the Festival of Tabernacles) in keeping with Leviticus 23:39–43.

**Talmud:** The Talmud is basically the exposition of the MISHNAH. However, the Talmud contains not only the discussions in the schools of learning of the religious legal aspects of Jewish tradition (*halachah*) but also homiletical exposition and legends (*aggadah*). There are two Talmuds, the Jerusalem (or Palestinian) Talmud (often referred to by the letters TJ) that records the discussions in the schools in the land of Israel until around the end of the fourth century CE; and the Babylonian Talmud (referred to by the letters TB), the record of the stronger and longer-lasting study centers in Babylon. Accordingly the Babylonian Talmud, written down around the year 500 CE and divided into thirty-six tractates (i.e., separate books; some are referred to in this work, e.g., TB Sanhedrin), is the principal and more extensive text serving as the main point of reference for the CODES and rabbinic ruling.

**Targum(s):** Literally, "translation(s)." The word refers to the Aramaic translations of the books of the Bible. Often in translating the text, the Targums expounded and in effect commentated on it.

**Temple (Temple Mount):** The sanctuary built for the service of God on Mount Moriah (Mount Zion) in Jerusalem.

**Ten Commandments:** Another name for the Decalogue in Exodus 20 and Deuteronomy 5.

**Tertullian (155–230 CE):** Church leader and prolific Christian author who lived in Carthage, North Africa.

**Tetragrammaton:** Greek for "a four-lettered word" and refers to the four-lettered Hebrew name for God, *YHWH*.

**Torah:** Literally "instruction." Torah usually refers to the Written Torah, i.e., the five books of Moses (PENTATEUCH). It is also sometimes used to describe Judaism as a whole, thus including the Oral Torah (Oral Tradition), which refers to the body of clarification and exposition of the Written Torah, as well as additional traditions that, according to Orthodox teaching, go back to the revelation at Mount Sinai (essentially contained in the TALMUD). Traditional Judaism has therefore taught that the Oral Torah as well as the Written Torah has divine authority.

**Trinity:** The teaching of the Christian church, both Protestant and Catholic, that God is one and yet revealed in three persons, Father, Son, and Holy Spirit.

**Triumphalism:** The tendency to fall into arrogant pride because of a conviction that the triumph of one's own person or one's own religious group is certain.

**Ultra-Orthodox Judaism:** Ultra-Orthodoxy (sometimes referred to as "fervently Orthodox") refers to those within Jewish Orthodoxy who seek to live in maximal isolation from non-Jewish culture and see modernity as a cultural threat. They tend to wear clothing from a few centuries ago and/or dress in black and white clothing.

**Universalists:** Those who believe that all people will be "saved," regardless of their belief or conduct.

**Vicarious Atonement:** The view that an animal sacrifice takes the place of sinners by which the debt of sin is cancelled. Christianity teaches that this was done when Jesus died on the cross for the sins of the world.

**Whitehouse, O. C.:** Late nineteenth/early twentieth-century British Bible scholar.

**Written Torah:** See PENTATEUCH.

**Yad Hachazakah:** Maimonides's codification of the corpus of *halachah*, Jewish practice.

**Yahweh (God the Redeemer):** The name of God that was given meaning at the time of the Exodus. See TETRAGRAMMATON.

**Zealots:** The Jewish religious nationalists who led the rebellion against the Romans in the seventh decade of the first century CE that led as a consequence to the destruction of the temple.

**Zionism:** The name given to the political movement that originated in the late nineteenth century with the purpose of restoring Jewish national sovereignty in the ancestral biblical land of the Jewish people.

# General Index

# Biblical Index

# About the Authors

DR. R. T. KENDALL was born in Ashland, KY, in 1935. He attended the undergraduate program at Trevecca Nazarene University in Nashville, TN, receiving an A.B. degree. In 1972, he received his Master of Divinity degree from Southern Baptist Theological Seminary in Louisville, KY, and an M.A. from the University of Louisville in 1973. He completed his Doctorate in Philosophy at Oxford University in England in 1977 and went on to serve as the Senior Minister of Westminster Chapel in London for twenty-five years. He has authored over forty books. He now lives in Florida with his wife, Louise. From there, he continues his career as a popular Christian preacher and writer. His best-selling books include *The Thorn in the Flesh*, *Total Forgiveness*, and *The Anointing*.

CHIEF RABBI DAVID ROSEN is the President of IJCIC, the International Jewish Committee that represents World Jewry in its relations with other world religions. He is Director of the Department for Interreligious Affairs and Director of the Heilbrunn Institute for International Interreligious Understanding of the American Jewish Committee.

From 1975 to 1979, he was the Senior Rabbi of the largest Jewish congregation in South Africa and rabbinic judge on the Ecclesiastical Court (Beth Din). He was also founder/chairman of the Inter-Faith Forum, the Council of Jews, Christians and Muslims.

From 1979 to 1985, Rabbi Rosen was Chief Rabbi of Ireland where he founded, together with the Christian Primates of Ireland, the Irish Council of Christians and Jews. He was a member of the Academic Council as well as lecturer at the Irish School of Ecumenics.

He returned to Israel in 1985 to take up the appointment of Dean at the Sapir Center for Jewish Education and Culture in the Old City of Jerusalem and subsequently became Professor of Jewish Studies at the Jerusalem Center for Near Eastern Studies.

At that time he also served as the Anti Defamation League's Director of Interfaith Relations in Israel and as the ADL's co-liaison to the Vatican. In 1997 he was appointed to the position of Director of the ADL Israel office.

Rabbi Rosen is a member of the Israeli Chief Rabbinate's delegation for interreligious dialogue with the Holy See and is a founder of the Interreligious Coordinating Council in Israel that embraces some seventy organizations in Israel involved in interfaith relations.

Rabbi Rosen is an International President of the World Conference of Religion for Peace (WCRP), the all-encompassing world inter-faith body (incorporating fifteen religions in over fifty countries); he is Honorary President of the International Council of Christians and Jews (ICCJ), the umbrella organization for more than thirty national bodies promoting Christian-Jewish relations (the ICCJ's Abrahamic Forum promotes dialogue between Muslims, Christians and Jews) and serves as a member of the Executive Committee of the World Congress of Imams and Rabbis. Rabbi Rosen is a charter member of the International Advisory Committee of the Council for a Parliament of the World's Religions (CPWR); and is a member of the World Economic Forum's C-100, a council of 100 leaders formed for the purpose of improving relations and cooperation between the Muslim and Western worlds. He was one of the initiators and participants of The Alexandria Summit, the first Middle East Interfaith Summit with the participation of the leaders of the three monotheistic faiths of the Holy Land, held in Alexandria, Egypt, and is a member of its Permanent Committee for the Implementation of the Alexandria Declaration (PCIAD); and he was a member of the Permanent Bilateral Commission of the State of Israel and the Holy See that negotiated the normalization of relations between the two.

In November 2005, Rabbi Rosen was named a papal Knight Commander of the order of St. Gregory the Great for his outstanding contributions to promoting Catholic-Jewish reconciliation.

Other Books by Dr. Kendall

———

*Out of Your Comfort Zone: Is Your God Too Nice?*

*The Parables of Jesus*

*The Sensitivity of the Spirit*

*Are You Stone Deaf to the Spirit or Rediscovering God?*

*The Anointing: Yesterday, Today, Tomorrow*

*Understanding Theology*

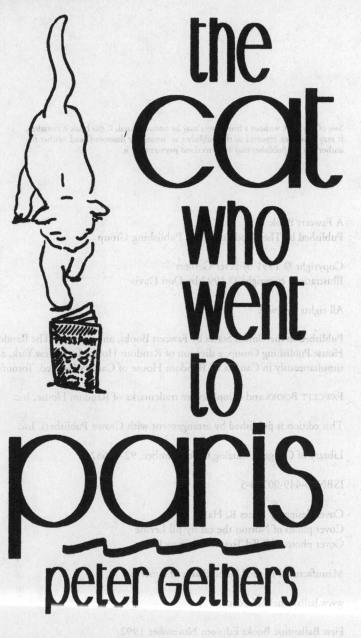

# the cat who went to paris

## peter gethers

**FAWCETT BOOKS    NEW YORK**

A Fawcett Book
Published by The Random House Publishing Group

Copyright © 1991 by Peter Gethers
Illustrations copyright © 1992 by Don Davis

Published in the United States by Fawcett Books, an imprint of The Random House Publishing Group, a division of Random House, Inc., New York, and simultaneously in Canada by Random House of Canada Limited, Toronto.

FAWCETT BOOKS and colophon are trademarks of Random House, Inc.

This edition is published by arrangement with Crown Publishers, Inc.

Library of Congress Catalog Card Number: 92-71682

ISBN: 0-449-90763-5

Cover design by James R. Harris
Cover photo of Norton the cat by Jill Levine
Cover photo of Eiffel Tower: Superstock, Inc.

Manufactured in the United States of America

www.ballantinebooks.com

First Ballantine Books Edition: November 1992

30  29  28  27  26

*To Dad.* You're missed.

*To Mom.* You're appreciated.

*To Janis.* I can't believe you let me do this.

*To Norton.* What can I say? You'll be hand-fed
Pounce as long as I'm around.

# contents

# Contents

# ACKNOWLEDGMENTS

First and foremost, thanks to Leona Nevler. All she did was come up with the idea for the book, think of the title, have confidence that I could write it, then come up with all the right suggestions to fix it. That's a good definition of a great editor.

Esther Newberg deserves a line or two (or a hundred) for convincing me that this was a good idea and, just generally, being the perfect agent.

Kathleen Moloney went through the manuscript word by word, as a favor. That was invaluable.

I wouldn't have Norton if it weren't for my brother, Eric. There's no way to even *try* to thank him for that.

Also thanks to everyone who let me write about them (whether they knew it or not).

# The cat who went to paris

The cat who went to paris

# Foreword

*A few weeks ago, I made out my first-ever will. At thirty-six, it left me feeling slightly melancholy, more than slightly middle-aged, and somewhat sentimental. Looking to share my sentiment, I mentioned to my mother that I had—quite magnanimously, I thought—left my New York City apartment to my brother Eric's one-year-old son, Morgan. Instead of the expected motherly glow of affection and pride, she looked at me as if I were an insane person.*

*"Can you do that?!" she asked.*

*I didn't understand her wide-eyed confusion, especially since, on the scale of human accomplishment, my mother ranks her small grandchild somewhere between Mahatma Gandhi, Thomas Jefferson, and Bo Jackson.*

*"Why not?" I said, just a tad confused. "I mean, I hope he doesn't get to use it for another forty or fifty years, but if he does, it'll go to Eric first and he can—"*

*"Did you say Morgan?" she interrupted.*

*"Yeah. Who else?"*

*"I thought you said* Norton," *dear old Mom told me.*
*"My cat? You thought I left my apartment to my cat?"*
*"Well," she said, in a particularly wise moment, and*
*shrugged, "with Norton, you never know."*

# 1. Before the cat who went to paris

This is a book about an extraordinary cat. However, the extraordinary thing about *any* cat is the effect it has on its owner. Owning a cat, especially from kittenhood, is a lot like having a child. You feed him, do your best to educate him, talk to him as if he understands you—and, in exchange, you want him to love you. He can drive you mad with his independence. He can, just as surely as a child, create a tremendous desire to protect him from anything bad. He is small, vulnerable, wonderful to hold—when he lets you. And he throws up on just about the same regular schedule.

Like children, cats exist on a separate and probably higher plane than we do, and like children, they must be at least partially defined by their relationship with their parents. And though they can do all sorts of amazing things such as hiding in the tiniest room imaginable and refusing to be found no matter *how* late you are for wherever it is you have to take them, they cannot write their autobiographies. That is left to humans. So this, as it must be, is also a book about people. And thus about relationships. And all sorts of other things cats have no business being involved with but can't seem to help themselves.

My involvement with a cat was strictly accidental. In fact, I had to be dragged into it kicking and screaming.

By way of example, a little over seven years ago, someone asked me to name ten things that I believed were truly self-revealing, deeply heartfelt, and absolutely irrevocable. This person, a woman I was going out with, asked me to do this, I believe, because she thought I was a person without much emotion, without a lot of passion. She had, I also believe, been through way too many years of Upper East Side New York therapy in which she had made way too many lists like this. The fact of the matter was that I had plenty of emotion and plenty of passion. I just didn't have much for her. People often seem to fall into this trap in their relationships. They seem to feel that if someone doesn't do what he is expected to do, then there must be something *wrong* with him. This is a much easier way of getting through life, I suppose, than having to think there might be something wrong with the expectations or oneself or the world. Or life.

I did, finally and over my better instincts, make a list of ten things I believed were true about myself. This is another trap that people fall into in their relationships (which cats *never* fall into): we do a lot of stupid things just so we don't have to be alone.

Anyway, this is the list that appeared:

1. I will never vote Republican.
2. Love does not usually hold up to close inspection . . .
3. . . . except for baseball. I *love* baseball—watching it, listening to it on the radio, talking about it, reading box scores. I am a baseball junkie.
4. Life is basically a sad thing, with an even sadder ending, so anything that brightens up a moment along the way is okay. Especially if it's funny.
5. I don't like being a part of anything—a religion, a regular softball game, a corporation, a government, you name it. As soon as some*one* becomes some*thing,* I tend to think he or she is lost.
6. Friendship must be earned. It is too important to fritter away on someone who doesn't want it, won't reciprocate it, or isn't worthy of it. As near as I can tell, people don't have all that much inherent value, but friends sure do.
7. There's very little cause for cruelty.
8. On the other hand, I'll pick entertaining and intelligent over nice any day of the week.
9. I don't care what anyone says: I think Meryl Streep's a lousy actress.
10. I hate cats.

In the years that have passed, a few of these irrevocable items have actually remained steadfast. Several have been altered somewhat, some bordering on the brink of unrecognizability. And there is one of the above that is so ludicrous it now seems inconceivable that it ever crossed my mind, much less made it through my mouth or found its way onto paper.

Numbers 1, 3, 6, and 7 remain absolutely unchanged.

Number 4 is basically sound, although I cannot be nearly so definite about the word "anything." There are terrifying things I did not conceive of when I made my initial list: oat bran, crack, *People* magazine cover stories on recovering alcoholic celebrities, wilding, sequels, and Abe Rosenthal's "On My Mind" column in the *New York Times*.

Numbers 8 and 9 are a little tricky. 8 now depends more and more on my mood and how hard my day was. And Meryl Streep's Australian accent really is astonishing.

Number 5 has changed somewhat. I have found something I am willing to join.

Number 2 clearly relates to Number 5, which will become much clearer as this book continues, and they both, amazingly enough, have changed because of Number 10.

Ah yes, Number 10 . . .

Well, now we've come to the youthful folly, a statement made in such ignorance it boggles the mind . . .

I, of course, have a cat now. Norton.

I treat this cat as very few animals—or people, for that matter—have ever been treated.

If he is asleep in the middle of the bed when it's time for my day to end, I sleep curled up in a corner of the mattress, happily braving stiff necks and bad backs so he remains undisturbed.

I take Norton everywhere I go. He's been skiing in Vermont, to a writers conference in San Diego, to the best restaurant in Amsterdam, back and forth on a regular basis to Paris. At one of that city's premier hotels, the Tremoille, when my assistant calls to make a reservation for Mr. Gethers, the desk clerk knows to ask: *"Avec son chat?"*

I bought a house in Sag Harbor, a real-life Bedford Falls of a town near the tip of Long Island, and though there were many other mitigating circumstances, the secret and overriding reason for the purchase was because my cat *loves* to run around in a yard.

I've had one girlfriend break up with me because she believed I liked Norton better than I liked her (which I did). And I once didn't go on a vacation with another girlfriend to my favorite resort hotel in America because they wouldn't accept small, very well-behaved felines.

I worry about him, I talk about him (and *to* him, I have to add) to the point of idiocy, and if he doesn't sleep within a crooked arm's reach of my pillow—which he doesn't about one day a week—then I don't sleep very well. I actually worry that I've done something to offend him.

I sometimes—and this is a particularly tough one to admit publicly—let him eat off my spoon. Usually ice cream or yogurt. Chocolate's his favorite flavor, and it's a pretty funny thing to watch when he decides it's time to lick that sucker clean.

It is hardly a one-way street, however. He does all sorts of things for me that are pretty wonderful for a cat.

He goes for walks with me. No leash. On a beach with no cars around to disturb him, he's gone up to two miles, walking anywhere and everywhere from ten feet behind me to three feet in front of me. His record in traffic is three blocks, which he does most Sunday mornings when I stroll to Sean's Murray Hill market in Sag Harbor.

Norton will wait for me anywhere, no matter where I

leave him. If I'm at a hotel, I can dump him outside by the pool or in the garden, and let him play there all day or night long. When I go to get him, he will be nowhere in sight, but when I call or whistle for him, he'll meow exactly once, then leap out of his hiding place to rush to join me. I honestly believe I could drop him in the heart of an African jungle, leave him for a year, reappear, and as long as I could find the bush he was last seen scurrying under, he'd be there waiting for me.

He likes to roughhouse. His favorite game is to pounce on my hand when it's moving tauntingly under a sheet, wrestle it, and try to eat it—but he will *never* bite or scratch any part of me that he recognizes as mine. If sometimes he gets carried away in the heat of battle and a claw accidentally isn't pulled in in time when my hand comes out from the linen, he will freeze at the sound of my yelp, put his paws over his eyes, and bury his nose under the pillow in shame until I pat him on the head and assure him I'm okay.

He sits on the side of the tub when I take a bath.

If I, as I sometimes forgetfully do, close the door to a room, leaving Norton on the other side, he will howl and meow as if possessed until I open the door. He does not like to be left outside of anything I am inside.

He trusts me.

He is quite a comfort when I'm sad and makes being happy much more fun.

He has seen me through broken hearts and illness and death.

I love my cat, if you haven't gotten the drift yet.

He actually forced me to change my list of irrevocable self-realizations.

In doing so, he changed my life.

When a small gray animal does a little thing like that for you, how can you *not* let him sleep in the middle of the bed when he's tired?

# 2. The cat who came to New York

Have you ever seen a Scottish Fold?

One cat book I read dared refer to the breed as a "mutation." What they are, in fact, are incredibly handsome cats whose ears fold over in half, forward and then down, giving them a vaguely owl-like look. Their heads tend to be rounder than regular cat heads, and their bodies, at least all the ones I've seen, seem to be short, firm, and trim. Officially they are a shorthaired cat, but I would unofficially place them somewhere in-between a long- and a shorthair. They feel particularly soft and nice. Their temperaments range from sweet to sweeter. All of the ones I've met and spent time with are intelligent, though of course none have risen to the heights of brilliance that mine has.

They actually do come from Scotland. Apparently, the first one was discovered in 1961 at a farm near Dundee, by

some people named William and Mary Ross. All of the fold-ear cats running around today can trace their pedigree back to Susie, which is what the Rosses named the first one they discovered.

The first time I ever heard of a Scottish Fold was when I got a phone call from my brother, Eric, who lives in Los Angeles. We talked about life (it seemed fine), work (since he's a screenwriter, it was hard, nasty, and full of deceitful intrigue), women (they were getting younger), and our health (we were getting older). The conversation seemed to have run its course when he dropped the bombshell.

"Oh, yeah," he said. "Did I tell you I got a cat?"

If this were a screenplay, the words *Long Pause* would now appear in parentheses, because there was a long one. A real long one. In that long pause my eyes rolled back in my head, my mouth dropped open as far as it could stretch, and I was certain the world had gone mad.

"You hate cats," I reminded him when I was finally able to speak.

"I know," was his response. "But this one's different."

I then heard the description of my first Scottish Fold, whom he'd named Henry. I have to say, I wasn't convinced.

"But you hate cats," I repeated. "We both hate cats. We loathe and despise them. We always have and we always will." By this time I think I was starting to whine. "We like *dogs*."

I could tell, even from three thousand miles away, that my brother was smiling that annoying superior smile he has when he thinks I'm saying something idiotic.

"You'll see," he said again. "This one's different."

I have to sidetrack here.

At the time, my girlfriend's name was Cindy Wayburn. We'd been going together for three years or so, having quite a nice time. At one point, about six months earlier, Cindy had casually mentioned to me that she was thinking of getting a cat. I, just as casually, mentioned that if she did she might think about spending her nights in someone's apartment other than mine.

We argued, we discussed, we argued some more. She cajoled. I brought up my "cats don't fetch" premise and we argued even more. She even took the tack that it would be good for *me* to have a pet. I'd made the mistake of mentioning to her once that I missed having an animal around the house, that it felt lonely without one.

"A pet, yes," I said. "A cat, no."

"But you travel so much," was her comeback. "You couldn't have a dog. It would die in about two weeks."

"I know," I said. "That's why I *don't* have a dog. But that still isn't convincing me that a cat is a good idea. A cat would die in about two weeks, too—because I'd kill it."

"You've never even been around cats. You'd like them once you got to know one. And it would be good for you. You spend a lot of time at the beach house—you could have company. You wouldn't have to spend so much time talking to the old ladies who hang out at the grocery store."

"How do *you* know I spend so much time talking to the old ladies? Who told you?" I thought this had been a well-kept secret. Every summer I spent a solid month writing at

a beach house I rented in Fair Harbor, Fire Island. Cindy, during the years it was Cindy, would come out on weekends, and I'd toil alone during the week, insisting that I loved the solitude. But after three days of slaving away over the typewriter (this was before I dared to punch away at a laptop), I'd begin to miss human companionship. I'd start to make a few more phone calls than usual, beginning around ten-thirty in the morning. After six days, my friends would start to keep their phone machines on since most of them didn't have the time to spend helping me avoid doing my work. At the ten-day point, I'd finally break down and start making three trips a day to the Fair Harbor market. It was only two blocks from my house, and there was usually a group of elderly housewives hanging out there, gossiping with the butcher and with each other. By my third season at the beach, I'd become a regular at the market. I knew everything there was to know about hundreds of people I'd never met. And best of all, I wasn't at the typewriter for half-hour stretches, three times a day.

"Have you ever lived with a kitten?" Cindy demanded, ignoring my pleas to reveal the Fire Island squealer.

"I've never lived with a snake, either. And I don't want to. I don't like them. Was it Frank, the butcher? Was he the one who told you?"

We went around in this adultlike manner for a reasonable amount of time—about seven hours—until eventually she decided that getting a cat for herself or for me wasn't going to be a plus in our relationship. To my great relief, our arguing ended and things went back on an even keel.

Until Cindy went to Los Angeles to visit her mother.

She wasn't particularly looking forward to the trip, since

she didn't much care for her mother. Once a year, however, filial guilt won out over common sense and Cindy would go west and pay a visit. Mrs. Wayburn—and I'll try to be as fair and objective as I can here—was an absolutely horrid woman who lived in some part of the outskirts of L.A. I'd never actually heard of, in a delightful little community called La Mobile Home Cité. If they'd had a slogan, it would have been "Come Spend a Few Depressing Years with Us Before Your Internal Organs Start to Fail." All in all, it was a great place to spend time if you didn't care about air, space, or ever looking at anything attractive.

This visit was worse than usual. After the second day, they had a huge fight. Cindy wanted to take her mother out to a fancy dinner, simply to be nice. Mom, in her typical upbeat way, said that all food tasted the same to her—like a lump of decaying, cold, gray clay—so there was no point in throwing money away on something as unpleasant as eating well. Cindy thought this was an unhealthy attitude, mentioned this to her mom, and the battle ensued. An hour after that, she was in my brother's house, crying and eating a delicious *tarte tatin* (my brother happens to be an excellent cook).

Eric was extremely nice to her, really cheered her up, and by the time she called me to say good night, she was in a terrific mood. Much better than could have been expected. So good, in fact, I should have been suspicious. She told me she was going to spend the next morning shopping with my brother, then would be on a mid-afternoon plane home. She'd decided she didn't want to see her mother anymore, and with no mother responsibilities, she didn't want to stay in L.A. The last thing she said before she hung up was,

"You won't believe how cute Eric's cat is. Wait till you see him."

I hung up, deciding I could wait a pretty long time.

At eleven-ten the next night, my phone rang.

"I'm at the baggage claim," Cindy announced. "Are you awake?" Her voice had that special singsong quality it had when she was feeling particularly affectionate toward me.

"I'm awake," I said, in much the same tone.

"I'll be there in thirty minutes."

"I can't wait," I told her. And, in truth, I couldn't.

Cindy had a key to my apartment and could bypass the various security buzzers and phones and TV cameras most people had to go through to get into my building. So thirty minutes later, I heard my front door open. When I came out of the bedroom, Cindy was standing by the door, grinning happily.

I went to kiss her.

"No," she ordered. "Stop."

I stopped.

"I have something to show you."

"You do?"

She nodded.

"Do I have to go to the hallway to see it?"

"No," she said, still with the biggest grin I'd ever seen on her face. "Stay there. Close your eyes. I'll tell you when."

I stayed, I closed my eyes. I heard her "when" and opened them.

Cindy was holding a little ball of fur in her hand. One

hand. It was so small, for a moment I thought she'd brought an extremely well-behaved mouse back from California.

But it wasn't a mouse.

It was a tiny, tiny gray kitten with a round head and funny-looking ears that folded forward and down. The kitten was sitting up in her palm, boldly swiveling his head around, gazing at all the sights in my loft apartment.

"You got yourself a cat?" I stammered weakly.

The kitten stopped swiveling his head, now stared directly into my eyes, and mewed. A quiet little mew right at me. And to this day I swear that he smiled.

"No," Cindy said. "He's not for me."

"Who's he for?" I asked quietly.

When she didn't answer, I said, again quite softly, "Cindy? Who's the cat for?"

When she burst out crying, I had a vague suspicion I knew the answer to my question.

I'd known for years that if I ever had a pet—I assumed a dog—I'd name him Norton. There wasn't even a close second choice.

My favorite name for an animal—and my favorite animal up to that point—was Yossarian, my brother's dog. Yossarian was, in my opinion, not just an incredibly cute cockapoo, which, for those of you who are strictly cat lovers, is half cocker spaniel and half poodle. He was also a genius.

He was never on a leash, not even in New York City. He would walk with you to the corner, stop, wait for you to cross the street, then trot along beside you. He would wait outside of stores for you while you shopped. He was also

extremely friendly and just generally had a kind of existential, world-weary air to him that made you believe he was capable of carrying on a very interesting drawing room conversation. In French.

I got to take care of Yossarian once, for a stretch of about six months, when Eric was living in Spain. I was living in a fifth-floor walk-up in the West Village, a divey little apartment, and Yossarian moved in with me. It didn't take long for me to realize that Yos wasn't wild about climbing up and down the five flights of stairs whenever he had to go for a walk. He especially wasn't wild about it in winter, when the snow and ice were already tough enough on his L.A.-tenderized paws.

I'd had him perhaps all of a week when, to my horror, the little guy started limping. I noticed it as we were strolling down Greenwich Street. His right front paw was definitely curled up in front of him, and he was favoring it. I went over to him, picked him up, and checked him out. I couldn't find anything wrong, but he was looking at me in such a pathetic way, clearly the dog was in great pain. I set him down just long enough for him to do his thing, then scooped him back up, carried him back to my building and up the five flights to my apartment.

I decided not to panic. I figured I'd give it a few days, then if the limping continued, I'd take him to the vet.

Yos seemed fine in the apartment, perhaps moving around just a bit slower than usual. Once he'd get outside, though, the limping would start up. I'd have to carry him around, set him down when he had to relieve himself, then pick him back up and return to my apartment with the dog cradled in my arms.

On the third day of this routine—he was now limping slightly even in the apartment and I was caringly carrying him up and down the stairs three times a day—we went for our afternoon stroll. I set Yosie down on the snow, and since I was with a woman friend, she and I walked on ahead to give him some privacy. After about half a block, I turned back to see how my ward was doing. He was doing just fine. In fact, he was doing so well, he was racing around the sidewalk in front of my building, playing with another dog. I couldn't believe it. I mean, this dog was *moving.* Full weight on that right front paw.

"Yossarian!" I called.

The dog froze. Didn't move an inch. Then he looked down at the snow on the ground, looked at me, looked back down at his paw, which was resting on the snow, one more look at me, and his paw shot up in the air in a desperate attempt to replicate the pathetic position he kept it in when he was feigning his limp.

"Forget it," I said. "The free ride is over."

If dogs can shrug, Yossarian shrugged, put his paw back down, and resumed his frolic with his playmate. That was the end of the limp.

I wasn't the only one who felt that Yossarian was far more human than the normal quadruped, by the way. A few years ago, when he was thirteen years old and getting sickly, my brother had a "roast" for him. About twenty people showed up with presents for the dog, Eric served food and drink, and everyone proceeded to tell their favorite Yossarian stories. I called from New York just to make sure that someone told my "limping" story, which was by then part of the Yossarian legend.

When, about a year after that, Yos died, I promise you, everyone who was there that day was truly happy that they'd gotten to tell him how much he'd meant to them over the years.

Ever since Eric had taken the *Catch-22* name for this brilliant little dog, I'd been trying to come up with a comparable name for my future pet, which I always assumed would also be a dog. Dunbar was a consideration, but it came from the same book, so I discarded it. McMurphy was a possibility, but then the movie version of *Cuckoo's Nest* came out and I hated it, so that was the end of McMurphy. I went further back in the annals of literature and quickly rejected everything from Falstaff to Tristram to Verloc, then moved on and rejected Malloy, Zorba, and finally even Snoopy.

I considered Steed (or Emma, if it was a female) from "The Avengers," but somehow those just didn't stay with me. Travis stuck around for about six months—that being the name of the character played by Malcolm McDowell in *If . . .* and *O Lucky Man!*—but then a friend of mine got a dog and named him Travis as in Travis McGee.

I switched to the sports field in a move of anti-intellectual desperation.

I couldn't name a pet Willie. What if some poor oaf thought I was naming it after Willie Davis or Willie Wilson or some other inferior imitation of the godlike Mays? I couldn't risk it. None of my other idols' names really lent themselves to being repeated over and over again while trying to coax a four-legged animal out from under the bed. Muhammad? Julius? Roger "the Dodger" Staubach? No.

Jim Brown? Forget it. I'd wind up with a pet who'd periodically throw me off a balcony. I was just about to settle for Clyde, figuring I would have a very cool pet who would never panic under pressure and would play great D, when, about two years before Cindy walked into my apartment with a cat, the name came to me.

I'm a television baby. I always watched it, I always liked it, when I grew up I even wrote for it. Sitcoms were always my fave (once "Bronco Lane" and "Sugarfoot" went off the air). From an aficionado's lofty view, there are only a handful of sitcoms that deserve the label "great." I'm not talking about campy "Gilligan's Island"–type garbage. I'm talking great writing, great acting, great characters. "Bilko" has to be near the top. Same with "The Mary Tyler Moore Show" and "The Dick Van Dyke Show" and, later, "Barney Miller" and "Taxi." But there's one that's in a class by itself. The others aren't even close. Best characters, best fat jokes, best sets, best straight man (or woman, actually), best Grand High Exalted Wizard, and the two best performances in TV sitcom history. Obviously, I'm talking about "The Honeymooners," and like a flash, I had visions of one day—and then every day for years and years—being able to come home from a hard day's work, call out, "Norton, pal o' mine, I'm home!" and see a little furry guy come leaping toward me, licking my face in a frenzy of joy.

As soon as this little cat mewed up at me from Cindy's hand, I knew that Norton had finally arrived.

I knew one other thing, too. And this came in just as much of a flash as the name.

It was love at first sight.

It doesn't make sense. There's no explanation. It's never happened to me before or since with man, woman, or beast, and I don't know if it ever will again.

I started to get angry at Cindy. I wanted to yell. I began to sputter and to say things like "How could you do this!" I was all set to pace and wave my arms around in the air like a lunatic. But I wasn't able to do any of those things. I didn't have the opportunity. Cindy was busy doing her impersonation of Lucy when Ricky comes home after finding out she disguised herself as a painter to get an audition at the club. "I thought you'd like him . . . *sniff* . . . Eric said you'd like him . . . *sniff* . . . I'm sorry . . . I thought . . . *sniff* . . . *Unaughhhhwaaaaaaaaa* . . ." I knew I wasn't going to get anywhere in that direction, so I turned to you-know-who. With my mouth still open, I looked into the little cat's eyes and I melted. Just dead away, gone, total mush.

Cindy, now switching to her Laura Petrie mode, trying not to cry but letting me know she might start again any moment, held out her hand, and I took the kitten from her. Having absolutely no experience with babies of any species—human or four-legged—I held him kind of awkwardly. Cupping him in my right palm, which I supported with my left, I brought him closer to me, raising him up to my face until we were nose to nose. I don't think he could have been more than six inches long or weighed more than two pounds. He was a light, soft gray with irregular patches of dark gray circling his body. Bits of white spread across the top of his paws and ringed around his little black-and-orange nose. Three startling lines of black began right between his eyes and streaked all the way down his back, broadening by his tail so that his back half was darker than

his front. His tail, even then, was very bushy, with black rings around it. It looked like a tail that could have belonged to a raccoon. His eyes were huge, twice too big for his head, oval and green. I had absolutely never in my life seen anything that was so cute, so independent, so smart, or anything that had ever looked quite so much as if it belonged to me. He never flinched or shifted his gaze away from me. He simply mewed once more and licked me more or less on my right eyelid with a sandpaperlike tongue the size of a small bristle on a paintbrush.

"He's six weeks old," Cindy said in a little bit of a hushed tone, drying her eyes. "And there's something very special about him. I don't think he's just a normal cat."

I switched him to my left hand and ran my right hand lightly over him, from his head to his tail, the first time I'd ever petted a feline.

"Of course he's not just a normal cat," I said. "How could he be? He's mine."

The shopping Cindy had done with my brother, of course, was to go out and buy this little cat, Norton. When she had seen what a Scottish Fold looked like, she flipped. She told Eric all about how she wanted to get a cat and how I wanted a pet but refused to consider a cat, and he, having known me for a much longer time than she had and knowing how I'd react when I saw a Fold, told her they'd go looking the next morning.

They drove out to the Valley, to the breeder where Eric had gotten Henry. The breed was, at the time, relatively unknown but already on the expensive side. Eric had paid

three hundred dollars for his. (Now, believe it or not, a good Scottish Fold will cost you up to fifteen hundred smackers.) He was a big believer in the theory that if you're going out to buy something, it's much better to spend as much money as possible and be as impractical as you can.

As luck would have it, the breeder had recently ushered in a new litter of Folds. She had too many Folds. Because they were so expensive, she didn't think she could sell them all before they got so big that they'd get underfoot. She knew Eric, she took a liking to Cindy, so she gave them one for seventy-five dollars, with the simple promise that they'd give the kitten the best possible home.

"Here, I'll give you my favorite," she told them.

She picked a six-week-old cat out of a cardboard box and handed him over. Along with his breeding papers, she gave them an article that had appeared the week before in the *San Fernando Valley Register*. The story was on exotic breeds of cats, and as an example of the exotic Scottish Fold, there was a photograph of the cat Cindy was holding. For the use of the article, the kitten had been named Baby, and the caption under his photo said, "Unlike some deceptively named feline families—Himalayans, for example, have no tie to the mountains—Scottish Folds like this kitten, 'Baby,' actually originated in Scotland."

"He's a star," the breeder said.

"I sure hope so," Cindy told her.

He certainly acted like a star on the trip home. Cindy was a bit nervous taking such a young animal on the airplane. She wasn't sure how he'd react, what he'd do to go to the

bathroom, whether such a long flight would make him neurotic the rest of his nine lives. She quickly found out he
wasn't the neurotic type. She had him in a little box, but
minutes into the flight, she lifted him onto her tray table just
to check him out. He yawned, lay down, and immediately
went to sleep. She figured she'd leave him there until either
the cat or the stewardesses started to freak out. Neither
happened. The cat sat or slept on the tray, happy as could
be, for the entire trip. The dread bathroom problem never
came up. (As Norton has proved on many a flight since, he
either has an abnormally strong bladder or an equally dominant sense of decorum. On this initial trip and on hundreds
to come, he simply waited until proper facilities presented
themselves.) Occasionally he would stretch, look around,
then sit back down. He meowed only twice. Both times
Cindy cooed at him and stroked him—and he made it very
clear that that was exactly why he'd bothered to speak. The
stewardesses fussed over him delightedly, brought him
milk, even picked him up to show him off to various passengers. Through it all, the little kitten acted as if he'd logged
as many miles as Chuck Yeager.

In the taxi from the airport to my apartment, he scrambled on the backseat over to the door handle, which he
stood on, stretching up to peer out the window as the car
drove him into Manhattan.

"It was weird," Cindy said, as I held him in my hand.
"Not only did he have absolutely no fear, he acted like he
knew where he was going—*and was looking forward to getting
there.*"

The cat now wiggled a little bit in my palm, so I gingerly
set him down on the floor.

"He'll be scared now," Cindy told me. "Kittens are always scared of new surroundings. This place'll seem huge to him and that's frightening to a cat."

Uh-huh.

My frightened kitten meandered over to a couch in my living room. Then he strolled over to the couch opposite it. Then he went back, halfway between the two, plopped down on the rag rug, and went to sleep.

I watched his little chest moving up and down while he slept. I'd never seen anything conk out quite so quickly. I knew I had an imbecilic grin on my face, but I couldn't help it.

"Norton," I called to him softly. "Norton . . ."

The kitten's eyes opened slowly. First they were just a slit, then they held at half-open, then his head tilted and he was looking up at me.

I smiled at Cindy.

"Look," I said. "He already knows his name."

# 3. The cat who went to Fire Island

Most people think that owning a cat is a lot less of a responsibility than owning a dog.

They're wrong.

They're especially wrong if a particular owner happens to decide that a particular cat is so sensitive, intelligent, and aware of what's happening that he has to be treated on a higher level than the owner's fellow human beings.

There actually is a certain logic to this. After all, people have *choices*. They do not have to be friends with someone they don't like or who mistreats them. They do not have to be alone if they choose not to be. (This is a general classification, remember: it does not necessarily apply to those people who don't use deodorant in the summer, think Sandra Bernhard is funny, or who idolize the Robert De Niro character in *Taxi Driver*.) They do not have to eat only

when someone remembers to feed them. And, most of all, if the person they live with comes home late, most people do not have to worry that that person has been eaten by a predator.

Cindy thought I was going a little overboard with this last comparison, but *she* was the one who gave me a book called *The Natural Cat.*

She gave it to me because it was rather immediately apparent that Norton was not only breaking down my resistance to *him,* he was breaking down a lifetime resistance to his entire species.

First of all, it's very difficult to resist anything that is so vulnerable. And there are very few things more vulnerable than a six-week-old kitten. Second of all, he didn't *act* vulnerable, which is even harder to resist. He scrambled, he clawed, he nudged; he took over my apartment is what he did. Third of all, he took over *me.*

His first sneak attack in this regard came in the middle of the night.

Cindy and I had a very particular sleeping order. I always slept on the left side of my bed, she on the right. I slept on my side; she curled around my back with her arms wrapped around me.

We weren't sure whether Norton should sleep on the bed. We didn't know if he'd wriggle around all night, keeping us awake, a prospect which didn't much excite me. We also didn't know if he'd even *want* to sleep with us. Maybe we were too huge and frightening. So we decided to leave it up to him.

His first night, we heard him sliding around the living room floor as we were falling off to sleep. It seemed as if

he'd made his choice—he'd find his own bed. Fine with me. No problem. Everyone knew cats weren't as affectionate as dogs, anyway. He could sleep wherever he damn pleased.

I awoke in the morning, as usual a few minutes before Cindy. With my eyes half open, I listened for the sounds of a small cat at play. Nothing. A bit worried, I strained to listen more carefully. It seemed natural that a newborn kitten should be awake causing trouble. Still nothing.

Then I felt a very light stirring from my pillow, and I rolled my eyes down to get a look.

What I saw was a small, gray ball of fluff, comfortably resting under my cheek and neck. He was awake, his eyes wide open, but he wasn't moving. Not an inch. He was staring straight at me, waiting for me to make the first move.

Without lifting my head, I slowly twisted my left arm, bringing it up so I could pet him. With two fingers, I stroked the top of his head, rubbing between his eyes down to his nose. He shifted, ever so slightly, stretching his neck so I could scratch under his chin. We stayed like that for several minutes, the cat stretched out luxuriously, the owner scratching away.

I felt pretty good.

He'd chosen me to sleep with. Not just the bed. Me. Not Cindy. *Me.*

It was *embarrassing* how good it felt.

I swiveled around to glance at Cindy. She was awake now, too, watching us and smiling.

Thus began a whole *new* sleeping arrangement. When Cindy spent the night, Norton would stay in the living room until we fell asleep. But every morning, when I awoke he'd be scrunched against my neck, partly under my

cheek, absolutely wide awake, waiting for me to scratch under his chin.

If it was just the two of us—me and the cat, not me and Cindy—Norton would take Cindy's place before the lights went out. He'd lie in her spot on the bed, head on her pillow, body stretched out like a person, usually under the covers. I'd turn my back to him, and he'd snuggle up there, exactly as Cindy did. In the morning he'd still be on her pillow, wide awake, staring straight at me, waiting for me to rise and shine. When I'd open my eyes, he'd move a few inches to me, lick my eyes or my forehead, then move to his under-the-cheek-and-neck position for five minutes of petting and scratching.

He never, ever woke me up. Never, ever meowed for breakfast. *A deux* or *ménage à trois*, he would stay quietly in bed until I was awake, wait until his morning petting, then he'd get up and join me for breakfast in the kitchen—one black coffee, one chicken and kidney in cream sauce deluxe.

His next sneaky little way of worming himself into my life was my own fault.

I wanted to show him off. (I knew that was a bad sign, but there you have it; there was nothing I could do about it.) So I started taking him places. Not far away. Just to friends' apartments. He was, needless to point out, quite a hit, proving to be as fearless in these apartments as he was in mine, prowling and hopping around from room to room. Some of these friends had cats of their own and were a bit worried about possible confrontations. I couldn't imagine how anything—even a rival cat—could object to Norton, and as it turned out, I was right. Most of the time, the cat whose turf we were invading would immediately hiss and circle Norton, whom I'd have plopped down in the middle of the living room. Norton would peer over at the tough king of the castle, give him a look as if to say, "Who are you kidding?"; then he'd roll over on the ground and look as cute as an animal could look. The grown cat would, more or less, have no choice but to come over and be friendly. Otherwise he'd look like a warmongering idiot in front of his owner.

It seemed like too much of a bother, on these goodwill tours, to lug his carrier around the city, especially when he was so tiny, so I'd simply put on a windbreaker or a raincoat and stick Norton in the pocket. Walking a few blocks was no problem. He'd sit calmly, occasionally sticking his head out over the pocket's rim to peer around, then retreat back inside. He actually got pretty good at this form of transportation. Even on long subway rides to the Upper West Side. The noise didn't seem to frighten him; rather it intrigued him. The sudden jarring stops and starts struck him as something of a fun game. The only drawbacks were (1) the bums who, thinking they might be hallucinating, would want to touch him to make sure he wasn't the step before the pink elephants, and (2) the garrulous strangers who were positive that a cat in one's pocket was an open invitation to tell life stories, tales of woe, or worst of all, adorable pet anecdotes of their own.

On Saturdays, I started to get into the habit of taking him with me on my errands. He never squawked about this; in fact, I think he liked it. Most shops were happy to see his little head pop out and swivel around. In my local bakery he came away with quite a few scraps of cookies and sweet rolls and he developed a serious taste for jelly doughnuts;

in the local grocery store he often lucked into pieces of cheese and the occasional chicken part. He'd even stay quiet—in an oversized pocket—for a relaxing brunch in a Village restaurant on a Sunday afternoon. A few waiters and waitresses wondered why I always ordered a glass of milk—a short, round glass if at all possible; if not, a tall glass and an empty saucer on the side—to go with my Mimosa or Bloody Mary, but no one ever said anything. To this day, I'm sure there are several maître d's and busboys who talk about the bearded fellow who always left little puddles of milk under his seat. You'll just have to take my word for it that I was actually quite neat. Norton, however, is one of the sloppiest lappers I've ever seen. When he's thirsty, his tongue reminds me of nothing so much as one of those machines that swirls paint around, nearly at the speed of light, on small canvases so kindergartners can create instant works of abstract art.

I got used to keeping my hand inside my coat on my travels about town, and constantly stroking this soft little cat. He got used to these hour- or two-hour-long adventures. When I'd leave the house without him—as I was forced to do far more often than I liked—he would look way too sad. As a result, it was taking me longer and longer to get out the door. (Have you ever spent five minutes explaining to a cat about your day's agenda and how it just wouldn't work if he came on your important meetings with you? Have you ever tried it when you have company? A word of advice: Don't.) Norton clearly didn't like being left behind. He much preferred being carried around in a pocket to spending the day dozing on the windowsill.

My only problem other than my five- and ten-minute

out-the-door soliloquies, was that summer was coming up. Even for Norton I didn't think I could wear an overcoat in the New York summer.

Meanwhile, since it was immediately apparent that Norton and I were joined at the hip (or the pocket, as the case may be), Cindy did two things. First, she got a cat of her own, a normal full-eared cat for whom she paid Bide-a-Wee five dollars. She named him Marlowe, as in Chandler and *The Big Sleep*, not the sixteenth century and *Tamburlaine*. I couldn't really object. I mean, here I was with my own cat who was sleeping on my head and for whom, twice in the first two weeks of our relationship, I'd stayed home from work so I could get to know him better. I no longer had a leg to stand on as far as cat-prevention was concerned. Besides, I liked Marlowe quite a bit. He was just as sweet as Norton. (In fact, in some ways, sweeter; it was clear from the beginning that Norton had a touch of the rebel in him. He liked to test me. Little things like scratching at the couch. To be perfectly honest, my attitude was that if scratching the couch gave him so much pleasure, let him scratch. It wasn't that big a deal to get a new couch every so often. But a horrified Cindy insisted that was no way to raise a kitten, so whenever Norton scratched, I would tell him "no!" just the way Cindy told me I was supposed to. He was definitely smart enough to realize he was doing something wrong and would immediately respond to my warning. He would stop scratching at once and move about three feet away from the leg of the couch. Then, watching me all the way, he would, inch by inch, slink back to the leg, stick his paw out, and give the thing one or two good rakes. I would clap my hands, say "no!" again, and he would

scamper those three feet away. I'd turn my back and, two minutes later, hear the familiar scritching of claws on canvas. I must admit I was proud of this James Dean–like adventurous streak and secretly encouraged it, whereas Cindy loved the fact that *her* cat wouldn't *dream* of doing anything to upset her.) Marlowe was quite handsome in his own way, too, a beautiful dark coat streaked through with black and brown, though even Cindy had to admit he wasn't in my guy's league. He was also a much better jumper than Norton. Marlowe could do something that never failed to amaze me. He could jump from the floor to the top of an open door and balance himself there. Norton used to eye this physical agility with some envy, I believe, though he soon realized his own limitations and comfortably settled for intellect over brawn. Overall, though, as truly nice as Marlowe was, he was *normal*. He was a cat. Norton was something more.

The second thing Cindy did was buy me the aforementioned book, *The Natural Cat,* so I could actually learn something about my animal. It's a wonderful little book, and I quickly studied up on such things as how cats clean themselves and how they adjust to litter boxes and all the things cat owners around the world already know and don't need to read about here. To me, it was all fascinating, much like discovering a whole new culture. I had never heard anything purr before, and I thought it was very possibly the most wonderful, soothing noise I'd ever listened to. I liked nothing better than having Norton stretch out on the bed or couch with me lying on top of him, the full weight of my head plunked down right in the middle of his body. He would purr and purr and purr in delight. I soon realized I

was passing up reruns of "The Rockford Files" in order to
spend an hour listening to this motorboat sound.

I had also never seen fur on anything's back stand straight
up or claws that retracted. I was particularly fascinated by
his claws because, as much as he loved to scratch, his claws
*never* came out when we were roughhousing. He made it
quite clear that such a thing was unthinkable, and I found
myself touched and moved by his instinctive gentleness. In
general, I was extremely interested in reading about the
whys and wherefores and history of all such behavior and
physical reactions.

In the last chapter of *The Natural Cat,* the psychology of
the feline is discussed. At some point in the chapter, it says
to watch and notice: if you come home from work every day
at six o'clock, when you arrive at the regular hour, your cat
will be dozing contentedly in some comfortable spot. He
will be relaxed and calm when he lifts his head up to welcome you home. HOWEVER: if you usually come home at
six o'clock, and then you don't come home until eleven or
so, when you walk in the door your cat will be pacing up
and down, nervously wondering if you've deserted and
abandoned him. This is because his fifty million years of
jungle instinct will have taken over, and the cat is sure that
you've been eaten by a predator. He has no idea you went
for a drink with a co-worker, then hit a ballgame with a pal.
The only thing he can conceive of is that you were minding
your own business, lapping up some water from a lagoon,
and some tusked animal weighing over two tons came along
and bit you in half.

I started worrying about this. Not obsessively, not day in
and day out. I wasn't that far gone. But if Cindy and I were

out to dinner and it got past nine o'clock, I would start to get a little edgy.

"What's the matter?" she'd say.

"Nothing," I'd respond. Then I'd glance at my watch nervously.

"What *is* it?" she'd want to know. "You're wriggling. You only wriggle when there's something wrong."

"It's nothing. Really. I'm just a little tired."

"Do you want to go?"

"No, no," I'd say. "Absolutely not. I'm fine. Let's stay."

Five minutes would pass and I'd nudge her under the table. "Maybe we should go *now,*" I'd whisper. And we would, much to Cindy's confusion and annoyance.

When we got to my place, Norton would be standing by the front door, looking, I was sure, incredibly stressed out. I'd pick him up, pet him for a while, reassure him that his dad had survived another day in the nasty jungle, tell him what a great dinner he was in store for, then sigh with relief and exhaustion that a crisis had been averted.

After a couple of weeks of this, Cindy figured out what was going on. She took *The Natural Cat* off my bookshelf and threw it away. She also forbid me to read anything or learn anything more about cats. She decided it was too dangerous.

The germ had already been forming, but this whole predator business put it over the top. I was beginning to think that, whenever and wherever possible, I should just take Norton with me. I would be a lot more relaxed, and I was pretty sure he'd enjoy tagging along with his dad rather than sitting around my apartment all day. The short pocket trips worked okay. Why not the more major excursions?

Cindy wasn't as supportive as I'd hoped. She told me I was crazy.

"You can't just take your cat on trips all over the place," she informed me.

I didn't understand why not. "He likes me. He's pretty calm. He goes to your house okay. What's the big deal?"

"The big deal is he's a *cat*. Cats don't like things like that."

"*He* does."

"He's a kitten. He'll go along with anything. When he gets bigger, he's going to hate it."

"I don't think so," I said. "I think he'll go for it."

"It just doesn't work that way," she said, shaking her head.

"Well, I'm gonna try it," I told her. "I like him. I like being with him. I don't see why he won't like being with me."

In fact, I had a place in mind I knew he would love to visit.

Fire Island is about an hour's drive or train ride from Manhattan. As mentioned, I rented a house there every summer, in the town of Fair Harbor. It was a wonderful little guest house, painted a deep sky blue; one room, comfortably furnished, with a Pullman kitchen and a sleeping loft. It had a cozy deck, which, even though the beach was only fifty feet away, I could rarely bring myself to leave. The entire island is approximately twenty-six miles long and about two blocks wide from bay to beach. There are many different little communities, each with distinctly separate rules and equally separate lifestyles. The rules range from *No Eating in Public* in one particularly crowded community to *No Campfires on the Beach* in a particularly cautious community to *No Rich People's Seaplanes Landing Here or We'll Blow Your Head Off* in one particularly blue-collar community. The lifestyles range from *Wild-Divorced-Heterosexual-Manhattanites-Discoing-the-Night-Away-in-Desperate-Search-of-a-New-Year's-Eve-Date* to *Boring-Please-Don't-Give-My-House-a-Funny-Name-I'm-Here-to-Relax-Not-Talk-to-Strangers* to *If-You're-Not-Gay-and-Haven't-Rented-*Can't-Stop-the-Music-*at-Least-Three-Times-Don't-Even-Bother-to-Step-Off-the-Boat.* I was in one of the Boring-Please-etc.-etc. communities and I liked it fine. In fact, I thought it was pretty close to heaven. There was one restaurant, which I dined in once a summer, a little grocery store, which, as mentioned, I went to a little too often, and a five-and-dime run by a woman who used to be a Rockette. (She was kicking when *The Men*, Brando's first film, played there.) There were a lot of nice families around me with a lot of nice kids. Best of all, cars aren't allowed on Fire Island. If you don't want to walk, you take a bike. If you don't want to do either of those, your only other choice is to sit in the sun and listen to the waves lap up to the shore. It seems like a place, with its wooden boardwalks and water taxis and everybody-knows-everybody-else feel, that time has forgotten. Above all, it is safe. Fire Island makes you feel that nothing bad can happen there, certainly nothing worse than, if you're a kid, falling down and skinning your knee, or if you're an adult, having too much to drink at a cocktail party and winding up in bed with a fat woman named Naomi. Which is why I thought

it was the perfect place for Norton to make his first excursion.

Once Cindy understood I was quite serious and that there was no way I was leaving my cat home alone for a whole weekend, she decided to give it a try with Marlowe. She didn't want him to grow up feeling like the neglected stepchild.

For our first trip *en famille,* we took Tommy's Taxi, a van service that picks you (and a lot of other yuppified weekenders anxious—and loud about it—to leave the city) up in Manhattan and drops you off at the Fire Island ferry. We bought a regular pet carrying case, a plastic one with metal bars on the top. Since both cats were so little, we figured one case would be plenty big enough.

We met the van at Fifty-third and First Avenue, loaded our bags on, then climbed aboard and made ourselves as comfortable as we could amidst the jewelry and designer clothes and exposed body parts. The cat case sat on my lap.

About fifteen minutes into the trip, I decided that it couldn't possibly be very comfortable curled up inside a portable pet prison, so I opened it an inch and stuck my hand in to reassuringly pet both guys. Marlowe didn't respond. His nose was buried in a corner, and he was trying his best to pretend he had been in a coma for about three weeks. Norton, however, scurried over to my fingers and began shoving his nose up against them. I stroked him for a minute, then when Cindy was looking away, staring rather horrifiedly at a pair of dangling gold earrings that spelled out a phone number—three numbers hanging from the left ear, four hanging from the right; I assume the woman wear-

ing them had the area code tattooed someplace I didn't want to know about—I lifted Norton out of the box and quickly shut it back up.

He looked up at me gratefully and meowed. At the sound, Cindy glanced over. When she saw the kitten on my lap, she rolled her eyes.

"I know, I know," I told her and tried to pretend that I sympathized with her hard-hearted approach to pet travel. "But he looked so unhappy in there."

"He wasn't unhappy," she told me. "He's a cat. *You* were unhappy because you weren't holding him."

I glanced down at Norton, who was curled up in a ball on my lap, his head resting on the back of my hand. I nodded at Cindy, acknowledging that her assessment was correct.

"At least move your hand," she told me. "You can't be comfortable sitting like that."

"I'm all right," I told her.

"You're comfortable?"

"Well . . . not exactly. But . . ."

"But what?"

"But *he* looks so comfortable."

"I think," Cindy said, "I may have made a mistake."

~~~~~

The rest of the trip went according to form. Marlowe cowered in the box, doing his best Helen Keller impersonation; Norton wound up inching his way up my arm and perching on my shoulder, watching the countryside slide by as we sped along the L.I.E.

One of the things I liked best about his position on my

shoulder was that it didn't ever seem to occur to him that he couldn't just push me out of the way or take up whatever space he wanted to take up. That's where he wanted to be, so that's where he belonged. And I had to agree. It only seemed fair. He was little; he was being lugged around not by his own choosing; he had no idea where he was going or why. If he wanted to sit somewhere and at least get a good view, how could I complain? I felt—and I think this is one of those clever things that cats somehow manage to do—*honored* by the fact that he chose me to be his piece of comfortable furniture.

In fact, not only wasn't I complaining, I was mesmerized watching Norton on his first trip in the van. He spent almost the entire hour staring out the window, hunched forward, his neck craning, his nose pressed against the glass. Something fascinated him out there, though I sure couldn't tell what. Every so often he'd turn to look at me and his eyes were full of questions. He'd stare at me until I felt ridiculously ignorant, and I'd whisper, "What? What do you want to know? *What?* Tell me!" When it became plain that I couldn't help him, he'd turn back to the window and continue his vigilant watch.

The thing is, it's not as if he were watching a flickering fire in a fireplace, unfocused and glazed by simple noise and movement. For Norton, this was hardly a vacuous way to pass the time. He wasn't *just* staring. His eyes were alert, constantly moving, his head shifting back and forth as if he were keeping track of a baseline-to-baseline rally at an exciting tennis game.

He was so *interested.* And it made me incredibly curious. I acted like a proud father whose son was about to win a

sixth-grade spelling bee. I kept nudging Cindy, not saying anything, just flicking my eyes toward Norton as if to say, "Will you look at him? Is he smart or what?"

Several people on the van actually stopped talking about themselves long enough to notice that there was a kitten perched on my shoulder, a kitten with folded ears who seemed to be unduly interested in the landscape of Long Island.

A couple of them reached over to pet him. Norton took the attention with what I would come to know as his typical laissez-faire reaction to adoring crowds. He didn't shrink away or scurry back into his carrier. Nor did he rub his nose affectionately against unknown palms or offer encouragement in any way. He simply sat there and took the cooing and petting and compliments as stoically as he could. At some point he turned to me, since we were basically at eye level to each other, and the expression on his face said, "It's all right. This is just the price I have to pay for being me."

I nodded at him knowingly, and when the petting stopped, he snuggled a few inches closer, turned away from the strangers, buried his face against my neck, closed his eyes, and went to sleep.

Marlowe, who in the van had certainly been, if not happy, quiescent, did not take well to the twenty-minute ferry ride from mainland Bay Shore to Fair Harbor on the island. He wouldn't move an inch in the carrier, and when Cindy went to pet him reassuringly, he drew away from her touch. I think, if he hadn't been as truly sweet as he was, he might

have hissed at her. But things hadn't quite reached that tragic level.

Norton, of course, only made matters worse because he took to the open sea (or, at least, the open bay) as if he were related in some way to the Popeye family.

As in the van, his nose went right to (and through) the metal bars at the top of his carrier, and he made it plain as day he wanted out. So, once again, I reached in, scooped him up, and set him on my lap.

Within a few experimental minutes, we found the position we both liked best: me with my left leg crossed over my right knee at a ninety-degree angle, Norton with his body on my right thigh and his head resting on my left foot. (For him, that's still his favorite traveling position, although as he's gotten older and bigger, his body and head now go from right thigh to left knee. For me, as *I've* gotten older and my joints creakier and creakier, it's less and less comfortable. Of course, I'm too well trained to change. I much prefer creaky joints to a disgruntled traveling companion.)

He also, about ten minutes into the crossing, decided the water was practically as interesting as the highway. With me holding the middle of his body as firmly as I could, he perched himself back on my shoulder, with his front paws resting on the ferry's railing.

Cindy was a little nervous seeing him in such a precarious position, and I must admit so was I. Believe me, I had visions of myself diving overboard in search of a floundering kitten. But I did have hold of him. And even more of a but, I simply had a very strong sense that this particular cat would not do anything as rashly crazy as jump off my

shoulder into the freezing bay. I don't know why I had such
faith in him, except to say that he more than justified it. I
expected him to behave in a certain way right from the
beginning, and he almost always did. I've left Norton in
cars with the doors open, in airport waiting rooms while I
went off to confirm tickets, in restaurant chairs while I went
to use their toilets. Not once do I ever remember him
running or jumping or hiding.

We got some awfully strange looks on that boat: a boy
and his seafaring kitten. Then in twenty minutes we were
back on land. We'd been on a taxi, a van, and a ferry. We'd
braved rush-hour traffic, the spray of sea salt, and crazed
sun-worshippers. The premier leg of Norton's first real
journey was complete.

# 4. The cat who commuted

Norton took to outdoor life immediately. It was a little frightening how easy it was to begin thinking of him as a country squire.

We took both cats into the little beach house and flipped open the carrier. Marlowe—poor guy; I hope no one ever reads this to him because he's going to get one hell of a serious inferiority complex—wouldn't come out. If I hadn't spent many more months in his company and *seen* him out and around, I'd venture to say he might *still* be in that box. Norton, on the other hand, had his new pad all checked out in a matter of minutes. He was the second coming of Tony Bill in *Come Blow Your Horn*.

He sniffed the miniature house out thoroughly—around the couch, over to the Pullman kitchen, up the ladder stairs to the sleeping loft. After exploring the upstairs, he stuck

his head over the edge of the loft to look down at us, and I knew exactly what he had in mind. When we made eye contact I shook my head only once, but firmly—and I'm convinced that's why he took the stairs back down to the living room floor, one little jump at a time instead of one great twelve-foot leap. I knew (and he knew) he could have done it. But I knew (and I'm sure he knew it, too) I probably would have had a heart attack.

Back downstairs, he checked out the bathroom, hopped onto the rim of the tub, slid down inside it. It was vinyl and very smooth, far too slippery for a kitten his size to easily leap back out, so when he began meowing impatiently I had to go fetch him. This became a fairly regular ritual until he grew to a more adult size and could get out of his own scrapes. At least once a day I'd hear a plaintive meowing echoing from the bathroom and have to go to the rescue. I must admit, partly to pay him back for dragging me away from work or fun or bed, partly because it was extremely funny to watch, I'd usually give him three or four tries on his own. He'd see me, try to scamper up the wall of the tub, not make it, and slide back down toward the drain. After a few unsuccessful attempts, he'd meow sharply, just once, to let me know the game was over and he wanted my help—*now*. He was not humiliating himself for my enjoyment any longer.

Norton particularly liked the walls of the beach house, which were covered with a burlap cloth. Quite attractive, no doubt, but also very handy for climbing.

While Cindy and I were doing our best to coax Marlowe out of the carrier, we heard a very quick ripping noise—actually five or six quick ripping noises—and turned around

to find Norton up near the ceiling, his claws clinging to the wall fabric.

I, of course, thought this was the greatest thing I'd ever seen. I was ready to rank Norton with Columbus, Tom Sawyer, John Glenn, and the first guy who ever ordered mail-order meat on my list of great adventurers. Cindy, luckily for my bank account, quickly pointed out how expensive it would be to completely refurbish every wall in the house. So we quickly pulled Norton down and tried to discourage this particular excitement, although it, too, became something of a regular occurence.

We next went out of our way to orient our adventurous cat. A litter box was set up in the bathroom, and we carried him to it so he'd be unable to use ignorance as an excuse for any accidents. (It turned out that in three years on Fire Island, he never *once* used a litter box. Outside, one giant sandbox was at his disposal, and I think he took great satisfaction in relieving himself in the freeing manner of his ancestors.) We also put food and water down for him and Marlowe—separate bowls, of course—but we figured Marlowe was *weeks* away from eating. Norton acknowledged the food with a quick bite or two of kibble, but his mind was elsewhere. He wanted the great outdoors.

Although he went straight for the screen door, he was still such a small kitten—not yet three months old—Cindy thought that, for health reasons, we shouldn't really let him loose outside. He was too young to be exposed to all those unknown germs and ticks and other strange things that abound in nature and that I couldn't even bring myself to think about. But he seemed so anxious to take off for parts unknown .

I had a solution. It was a perfect summer day, so we quickly changed into our formal Fire Island wear—shorts, no shoes, no shirt for me, tank top for Cindy—made ourselves some iced tea, and began Step One of turning Norton into an outdoor cat. We put a blue collar on him—quite distinguished-looking nestled in his gray fur—and got a long, long string, maybe thirty feet long, from the Rockette lady. We used the string to make an impromptu leash, carried Norton onto the porch, and tied him to the handle of the door.

Minus Marlowe, who still hadn't budged from his portable prison, Cindy and I took our iced teas—by the way, these were nonalcoholic iced teas; this is worth explaining because we'd learned that, for some unknown reason, in bars and restaurants anywhere on Long Island, if you just order iced tea, they give you something with enough alcohol in it to topple an elephant—sprawled into our madras beach chairs, and waited to see what would happen.

We didn't have to wait long.

Norton needed a few seconds to get his bearing. This was a little different from being transplanted into a strange living room. This was like being picked up by Brian Dennehy in *Cocoon* and going for a stroll on a strange planet.

First he went into a crouch. He glanced around nervously, as if waiting for something to pounce on him. Then he relaxed a bit. He took a step forward, still staying fairly alert to the potential for danger. His nose twitched, taking in the hundreds of brand new odors, and his folded ears switched from side to side, hearing all sorts of things, like birds and crickets and bees, that he had had no idea ever existed. Then a great thing happened.

Norton suddenly sprang into the air in a joyous leap. Baryshnikov would have been jealous of his form. He landed on his padded feet and went right back up, this time swatting at the string, which lay stretched out before him. A meow came out of him, but not a normal meow. This one sounded suspiciously like "whooooppeeeee!"

It took maybe thirty seconds for my cat to race exhilaratedly all around the deck. It took me maybe thirty *minutes* to unwind the string—which was now tangled up under a chair, around a square outdoor table, around another chair, twice around Cindy's ankles, over and then back under a third chair, somehow wrapping around the table again before coming to a sudden stop somewhere in the middle of the deck as the leash ran out of slack.

Norton couldn't move an inch. By the time I'd managed to straighten things out, he was raring to go again. And go he did. Another thirty seconds later, I was doing my best to unwrap him from his string straightjacket. Cindy couldn't stop laughing, Norton couldn't stop running, and I couldn't stop unwinding. All three of us were as close to happy as it's possible to get.

Within a couple of weeks, we had the routine down cold.

Thursday evenings, pack one bag each, load each kitten into his own carrier—we'd splurged for comfort's sake; *their* comfort—catch the five-thirty Tommy's Taxi and the seven P.M. ferry to Fair Harbor. Marlowe would hunker down in his carrier, emerging only when he was safely inside our house. Norton would spend the van ride on my shoulder, staring out the window, and the ferry ride on my lap, lean-

ing up against the railing. Once we hit land, he was beginning to squirm and think seriously about jumping out of his
carrier. I knew it wouldn't be long before he'd be prowling
the island on his own.

I'd bought a new travel case, perfect for him, easy for me.
It was really meant for dogs, but he was quite comfortable
in it and seemed to like it better than the old one. It was
a soft cloth shoulder bag with a hard strip underneath it for
support. There was a mesh patch in front so the animal
could breathe and see out. Norton didn't need the mesh to
see or breathe, because I never zipped the thing closed. I
just stuck him in and hung the bag on my left shoulder while
he sat there, head swiveling in every direction, taking in
every single sight, sound, and smell. It wasn't long before
I didn't even have to pick him up and put him inside. When
it was time for us to take a trip, I'd simply lay the bag on
the floor and he'd step right in and settle himself there.

After a month of weekends spent mostly trying to untie
string from every available item on our deck, we decided
it was time to turn the cat loose. My landlord, whose family
shared the front deck with us, was complaining. Their bicy-
cles were so tightly wrapped in string by this point, they
looked as if they were bike mummies excavated from Tut's
Tomb.

On the chosen weekend, Cindy and Marlowe had to stay
in the city. One of Cindy's best friends was in from out of
town, and they decided to have an official GNO (Girls'
Night Out). The whole wild works—non-diet Cokes, oil on
their salads, loud public discussions of bladder infections.
Norton and I were on our own, bacheloring it up.

Friday night, on Tommy's Taxi, I happened upon a star-

tling and, in years to come, useful revelation. It had always struck me as quite odd that none of the reveling weekenders in the van or on the ferry ever paid much attention to the fact that there was an incredibly cute cat on my shoulder, doing incredibly cute things. I didn't expect banners or original songs about "A Cat Named Norton"—

> *Who's the cat with the floppy ears?*
> *Who's the cat who ain't got no fears?*
> *Who's the cat doin' all the cavortin'?*
> *That ain't no cat—that's Norton!*

—or anything like that, but I did expect the occasional "What a cute cat!" or "Is he always this good?" or "What happened to his ears?" No. Usually I got nothing.

Well, this Friday I was riding along as usual, immersed in the *Post* sports section, cat on my shoulder studying the L.I.E. landmarks, when a woman behind me, wearing a sweatshirt that read "Life's a Beach," said, "What kind of cat is that?"

"A Scottish Fold," I explained. "His ears fold in half. See?"

"He's amazing."

Smiling, I went back to the sports section.

"Excuse me," the woman sitting next to me said. She had on a T-shirt that said, "Life's a Beach." "What kind of a cat did you say he was?"

"Scottish Fold," I repeated. "See? His ears fold like this."

"He's beautiful."

"Thank you."

"Is he always this well behaved?"

"Always," I said proudly.

Back to the sports pages.

"Is that a Scottish Fold?" the woman in front of me asked, turning around to smile at me. She *didn't* have on a T-shirt that read "Life's a Beach." But the guy sitting next to her did.

"Uh-huh." I nodded.

" 'Cause his ears fold like this."

"Uh-huh."

"He's so *cute.*"

"I know."

"Is he always this good?"

As a person who's always prided himself on being an acutely sharp observer of human behavior, naturally enough I had absolutely *no* idea why, all of a sudden, Norton's ears were the main topic of the car ride. I had zero concept of what was different from past rides.

It wasn't until I was on the ferry that it hit me.

We were on the upper deck. Norton was peering fixedly at the gulls swooping around the waves. I was munching on a take-out order of fried clams, a specialty of Porky's, the wonderfully divey pub by the ferry.

*I was single this trip.*

That was the difference.

No one wanted to bother admiring my cat when I was sitting next to an attractive woman I was obviously attached to. But this night there was no Cindy. So all of a sudden, Norton was the perfect conversation starter.

I was mildly stunned. I'd never really seen myself as the object of a van-ful of women's lust and desires. And I'd certainly never viewed Norton as bait to be trolled. Were

times so bad that people wouldn't even *talk* to someone unless they wanted something? Like a mate for life? It was amazing. It was . . .

As if on cue, a hand swooped down in front of me and plucked a clam—*my* clam—from the styrofoam plate.

I looked up to see a reasonably attractive woman, late twenties, holding the clam in her fingers. She was wearing—remember, this goes back a few years now—a *Flashdance*-type T-shirt. Over the course of the summer, I was going to become far too familiar with this look. (One of the amazing things about a sleepy little place like Fire Island being so close to Manhattan is the way fads sweep in and take over the entire island. My own personal favorite fad is a game called Kadima. It might also be called The Stupidest Game Ever Invented. It consists of one wooden paddle per player—of which there are usually two or three—and a hard black rubber ball. The object of the game is to stand ape-like on the beach, preferably in the middle of a particularly crowded section, where you can annoy people who are trying to mind their own business and have a good time. One player hits the ball to another person, not letting it touch the sand. There's no net, no out of bounds, no points, no rules other than what I've reported. What there *is* is a really loud, annoying noise that echoes every time ball hits paddle. Sounds like a lot of fun, doesn't it? Believe me, that summer Kadima was good for *hours* of entertainment on the ocean's edge.)

Anyway, back to the clam thief.

Her T-shirt was intentionally torn at the neck, revealing a darkly tanned shoulder (with a lot of flesh to tan) that had a tiny tattoo on it. I had an irrational fear that if I got too

close to the tattoo, it would say, in micro letters, "Life's a Beach." So I averted my eyes, or at least refocused them on the clam.

"I knew that anyone with such a cute cat," she began, "wouldn't mind sharing his food. I'm *starving.*"

She showed me all her teeth in the friendliest smile I'd ever been on the receiving end of. It would have been more effective if her gums hadn't gone from her forehead nearly to her knees.

"May I have my clam back, please?" I asked her politely.

Her teeth sparkled again, only this time she popped the little fried sucker right in between the uppers and lowers.

"What kind of cat is that?"

I didn't answer. I was too busy watching her chew.

"How come his ears are down? Is he afraid?"

I shook my head. She swallowed. I watched the little bulge in her throat slide down out of view.

"Did you sedate him? How can he just sit there like that?"

Then she moved. Her bejeweled, tan fingers reached toward my plate again. This time my hand went up to meet hers. To her surprise, our fingers locked for a moment. But she managed that dazzling smile again. The smile faded somewhat when I said the words "Touch another clam and die."

I'm pretty sure she thought I was kidding, because she tried to disentangle her hand and make another go at my dinner.

"I don't want to be rude," I said, in my best quiet Clint Eastwood impersonation, "but I'm extremely hungry. I bought these clams so I could eat every single one of them, except for the ones I give to my cat. I don't mind if he reaches down and takes one because I know him. But I don't know *you*. So if you try to get to them, I'm afraid I'm going to have to find out where you live, sneak over in the middle of the night, and break your thumbs."

I did everything but say, "Are you feeling lucky, punk?" It seemed to do the trick.

She backed away slowly—clearly she'd been flirting with the Ted Bundy of the ferry set—and disappeared into the crowd.

I looked down at the cat draped over my shoulder. He looked back at me and meowed.

"I know what you mean, pal," I told him. "I don't think we're ready for the singles scene."

The next morning was D-Day. Norton was about to hit the shore.

He knew it, too. Don't ask me *how* he knew, but he did. I've come to expect this from him. He always seems to know when a big event is upon us: if I'm going on a trip, if *he's* going on a trip, if something particularly sad has happened, if something particularly festive is about to happen. If I didn't know better, I'd swear he keeps a calendar hidden somewhere in the apartment. Because as he got more and more used to going away to the beach for the weekends, his morning routine even changed. Mondays through Thursdays, we'd go through our wake-up cuddling, and then, as I dragged myself out of bed, Norton would race to the kitchen, jump up on the counter, and wait impatiently for me to feed him. On Fridays, he'd race along

the same path—off the bed, through the bedroom door, around the corner, sharp right, cut through the living room, past the front door, into the kitchen—only he'd skid to a sudden stop at the front door and wait there eagerly. On Fridays he didn't even care about breakfast. He just wanted to hit the open road.

On the day of his first outdoor solo expedition, the moment my eyes popped open in the morning, my guy was out of bed, waiting at the front door of the Fire Island house, glancing back repeatedly to see what was keeping me.

Still rubbing sleep out of my eyes, I pulled on a pair of shorts, climbed down the stairs of the loft, and met him at the door. I hesitated. For one brief melancholy moment I had a vision of Norton on the side of an endless road, thumb out, heading far away in search of fame and glory. I composed myself, remembered that he didn't *have* a thumb, then I swung the screen open. Norton *didn't* hesitate. He scooted outside. In the blink of an eye, he was gone, racing across the yard, racing right back, disappearing in a flash under the deck.

I realized I had two choices. I could act like a total lunatic and tail him outside, try to follow him around wherever he went and keep an eye on him. Or I could be a rational, sane man: relax, make myself a pot of strong French Roast coffee with just a dash of cinnamon, get the newspapers, read about the fascinating events of the day, then go for a healthy, invigorating morning swim. It seemed like an obvious choice.

I decided to follow Norton.

He was having the absolute time of his life. Frolicking, chasing birds and squirrels—not catching, just chasing—

crawling through the grass on his belly, chomping on flowers, and generally enjoying his new role of jungle beast on the prowl.

After half an hour or so, I decided he was safe and sound, more than able to cope on his own with the great outdoors, so I went back inside to attend to some people-related chores such as trying to write a book and earn enough money to pay for Norton's summer house.

I never *really* worried. I knew he'd stay fairly close to home or, at least, wouldn't go so far away that he couldn't find his way back. Periodically, I'd step to the front door or back window and call his name, just checking up. I'd hear one crisp meow in response, letting me know all was well, then I'd go back to work.

At lunchtime I decided to head to the market (I'd forgiven them for ratting on me to Cindy). Going for the surprisingly mature route, I didn't even check up on Norton. I figured he wouldn't miss me for the twenty minutes I'd be gone, so why bother him? I didn't want him to think I was an overprotective dad. Feeling as proud as a father whose son has just gotten his driver's license and is driving away on his first date, I made a list of what I needed to buy and took off.

I was three quarters of a block toward the market when I first heard it. A faint growling of a meow, a little whiney in fact. I took another two steps, heard it again. *Brrrrrrmeowwwwww.*

I stopped, turned my head. Norton was in the middle of the sidewalk, twenty feet behind me. He was trying to follow, but I was walking too fast.

"What are you doing?" I asked. "Go back to the house."

Again I headed for the store, managing to take all of two steps before hearing a much more insistent meow. When I turned, Norton had scampered a few feet closer.

"Then come on," I called. "Let's go."

And much to my astonishment, he ran up until he was about five feet behind me. Then he stopped. "Come on," I told him. "I'll walk slow." But he wouldn't budge any farther.

I took a few more steps, glanced behind me. He was following—but he stopped when I stopped. I went a few more steps, glanced. He'd kept pace.

I walked the rest of the three blocks to the market, and Norton followed, always staying five feet behind, every few feet meowing to let me know he was still there. Several Fair Harborites passed by and stopped to stare in amazement. I acted as if there were nothing at all unusual about the world's cutest kitten going for a lunchtime promenade with his favorite person.

Twice, people on bikes zoomed past and Norton froze. But he never panicked. Once they were gone, I just had to reassure him that everything was okay, that bikes were only an occasional hazard here in the real world; then he'd resume his faithful trot, taking my word that I was watching out for his best interests.

In a few minutes we were at the entrance to the market, where there were about ten times the number of people Norton had ever seen in his entire life. Kids were racing around playing tag, bikes and skateboards were skidding to and fro, several people with "Life's a Beach" T-shirts were trying to impress several other people with *Flashdance* T-shirts. Even for Norton it was a bit much.

As we approached, I wasn't sure what to do with him. See if he'd stroll inside and peruse the aisles with me? Pick him up and carry him? Ask someone to keep an eye on him while I shopped—a ten-minute cat sitter?

Norton ended my pondering and took matters into his own paws. After sizing up the situation, he darted past the door to the market, sprinted ten feet or so toward the dock, then disappeared into a thick row of bushes.

I had a feeling that most of my afternoon was going to be spent coaxing him out from under the greenery. After twenty minutes of trying, I figured there was nothing to be done about it. I could see him and he clearly wasn't going anywhere, so I decided it was safe to leave him while I shopped. I went into the market, bought the makings for a delicious lunch—two juicy knockwurst, some German potato salad, a dark Heineken, a can of Nine Lives Turkey Giblets—then trooped back outside to assess the cat situation.

The situation was this: the cat was gone.

Standing in front of the bush he'd been hiding in, I called his name. Nothing. Not a sound, not a stirring. I got down on my hands and knees and peered through the thicket, but there was no sign of gray fur anywhere. My throat felt as if I had a two-ton chunk of granite stuck in it; my stomach was flip-flopping to beat the Seven Santini Brothers. I couldn't believe it. How could I have left him alone outside? What was I thinking of? As smart as he was, he wasn't human. He wasn't even a dog. He was just a cat! A cat who'd never been outside on his own before, and I'd deserted him, left him stranded! And now he was either hiding somewhere, shivering in total terror, was hopelessly

lost, never to be found again, or had been kidnapped by two brothers named Rick and Mick who had already tied the first firecracker to his tail.

Forcing myself to be calm, I took a deep breath and called Norton's name a second time. There was only a terrible silence. For one long second. Then two seconds . . . then . . . *brrrrrmeowwww.*

A gray head with folded ears poked its way out of the bush—exactly where I'd last seen it. The rest of the body followed. Norton stood on the sidewalk, looking up at me with one of his "What's the problem?" looks.

I didn't want him to see that I'd completely lost faith in him and panicked, so I only allowed myself a minute sigh of relief. Then I turned and walked past the market, not stopping until I was on my own front deck. There was no need to look behind me: Norton, of course, had kept pace, trotting briskly five feet behind the entire way.

Over the course of the summer, Norton's little jaunts turned into a wonderfully pleasurable routine. Cindy was having to work more and more on the weekends, so Norton was, every two or three weeks, my only beach companion. He always walked me to the market in the morning, he usually walked me there at lunchtime, and he sometimes deigned to come along at dinnertime. Rarely did he walk by my side. He was most comfortable lagging those five feet behind. He would meow periodically just to let me know he was still tagging along. Once I got used to this, I stopped even bothering to turn around to check on him. I'd simply walk merrily on my way, hear him alert me that all was well, and I'd call back, "Okay, okay, let's try to keep up." I got quite used to, as people passed us by, someone turning to a friend, whose eyes would be bugging out, and saying, "See, I told you."

As we both got comfortable with our walking patterns, he (and I, I suppose) got more adventurous.

My writing partner is named David Handler. We do most of our television and film scripts together; the business is so filled with sharklike monsters whose greatest pleasure is chomping their sharp teeth down on helpless writers that we feel, erroneously no doubt, there's safety in numbers. David and his girlfriend, Diana, had a house four or five blocks north of mine. On the days we worked there, Norton took to accompanying me. He got to know the route well: straight for several blocks, left, then go all the way to the bay. He got to know it so well he began making the excursion on his own. Not infrequently, Cindy and I would be cooking dinner and David would call, saying Norton had been visiting for a couple of hours but he'd just trotted away, so I should expect him home soon. Sure enough, twenty minutes later there'd be a meow at the door, and a certain wandering feline would make it very clear he wouldn't mind eating a can of Cheese and Chicken Chunks and eating it *right now*.

One thing I learned early on is that I never had to worry about losing Norton along the way, no matter how far we traveled. Taking Central Walk—the erratically paved path that went for several miles along the center of the island—to David's, Norton would periodically get distracted or frightened or simply playful. If a squirrel happened to cross his path, Norton would scamper after him, sometimes into the bushes, sometimes under someone's house, sometimes up a tree. If a dog decided to act doglike and bark or growl, Norton was outta there. Same if a bike came clanging along and cruised too close. At first I would simply wait impatiently until he'd reappear, which sometimes took as long as fifteen minutes, or I'd spend the same amount of time crawling around trying to find and catch him. Once, I was in a particular hurry. David and I were to be on the receiving end of a conference call from a producer in L.A. who felt he could just as easily humiliate us over the phone as in person. So I just left Norton where he'd sprinted away to, hidden under someone's deck. I went to my conference call, spent forty-five minutes trying to iron out the intricate plot elements of a super-realistic sitcom episode (involving a college student who broke out in a rash whenever the girl of his dreams kissed him), then convinced David to come and try to look for my kitten. We went to the spot where I'd last seen him, I called his name, and presto, there was Norton, popping out into the sunlight, happy to follow us back to David's, where he could spend the rest of the afternoon playing in the tall reeds by the bay.

It became obvious I could leave Norton anywhere, and for any length of time. Even if we didn't want him, he'd often follow me and Cindy when we left the house. If we were walking over to someone's place for dinner, he'd stay with us until he got bored, meow loud enough so I'd be sure to turn and see where he was, then dash off to have fun on his own. Hours later, after dessert and coffee, I'd make my way back to the spot, call his name, and with one of his *brrrrmeowwwws*, he'd be ready to head back home.

Norton clearly liked the combination of his freedom and

my company as much as I did. It got to the point where it
was rarely necessary to stick him into his shoulder bag/
carrying case. He wanted to walk everywhere instead. Leaving for Fire Island from my apartment, he always hopped
right into the bag because, even for Norton, asking him to
walk on a crowded Manhattan sidewalk was a bit much.
Then, when Tommy's Taxi hit the ferry dock, he'd also
willingly slip off my lap or shoulder back into the bag—
there was too much foot and car traffic, not to mention the
general sense of hysteria from the hordes of city dwellers
overly anxious to drink frozen daiquiris, get skin cancer,
and exchange phone numbers with members of the opposite sex who either owned or looked as if they would
soon be able to own a two-bedroom co-op in a doorman
building.

But once the ferry was headed across the bay, forget it.
Norton was on his own.

As soon as were seated, he was out of the bag and either
on my lap or propped up against the railing, checking out
the fascinating movement of the waves. He would race to
the door the moment we were tied up to shore and hop
onto the dock's wooden planks himself. He'd wait impatiently for me and Cindy to make our way through the
crowd (Why New Yorkers line up for five minutes—on a
boat! Which you can't get off because it's still in the
water!—then push and shove so they can get somewhere to
*relax*, I'll never know), then race ahead of us toward the
house, stopping every ten or twelve feet to make sure we
were following. If he was hungry, he'd deign to come inside
long enough to chow down, then he'd meow or scratch the
screen door until we let him out. I didn't like the idea of

his staying out all night—okay, okay, so I had a *touch* of Jim Backus in *Rebel Without a Cause* in me, get off my back— and, to his credit, he always came inside when it was time for me to go to bed. Even having glimpsed the world beyond, he didn't alter our regular sleeping arrangements.

Sunday night or Monday morning, when it was time to head back to the concrete jungle, he would walk with us to the ferry, stopping right before we reached the dock, where he'd hop into the bag and allow me to carry him until we were seated on the boat.

The more comfortable I got traveling with him, the more I realized how much I could trust him.

At the ferry stop was a great divey restaurant/pub, Porky's, whose desirable fried clams were mentioned earlier. Porky's had a take-out window, and I soon got into the habit of leaving Norton's bag—with Norton in it—on one of the benches by the boat while I went to get food before boarding. (I highly recommend their toasted homemade blueberry muffins, washed down with a long-necked bottle of ice-cold Bud.) I wouldn't be gone long, maybe ten minutes, but it would usually be long enough for a small crowd to have gathered round the gray cat with folded ears who was lying nonchalantly on top of his bag, taking a snooze or checking out any interesting fellow passengers.

He was quite relaxed and extraordinarily obedient when told to stay put. Eventually, as his modes of transportation and range of travels broadened, I was able to leave him in airport lounges for as long as twenty minutes while I went magazine or upgrade shopping, and in restaurants, sitting in his own chair while I ate peacefully in mine.

One of my proudest accomplishments, leading to one of

Norton's shining moments, was getting him to walk on the beach. For some reason, cats don't like the sand. Maybe it's too hot for their padded paws; maybe the water scares them; maybe they're put off by all the "Life's a Beach" shirts, umbrellas, and towels. Anyway, Norton was no exception.

Here was Norton walking along the boardwalk *toward* the beach: cocky swagger, confident gleam in the eye, the look of someone who'd been parading around town pointing his finger at a neighbor, saying things like "Howdy, Bill, we missed you at the town hall meeting last night."

Here he was when I'd plop him *in the middle of the beach*: cowering, shaking, racing as far away from the waves as he could get to huddle terrified against the dunes. Picture Jimmy Cagney on his way to the chair in *Angels with Dirty Faces. Norton Dies Yellow!*

I decided this simply wouldn't do.

When a kid takes horseback riding lessons and tumbles off, what's the very first thing he's told? *Get right back on.* I knew I'd never get Norton to go for a horseback ride— well, there's no point in saying *never*—but I couldn't see any reason for him to stay off the sand.

In my own defense, let me say right here and now that I'm not one of those pushy stage parents. I mean, if Ethel Merman were alive, she wouldn't play me in a musical. Although Norton is a show-quality cat, I'd never even *think* of displaying him or training him to do tricks. Those things are for *other* people. This was for me and him. He'd *enjoy* having new areas to roam and explore. Why should he limit himself when he could be frolicking with some beach bunnies down by the water's edge? To end my own defense, let me say that I felt then, and I feel now, a little too much

like the parent of a nine-year-old boy who's making the poor lad take piano lessons and says, "Believe me, he'll thank me for this when he's older."

The first few times I let Norton loose in the sand, he was gone the moment I set him down, running for the protective safety of dirt and boardwalk. The next few times, I put him down and held him, letting him get used to the feel. He didn't struggle and he didn't appear too miserable. When I let go, he'd hesitate, realizing that perhaps this whole beach thing wasn't as terrible as he'd assumed—as I'd been telling him repeatedly—but then he'd hunker down and skulk back to real land. Not sprinting exactly but not stopping to admire the view either.

After that it got easier. His instinct was to follow me. I'd never led him astray before; there was no reason for him to believe I was starting now.

Within a week, Norton was walking comfortably on the beach, his usual five steps behind me, meowing a lot more and a lot louder than usual, but he was there. He wouldn't go all the way to the water, but he *would* walk about halfway there, wait while Cindy or I shook loose a towel to lie on, and stick around for half an hour or so, especially if he got to share any of our picnic lunch. I still believe he would have spent more time relaxing there if it wasn't for the constant *thwapp-thwapp-thwapp* of the Kadima balls.

One day, toward the end of August, Cindy and I were invited to a cookout in Seaview, one of the other beach communities. Cindy had a girlfriend who was in a "share" there, a share being when six people share the cost of a three-bedroom house, figuring out such complicated schemes as alternate weekend visits, splitting food costs, and prorating the fee for the largest bedroom or the one with the ocean view or the one closest to the refrigerator.

On this particular weekend, all the sharers were stuffed into the house because it was the weekend of the annual Seaview Clam Bake. Every year, everyone in the small community brought food and drink to the beach—clams, lobsters, burgers, hot dogs, kegs of beer, pitchers of margaritas—dug pits for barbecuing and steaming, and cooked out, drank, and generally made merry. This went on all day and a goodly portion of the night. There was usually music and volleyball games and three-legged races and other Andy Hardyish events; all in all, it was awfully hard to think of a much better way to spend a ninety-degree day in the heart of a New York summer.

Cindy went early to help prepare. She thought it would be fun to be in on the beginning of the festivities. As much as I always enjoyed the Seaview bash, my antisocial theory about large gatherings of human beings always was and is "less is more."

I puttered around until the late morning, did a little work, and, since Cindy wasn't around, caught up on my Rotisserie League stats. Rotisserie League, for those of you in the baseball dark ages, is sometimes called Fantasy Baseball. The game has swept the nation—*USA Today* estimates that 750,000 people now play it—and I'm proud to say I'm one of the cofounders of the original league. The premise is a simple yet immensely gratifying one. You put together a team at an auction, bidding against nine or eleven other "owners," depending on whether you're in the National

League or the American League. The structure of the team is specified: two catchers, three cornermen, five outfielders, nine pitchers, and so on. If you buy Darryl Strawberry— God forbid!—and he hits a home run for the Dodgers, he also hits one for your team. Being a total maniac about the game, I have *two* teams, which makes it nearly impossible to get any real work done during the summer months. My American League team is called the Gethers YeRosebuds, my National League team is the Smoked Fish. (I am respectfully referred to by my National League *compadres* as the Sturgeon General. And believe me, I'd way overpay if there was any way to get Steve Trout on my pitching staff.) I liked to do my stats when Cindy wasn't with me because she thought it was rather scary that a reasonably intelligent person would actually *want* to spend two hours a day totaling up the Hits and Walks Per Inning Pitched ratio for people who toiled in such places as Memorial Stadium and Chavez Ravine.

Satisfied that the Rosebuds were sprouting up for a big stretch run and a little depressed that I saw no end to the Fish's floundering, I decided it was time to head off to the Seaview bash.

Norton was lazily sunning himself on the porch as I stepped outside. His half-ears twitched in idle curiosity when I passed him by. I think he was wondering why anyone would bother leaving such a perfect spot.

"Whaddya say," I asked him. "You up for a stroll?"

Now, Seaview was two miles from where we were in Fair Harbor. The only way to get there in a reasonably straight line was by walking on the beach. Norton had never gone more than about thirty feet on sand. This had the potential

for disaster. But I thought Norton would like the cookout once he got there. It seemed worth a shot.

My pal was ready to give it a go. He lifted himself up from his sprawled position and began trotting after me. When it came time, half a block later, to descend to the beach, he meowed loudly.

"Come on," I coaxed gently. "What have you got to lose?"

If I'd been by myself, I probably would have made it to the party in twenty-five minutes. With Norton, I got there in thirty-five. He was perfect—never slowing down, never letting himself be distracted, always keeping pace right behind me, except for when he got frisky and raced ahead of me. He meowed a little more than usual, but he didn't seem to be complaining. He was just feeling gabby.

The way Seaview is set up along the beach, you have to climb up a small incline to get there. When you've climbed, you're standing on a dune overlooking the town's entire stretch of beach. It's not the Grand Canyon or anything, but it's quite nice, especially on a day when there are a couple of hundred people happily cooking and serving and playing.

I climbed, stood there for a moment enjoying the view, and spotted Cindy. She waved; I waved back. I swiveled my head back behind me to check on the walking wonder and said, "Let's do it."

Norton meowed once and followed. Up the incline, down into the laughing hordes. Within moments, the noisiest event of the season was eerily quiet. One by one, heads turned, eating stopped, music ceased. These sophisticated Fire Islanders had seen Frisbee-playing dogs in their midst.

They'd seen a spider monkey with a pail and shovel digging holes in the beach. They'd even once seen a female member of the singles-oriented Kismet community who *wasn't* wearing an ankle bracelet. But they were all staring at the kitten who'd traversed the sandy shores to help them party hearty—Norton of Arabia.

"Where did you come from?" the first person I passed asked.

"Fair Harbor," I told him.

"Your cat walked *two miles* like that?!"

I nodded. By the time I reached Cindy and her friends, I was nodding like a madman, my head bobbing up and down, and I was repeating all the familiar phrases: "Yup, does it all the time . . . Scottish Fold. See the ears? . . . Norton . . . Two miles . . . Fair Harbor . . . Yup . . . See the ears?"

Gradually the cookout went back to normal. The band started up again, backgammon games resumed, shrimps were skewered. Norton, after sampling some grilled tuna, went to play in the grass, away from the sand. I went with him to the steps leading away from the beach, told him I'd come get him in a few hours. I picked him up, kissed the top of his head, then I watched him disappear, knowing he'd be waiting when it was time to go home.

# 5. The cat who went to california

My Fire Island landlord was nice enough to extend our summer season until the end of September. But over the Labor Day weekend it hit me: What was I going to do with Norton when I didn't have a summer home where he could frolic the day away? How was he going to adjust to being an indoor cat? Especially—since I had recently learned that the biggest cause of fatalities in New York City cats was their leaping to their deaths out of apartment windows—an indoor cat whose father wouldn't ever again open a window so much as a crack.

By October 1, I hadn't come up with any intelligent solutions. Norton's travels were relegated to going back and forth between Cindy's and my apartment. When she spent the night at mine, Marlowe would come along. He was perfectly comfortable at my place, so it seemed only right that Norton should be their houseguest when the sleeping arrangements were reversed.

I was starting to do a fair amount of business-related traveling. (I should probably explain that the traveling was complicated because my business was complicated. I should say business*es*—and perhaps "confusing" is a better description than "complicated" since I don't actually have one job, I have several, none of which makes all that much sense. One part of me runs a publishing company. That part allows me to make honest-to-goodness grown-up financial decisions, meet anyone interesting I can think of who might like to write a book, and work with very talented and very temperamental authors and personalities. Another part of me writes and produces television and movie scripts. That part allows me to wear sunglasses and hate actors and get really aggravated when producers say things to me like, "I love it! It's perfect! And don't worry, I know exactly how to fix it!"—which actually *was* said by the executive producer of a TV series I worked on. The third and final part of me—probably my favorite part—writes books. This is the part that allows me to sit alone in a room and torture myself trying to invent characters and plots that most people will never read or hear of. It also gives me a chance to create some meaning out of all sorts of otherwise meaningless things. None of these jobs particularly fits together, and I never actually meant to turn into a compulsive workaholic—but somehow it's happened and I kind of like it.) My publishing job—at this point I was helping to start a new imprint within the large and still growing Random House complex—would take me away for a sales conference here and there, a trip to San Francisco to see agents, a quick

sojourn with an author to make sure he or she felt loved and appreciated. My writing career was also keeping me busy and on the road. When you live in New York and write for Hollywood, you've constantly got to prove to the networks and studios that living three thousand miles away from the people paying you—and usually paying far too much money to write things that never get made—isn't anything they should worry about. The only proof is visibility, which meant my partner, David, and I had to hop on a plane on a fairly regular basis and show our faces around town.

Norton and Marlowe were great pals; thus it was never a problem figuring out what to do when I went away: Cindy would take him. She was nearly as crazy about my guy as she was about hers, and she truly enjoyed watching the two cats play and stay together for three or four days in a row. All three of them had fun when I was gone.

Everything seemed perfect until this pleasant and easy routine was forced to change. Cindy broke it to me that she was having a little *too* much fun when I was gone.

We had a strange relationship, Cindy and I. I had been smitten the moment I saw her; she had hated me on sight. She thought I was smug, egotistical, and watched too much baseball. But I was persistent—writing, sending flowers, calling, doing everything but watching less baseball—and eventually won her over. We couldn't have been more opposite. She was wary of relationships and hesitant to get involved, positive that she'd be wounded irreparably just at the moment she relaxed enough to decide our particular relationship was a permanent one. Although I didn't believe in or even consider the possibility of permanence, I was an incurable romantic and was more than happy to rush

in with my chin jutting and get knocked out with the first straight right hand that came my way. She didn't believe in spending money unwisely and thought it was almost sinful to spend it on one's immediate pleasure and comfort. I believed in spending any money I received as soon as possible—and *only* on things that would bring me pleasure and comfort. She thought she was a terrible human being—which she most certainly was not—while I, on the other hand, couldn't imagine anyone being a better, nicer guy than I. She got depressed all the time; I was almost always happy. She was always cold; I was always hot. She thought it was important to be serious—that times were bad and only serious thought and behavior might improve them. I was of the *Sullivan's Travels* school of behavioral thinking—times *were* bad, so let's laugh it up and try to find amusement in everything. She was searching for meaning. I hoped I'd *never* find meaning in *anything*—or I was in big trouble.

What really brought us together was the fact that we had *one* thing in common—we both wanted to stay independent.

The only thing we could agree on was that we didn't believe in a standard, old-fashioned, monogamous relationship. We didn't believe in marriage. People should stay together because they *want* to stay together—not because a piece of paper tells them they've made a legal commitment. We wanted to be free, unrestricted. If we felt like spending Saturday night together, fine. If we didn't, fine again. No problem. And no ties.

We never actually came out and said the words "I love you." We danced around it with clever phrases like "I

really love being with you" and "I love the way we don't have to say 'I love you' and we still know how we feel about each other," but once we realized we liked each other a whole bunch and that we didn't *have* to be in an old-fashioned relationship where we saw each other every Saturday night, we fell into a very comfortable old-fashioned relationship where we saw each other every Saturday night and generally took good care of each other. Neither one of us ever really thought about making more of a commitment than we had to make. In retrospect, it seems obvious that neither Cindy nor I truly understood the nature of commitment. Although, I realize now, I was in the process of learning. It just wasn't with Cindy.

Toward the end of the previous summer, Cindy and I had spent more time apart than usual, but I had attributed that to Cindy's new job and the fact that she was working long and hard hours. It turns out I should have attributed it to the fact that she'd fallen in love with her doctor.

She'd switched to him sometime in the spring. I remembered that she'd mentioned how great he was—and how cute. I also remembered that sometime around the Fourth of July, she'd started saying things like "You know, you really shouldn't eat popcorn. It tends to clog up your intestines" and "Did you know that by the year 2020, the average doctor will spend nearly a million dollars to go to medical school? Doesn't it steam you that people think of doctors as selfish and unfeeling when they have to risk so much to do what they do?"

I'd usually say things like "Oh yeah?" or "*What?*" and then not give it any thought. But I gave it a lot of thought when she told me I was getting dumped for the doc. Espe-

cially because it came right after I had invited her to England—the week's vacation was to be a present for her birthday.

"I just can't live a lie anymore," Cindy told me.

I readily agreed that she shouldn't have to live a lie, although I wished she could have lived it until after we'd been to a couple of farmhouse bed-and-breakfasts in Devon. She also wanted me to agree that it was a sad thing that it hadn't worked out between us. I managed to say that I thought it *had* been working out between us.

"No," Cindy said. "I don't know if you're capable of the kind of feelings that I need."

"You mean the kind of feeling where it's okay to dump someone who tries to do incredibly nice things for you like taking you to England?"

"No, I mean abandoning yourself to love. You're an observer," she told me. "I don't know if you're a participant in life."

This stopped me short. I'd always thought I was a good participator. Granted, my idea of a good time was watching *On the Waterfront* for the sixty-second time and then calling Sports Line to find out how the Mets had done, but I'd stack my life experiences with anyone's.

"Oh, you do participate," Cindy now said, "but you hold back. It's as if you're waiting for something."

"For what?"

"I don't know. For something better. Something *different*. Something you don't have. And you're holding back your true self until you find it."

"This *is* my true self," I tried to tell her. "You may not

like it as much as Dr. Polaro's true self, but it's mine."

"You don't understand," she said. And with that I had to agree. I had thought Cindy and I were on the same wavelength. I'd thought we were giving each other what we both needed. I'd thought there was a bond of honesty and trust between us. I'd thought we were finally at the comfortable stage, something men and women have an awfully difficult time reaching together without being in a rest home. Obviously I'd thought wrong.

I didn't stick around for too much longer. For one thing, I was getting awfully sad. For another, I was fairly certain Dr. Polaro's true self would be coming over soon, and I didn't particularly want to be there when it did.

It wasn't easy saying good-bye to Cindy. In a weird way, it was even harder to say good-bye to Marlowe. I'd really gotten to like the little guy. And with Cindy, at least I could hate her a little bit. I knew that wouldn't last, but it was some comfort at the moment. I had no reason to hate Marlowe. He'd never done anything to me but make me laugh and make me feel good. I'd even gotten him finally, on our next-to-last weekend on Fire Island, to go for a short walk with me and Norton. He made it almost all the way to the market. Now I picked him up and scratched his full, standing-up-straight ears. "You can come over anytime," I told him.

Norton was surprised we were leaving so soon. Once I'd lugged him over there, he was prepared to spend the night. He meowed, a tad annoyed, when I put him back into his bag. Cindy didn't pet him or say good-bye to him. In fact, she wouldn't even look at him. I think she felt too guilty.

Or else she thought that *his* true self might ask her what the hell she was doing dropping us for a guy who wouldn't eat popcorn.

The last thing Cindy said to me was, "You won't be sad for long. You don't really love me. You don't know what love is."

The next few weeks were a little rough. I felt funny watching *On the Waterfront* by myself on Saturday night, and Norton didn't understand why (1) he hadn't been out of the apartment at *all,* not even across town to Cindy's, and (2) if he wasn't going to be able to leave, where was his friend Marlowe to keep him company?

Most of my time was taken up working and feeling sorry for myself. I found comfort in little things: I remembered that Cindy once actually told me she thought the ending to *On the Waterfront* was *stupid*—that Brando shouldn't have had to stand up at the end for the men to go back to work; he was risking serious injury (and this was *before* the doctor). I remembered that she liked to sing the theme song to "The Brady Bunch" when she cooked. And I realized, at last, I could now take taxis everywhere without someone trying to make me feel as if I were personally responsible for famine in Pakistan. In fact, within a day, I'd managed to make a list of things about her that so infuriated me, I had almost forgotten about going back to her to beg and plead for a second chance.

Luckily for my sanity (and the sanity of those around me), I was distracted by the need to prepare for a week-long trip to California. I kept busy making appointments, figuring out what I was going to do and say . . . . It was only three days before I had to leave that it occurred to me I had to do something with Norton.

I considered calling Cindy to see if she'd still take him. I was fairly certain she would, but I didn't feel it was quite the appropriate thing to do. I didn't like the idea of her knowing I couldn't manage without her. I also had visions of Dr. Polaro, whom I could no longer separate from Son of Sam when trying to imagine what he was really like, performing some strange surgical procedures on Norton's fragile and vulnerable body. So Cindy was out. I called almost everyone else I knew—and not one of them could cat-sit for the week. Either they had a cat of their own and felt it wouldn't work, or their apartment building had a strict no-pet rule, or they were allergic to cats, or they were too nervous because they knew what I'd do to them if anything happened to Norton while he was in their care. By the time I'd run through my phone book, I had two days left to come up with a plan.

The reason I was going to California was that I'd agreed to speak at a writers conference in San Diego. I was going to spend three days there, then go to L.A. for the rest of the week to work, see a few people, have a few meetings, and spend some time with my family. Nothing too hectic, nothing too formal, nothing too intimidating—in other words, absolutely nothing that would preclude taking an extraordinarily well-behaved and well-adjusted cat.

I got on the phone immediately. San Diego was a breeze. The conference had booked all the speakers and would-be writers into a large motel near the UCSD campus. The motel was delighted to have a cat spend a few nights in their

care. I had a sudden and brand new appreciation for the laid-back, Southern California lifestyle.

Los Angeles was more difficult, however. My regular hotel wouldn't hear of it. Out of the question. The next five hotels also wouldn't consider having Norton as a customer. But then I struck pay dirt.

The Four Seasons had just built a new hotel in L.A. It was in a very convenient location, was the right price, and was supposed to be terrific. This was their first week open for business.

"How big is he?" they wanted to know.

"Little," I said. "He's very little for a cat."

"Over forty pounds?"

"No. I said he's a *cat,* not a *lion.* I think he weighs *six* pounds."

"Claws?"

"Yes," I said, then realized I should have lied my head off. "But he never scratches anything!" I added immediately. "And if he does, I'll happily pay for any damage." At those last words, I rolled my eyes to the heavens and prayed if there were a god that he hadn't given the Four Seasons a decorator who had a fetish for burlap wallpaper.

"Let me check with the manager. Hold on."

I held on, a wreck, preparing all sorts of arguments for the manager in favor of allowing cats in their rooms. I decided I was even prepared to audition him. "How's this for a deal," I was thinking of saying. "I'll pay for a separate room for Norton for one night, put him in there for an hour. Then you can check him out . . ."

"Hello?"

"I'm still here," I said quietly.

"We'd be pleased to have your cat stay with us," the reservation clerk told me. "What's his name, so I can add him to the guest list?"

That was the first moment I realized I might be able to survive without Cindy. If I was going to marry this wonderful woman on the other end of the phone, I *had* to survive.

The day of the flight, I was totally unprepared. I had no idea how to make a cross-continental airplane trip with a cat, so I was forced to improvise. I assumed that if I were doing anything wrong, some right-thinking airline employee would set me straight.

I was flying with my agent, Esther Newberg, who was also speaking at the conference. Esther happened to have two fears—flying and cats—so when I picked her up at her apartment and she saw Norton, she was ready to call the whole trip off. But Fear Number Two was eradicated by the time we reached the airport. Within thirty minutes, Esther, whose mind is about as easy to change as Attila the Hun's, decided Norton was the greatest animal she'd ever seen. She couldn't get over the way he sat on my lap and peered out the window for the entire drive.

"I'm hoping he does that on the plane, too," I told her.

"What's he done on other flights with you?" she asked.

I decided I wouldn't break it to her. Esther's the nervous type.

When we got to the airport, I put Norton in his bag, slung it over my shoulder, and went to check our bags. At the ticket counter, the woman gave me a boarding pass, tagged my suitcase and sent it slithering along the conveyor

belt, then looked Norton right in the eye. She smiled at him, said nothing, and returned my ticket to me.

Next we went to the security checkpoint. Esther went through with no problem. When Norton and I stepped through, I expected alarms to go off to beat the band. But no. I guess those things are a lot more sensitive to steel and explosives than to fur. All that happened was that one of the female guards patted Norton's head when he stuck it out of the bag to check out his surroundings.

When we got to the gate, I began to have serious doubts that anyone was ever going to say anything about my flying with a cat. Perhaps it was a lot more common than I thought.

Boarding, Norton snuggled down into his carrier when I showed my ticket to the stewardess. All she said was "Seat 8C." Not a word about you-know-who.

Esther and I took our seats, and Norton hopped out of his bag and settled onto my lap in his favorite position—lying straight along my crossed legs, head resting on my left foot. I got a blanket and laid it over him, figuring it would make it easier to hold on to him when we took off.

We saw a short film, instructing us how to correctly fasten our seat belts. (I must say, my theory is that if you're a grown-up human being who can't figure out how to fasten your seat belt, the odds are that you wouldn't have been able to make a plane reservation and actually get to the airport, which means you wouldn't be in a position to enjoy this superb cinematic experience.) Then a stewardess passed by, checking to make sure everyone had managed to understand the film and do the fastening correctly. She looked straight at my lap—upon which sat the cat—smiled,

said nothing, and passed by to look at the next lap. Still no one had said a word about Norton.

For two hours, Norton sat there, the perfect gentleman, staring out the window, fascinated by his first adult close-up glimpse of clouds. He didn't stir; he didn't make a peep. I began to relax.

Two hours and one minute into the flight, someone finally said the very first thing about the fact that there was a cat on board. It was the head stewardess, a woman of about fifty, who had the delicate good looks of Marie Dressler and the charming personality of Nurse Ratched.

"You've got a cat!" were her exact screaming words.

I looked up from my book. Norton turned away from the window to see who was making so much commotion.

"Get him *out* of here!" she hissed.

I looked over at Esther, glanced back to the stewardess.

"Where would you like him to go?" I asked.

"I don't care!" the woman said. "Just get him out of here!"

"Why don't you open the door," I suggested, "and I'll toss him out over Cleveland."

I didn't have a moment to even admire my own calm and wit, because at this point, things accelerated. The man behind me stood up and said, "Oh, my god! There's a cat! I'm allergic to cats! Get him out of here!" The guy started sneezing like a lunatic.

"The cat's been right here for two hours," I said, trying to be a sane voice in the wilderness. "What the hell are you sneezing *now* for?"

The guy couldn't answer me, unfortunately, because he was too busy sneezing, wheezing, coughing, and struggling

to get out of his seat belt so he could escape from the dread cat hair. I thought of suggesting to the stewardess that they should show a short film about how to *un*fasten your seat belt but decided against it.

"Get that cat under the seat!" the woman snapped at me.

"I don't think you want me to do that," I told her.

"Did you hear what I said?!"

"I did. But if you'll just listen for a second—"

*"Put him under the seat!!"*

I picked Norton—who was responding to the crisis by acting particularly docile and cute—up off my lap and put him on the floor under my seat. When I told him to "stay," the stewardess flew into an absolute rage.

"In his box! Put him in his box!"

Now, I'm not big on public scenes. I'd place them somewhere right below walking on hot coals and sitting through Bette Midler movies on my list of least favorite experiences. But I was starting to get annoyed.

"I *can't* put him in his box. He doesn't *have* a box. That's why I told you you didn't want me to put him under the seat."

This charming woman could not have had a stronger response if I'd said, "I'm carrying a bomb. Give me all your money or this plane's confetti." As far as she was concerned, I was the Salman Rushdie of passengers and she was the Ayatollah.

"What do you *mean* you don't have a box?!" she demanded. At this point I realized there was no way to stop this whole thing from getting completely out of hand, so I figured what the hell and decided to go for it.

"You know those little cages that cats go into? The ones

that fit under the seat? I don't *have* one of those. *That's* what
I mean!''

By now, I didn't think it could get any worse. I was
wrong. Esther decided to get involved.

"Look,'' she said—and when Esther says "Look'' at the
beginning of a sentence, the only thing that comes to mind
that *might* be as scary is the moment in *The Godfather II*
when Al Pacino hears that Diane Keaton got an abortion—
"one of the other stewardesses saw the cat on his lap earlier.
She didn't seem to think it was a problem.''

"Stewardess?!'' The woman was now in an apoplectic
fury. *"Stewardess?!!!''*

Esther and I looked at each other, not sure what the
problem was now. Esther, ever the forceful agent, took a
stab at it. "That's right. The other stewardess walked right
by and—''

"We are not stewardesses! We are *flight attendants!''*

The next five or ten minutes is a blur. I remember gig-
gling. Then I remember the stewardess . . . er . . . attendant
accusing me of smuggling Norton aboard. I have a vague
memory of trying to explain that she was mistaken, of her
telling me I was breaking the law, of me telling her to go
ahead and throw me in airplane jail. I definitely remember
Esther rising to Norton's defense and unleashing a string of
expletives that would have made John Gotti blush. They
didn't seem to have much effect on the Dragon Lady,
though.

Other than the fact that there was a wild, untamed jungle
beast running free, able at any moment to terrorize the
passengers—if you believed what our attendant was saying,
the flight was quickly turning into one of those disaster

movies starring Helen Hayes and George Kennedy—the biggest problem seemed to be that they were about to serve us some of their scrumptious airplane food. Apparently, health regulations make it illegal on American planes for a pet to be out of his cage during mealtime. Is this a great country or what? We can't lick the homeless problem, but the FAA has made damn sure that we're able to sit in really cramped little chairs and eat microwaved teriyaki chicken in peace and quiet.

We did eventually work out a compromise, which unfortunately didn't involve my being able to staple our attendant's lips together. I simply agreed to forgo the delicious meal, as did my loyal agent. In exchange, I didn't have to toss my cat out and let him parachute his way to safety. He could stay on my lap. The guy behind me could switch seats with another passenger sympathetic to my plight. And our plane could continue on to San Diego without any more hysteria.

Which is exactly what we did. Norton stared out the window, perfectly content, until we landed. Mr. Allergy moved to the back of the plane and spent the rest of the trip breathing clean, cat-free air. Esther was so furious about Nurse Ratched's behavior that she forgot to be afraid of crashing and dying; she even allowed Norton to sit on her lap for a while. The evil stewardess—on principle alone I refuse to call her an attendant—steered clear of us for the rest of the trip, even refusing to bring us coffee or little Wash 'n' Dries.

The final three hours of the trip were calm.

The hysteria didn't begin again until we landed.

By the time we got our bags, rounded up two other publishing people who needed a ride, waited on line at the rental car desk, found our car, and got directions to the conference, we'd been traveling for nine hours. This is the second lesson I learned (after the one about buying a carrier that will fit under one's seat) about transporting a cat across state lines: nine hours is too long to go without a litter box.

Four people and one cat crowded into a shiny Oldsmobile. The people immediately started grumbling about being hungry and hating Southern California. The cat uncharacteristically started meowing like a lunatic. Norton perched himself on the shelf under the rear window and howled. He kept this up for fifteen minutes or so. I think it took that long for him to realize we still had a ways to go to hit the motel. But once the realization set in, he decided to do something about it.

He urinated all over the backseat.

Needless to say, this didn't go over all that well with my traveling companions. Especially because we couldn't get him to stop. I'd never seen an animal—two- or four-legged—pee for quite so long.

I didn't get angry. I couldn't. It was awfully hard to blame Norton. And from the miserable way he looked, he clearly didn't like it any more than we did. He just didn't know what else to do.

As we stopped at a gas station, in a desperate attempt to clean things up, I realized that I was totally unprepared to have a cat with me for the next week. Not only didn't I have a litter box, I didn't have any litter. I also didn't have any cat food, any cat food dishes, or any little cat treats. Basically, I realized that because of my selfishness in wanting him to travel with me, I'd just put my beloved cat through a crash course of Cat Torture 101.

Norton was clearly mortified and humiliated about his public . . . ummm . . . accident. He didn't seem to understand that it wasn't his fault. He hid under the driver's seat until we pulled into the motel. And once I had let my disgruntled passengers out of the car, I took immediate action to rectify my thoughtless ways.

The first thing I did was drive to a market, where I got a large cardboard box. (I've since gotten *much* more sophisticated about this potentially awkward problem. I now stock up on portable, folding litter boxes, twenty at a time. Any pet store sells them; they're sturdy enough to last a week or two, and they easily slip into my briefcase or traveling bag. I can't recommend them highly enough.) I bought some litter. (Again, years later, I've now gotten this all down to a science: two small five-pound bags of litter easily fit into my suitcase. The moment we hit the rental car, I open up the folding litter box, rip open one of the bags, and *voilà,* Norton's got everything he needs, *immediately* laid out on the floor of the backseat. There's no need to torture him for the entire drive to our final destination, and it makes it a lot easier for me to drive him around town for the rest of my stay. Once I get to my room, I take out a second box and tear open the second bag of litter. Not only does Norton appreciate the extra facilities, I'm sure the rental car company and the hotel are a lot happier. I know the bellboys are. The first time I thought to put a litter box in the car,

I didn't have a second one. So when I checked into the
hotel, a not-very-happy guy in a uniform had to lug a used
cat box up to my room.) I also bought a scooper at the
market so I could clean the box out, a week's worth of food,
and a container of cat treats.

Back at the motel, I checked in and set Norton up in fine
style. Two ashtrays made perfect food and water bowls. I
fed him, showed him that I was setting up his litter box next
to the sink, then set him on the bed and started petting him,
telling him with the utmost sincerity that he was, very possibly, the greatest animal who'd ever lived. It wasn't too long
before he was purring. After half an hour, I decided it was
safe to unpack. I was pretty sure I'd been forgiven.

Part of the deal with the conference was that I would spend
a portion of each day critiquing manuscripts. Any student
who wanted my opinion could leave fifteen to twenty-five
pages for me to read; then I was to spend several hours
sitting by the pool, and each of the students could spend
fifteen minutes with me discussing his or her writing ability
(or, at least, my educated opinion of his or her writing
ability). I always like this part of every writers conference
I go to. It's always interesting to see what people are trying
to write and to hear what they *think* they're trying to write.
Sometimes, however, these sessions can get a bit hostile.
Many editors go right for the throat and actually tell the
truth. This is not a recommended course of action. Many of
the student writers don't take kindly to even the remotest
criticism of their precious words. One has to delicately
balance truth with encouragement. It's not always easy.

(Imagine trying to critique, without offending the writer, an Oklahoma dentist's true account of the hilarious world of tartar control, called *Open Wide.*) I try to be gentle since, for the most part, I'm not dealing with professionals. With a pro, an editor can actually come out and say, "This paragraph stinks. Cut it." The pro will usually reexamine the paragraph with an open mind and, if it does indeed stink, get rid of it, or at least rewrite it. With an amateur, such a blunt response can produce anything from tears to guns. So I try to look for positives as well as negatives. Basically, I try to give the would-be writers their money's worth.

Along the same lines, I thought I should try to give Norton *his* money's worth. As long as he'd made the trek across country, it seemed foolish to keep him cooped up in the motel room. So the day of my first poolside sessions, I carried Norton with me, set him down by my chair, and told him to have fun for the next few hours.

As soon as he was free to go where he wanted, he took off for the far side of the motel, where there was a lawn and bushes to prowl through. Before he rounded the corner and disappeared from sight, he meowed once, loudly. I looked up, our eyes met (I'm not making this up, I swear), he made sure I took notice of where he was, then he was gone.

A New York editor who was also teaching at the conference came over to me and asked if I knew there was a freeway on the other side of the motel. I told her I wasn't in any hurry to go anywhere, and she then told me she wasn't all that concerned with my travel plans, she was concerned that my cat was going to end up as road kill. I assured her that he was all right, that he did this kind of thing back on Fire Island all the time, and forgot about it.

I began my first session, a critique of what was supposed to be a novel but what was obviously a thinly disguised true story, about a tumultuous love affair between a young Jewish girl and an older Italian man in the 1930s. The book was poetically titled *Matzos and Spaghetti*, and the author was a seventy-year-old woman named Naomi Weinblatt. My helpful comments ("The dialogue is strong, but are you really sure it has a contemporary feel to it?") were interrupted by the worried editor, who stopped by to tell me she'd just been looking for my cat and he had clearly jumped ship. She'd tried calling his name, but he was nowhere to be found. Once again, I told her to relax and went back to my student, who was defending her novel by saying, "But this really happened!"

While I was commenting on the next manuscript, a Civil War novel about a beautiful, tempestuous woman named Scarlett who was in love with a handsome, brutish rogue ("You have a good feel for the era, but it seems a bit derivative"), I heard the editor's voice calling "Norton . . . Norton . . ." I glanced over, and sure enough, she was thrashing through the bushes near where he'd disappeared, trying to coax him out. I shook my head and went on to my next eager writer.

An hour and several manuscripts later (one science fiction novel in which computers that are really human beings create human beings who are really computers; one series of uplifting essays meant to convey the simple pleasures of life, called *Hey, It Doesn't Matter If You're Fat;* one short story by an extremely clean-cut woman named Joy about an extremely clean-cut woman named Jill who's raped by the side of a muddy road, then crawls for miles until she reaches a garbage heap, which she staggers into, buries herself in filth, then dies, wanting only to know the name of her rapist so she can forgive him—my extremely helpful insight: "Write what you know."), my editor friend had organized a little search party. There were now four or five students crawling around the lawn screaming Norton's name, begging him to come home.

By the end of the next hour (a screenplay in which screen time mirrored *real* time—in other words, *nothing* happened; a dozen poems about everyday life, of which the only thing I remember is that the author actually rhymed "June" with "spoon"; and a thriller that had this for an opening line: "The bullet creased his forehead and he felt faint, barely having the energy to remove the pin from the grenade which was hidden in his coat, which he threw at the onrushing Krauts, knocking them to hell and gone, which they deserved." My only comment on this one was "Did he throw the grenade or the coat at the Krauts?"), I couldn't stand watching what had now become a dragnet for Norton. It seemed that most of the San Diego community was searching the grounds for my lost cat. I have to say that although outwardly I was cool, calm, and collected, inwardly I was beginning to get pretty worried. What if Southern California *wasn't* like Fire Island? What if Norton decided to *find* Fire Island and decided the freeway was his best and quickest bet? What if . . .

I decided these musings were getting me nowhere, although I was quite sure one of my students could turn the situation into a bad prose poem. I decided to find out for myself if my faith in Norton had been misplaced.

Never showing my fear, I strode over to where I'd last

seen him meow and called his name once. Without even a moment's hesitation, my little gray cat leaped from the bushes and meowed excitedly, happy I'd come to rescue him from all this noise. I petted him proudly, then turned on my heels and headed up the stairs toward our second-floor room. There was nothing but silence from around the pool as Norton trotted after me, ready for his pre-cocktail nap. When I opened the door to usher him inside the building, there was a spontaneous burst of applause.

As Norton scampered inside, I wondered if it would be possible to teach him how to bow. I decided it was probably worth spending a few minutes working on it.

The rest of the conference went smoothly. Norton, depending on his mood, spent part of each day in the room snoozing and part of each day by the pool prowling. He did attend one of my seminars, spending most of it asleep on the podium, directly on top of my notes.

When the readings and seminars and lectures and poolside sessions were over, reaction to my participation was decidedly mixed. Some people thought I was too harsh; some thought I was a welcome dose of publishing reality. I judged my chances of being invited back the following year at about fifty-fifty. The response to Norton was far more one-sided. It was quite clear he was welcome back whenever he wanted to come.

Before he could return to San Diego, however, Norton had to be introduced to the unique town of Los Angeles. He, Esther, and I got back into our rental car and headed up the coast. Our only stop was at the first market we came

to before we hit the freeway. I explained to the manager why I needed two empty boxes, and he was nice enough to oblige without charging me. The trip went quickly, memorable only because Norton decided to spend half of it perched on my shoulder with his head sticking out the open front window and because Esther decided to spend *all* of it complaining about the fact that the car still smelled decidedly from our last trip with Norton.

I dropped Esther off at the Beverly Hills Hotel, and I went on to the Four Seasons. The Beverly Hills is just a little too show-bizzy for my taste. It's extremely difficult to walk through the lobby or make it through a meal without hearing such charming words and phrases as "fuck *them* if they think I'll go for a step deal" and "the idea is great, but the concept is way off" and "sure, I can get it to Dusty, but is he right for it?" All these things are usually uttered by people who would, in fact, kill for a step deal, have no idea what a great idea actually is and would be terrified if they actually heard one because then they'd have to make a decision, and could only get something to Dusty if they bumped into him on the street and began the conversation with the words, "Excuse me, Mr. Hoffman, you don't know me but . . ."

I dropped Esther off at Show Biz Central and went on over to my hotel. Still a little wary from my encounter with our flight attendant, I was much relieved to hear the desk clerk say to me, with a huge smile on her face, "And this must be Norton."

While he sat on the registration counter, we got checked in quickly and easily, and then we were shown to our room.

I was happy and, as soon as I'd set up the litter box and ashtrays for food and water, so was my cat.

Norton quickly took a liking to L.A. His only problem was at my parents' house. I should say his only problems.

The first problem was an unsolvable one. My parents' house was up in the hills above Coldwater Canyon, and they had coyotes roaming the countryside. Once, when the folks came home from a dinner party around midnight, two coyotes were actually standing in the driveway right in front of the garage. Luckily, the beasts were as frightened of my parents as my parents were of the beasts, and nobody was eaten. But a lot of little animals in the area *had* been eaten. The people who lived next door to my folks had an adorable little poodle. They wouldn't let the dog out at night, fearful that the coyotes would attack under the cover of darkness. But they figured it was all right to let the dog romp around during the day. One morning they let the pooch outside at ten A.M. At noon, they went to find him— and all that was left was the head and the four paws. It was pretty gruesome.

It's difficult to feel sorry for coyotes, as they're unattractive and unappealing animals, but one has to, just a bit. There's so much construction and upheaval around Los Angeles that the coyotes have basically been displaced. Their land is gone and they have nowhere to live or hunt. They are left with little choice but to hang out around rich people's homes and go after their garbage and their pets. I tried explaining all this to Norton, but it didn't go over too well. He didn't care much about the plight of the coyotes. He only cared that he wasn't allowed to venture

into the backyard, which looked incredibly inviting to him. But I decided better he be frustrated indoors than coyote food outside.

The second problem was that my parents had two golden retrievers who had the size and intelligence of dinosaurs. Dolly and Rewrite are as sweet as dogs can be. But being around them is like being around two of the Three Stooges. They wag their tails, and expensive crystal goes crashing to the floor. They jump up to greet you, and white linen suits are covered with muddy paw prints. Go to pet them and you spend the next ten minutes trying to wash several gallons of dog slobber from your hands, arms, and even your neck. My parents were wild about these dogs. My father had taken to calling them his "children," and when I called from New York to say hello, if I didn't ask about them, I was severely chastised. I was fairly sure that, by this point, Dolly and Rewrite stood to come out a little ahead of me and my brother in the will.

While I will admit to liking my four-legged "brother" and "sister," it was difficult for Norton to warm up to them—mostly because their favorite activity was chasing him at full speed up the steps, cornering him under my bed, and barking as loud as they could possibly bark, which is about as loud as anything I've ever heard outside of a Who concert I went to in 1972.

Norton got along with the few dogs he encountered on Fire Island. He was usually cautious around them but would give them the benefit of the doubt. I wouldn't say he had any dogs as his best friends, but I had seen him on more than one occasion in my backyard, lying peacefully right next to one of my Fire Island neighbor's dogs. Dolly and

Rewrite, however, were another matter. There was no peace at all when the three of them were in the same house.

The matter settled itself fairly easily. When Dolly and Rewrite were outside (the coyotes willingly stayed away when these two lummoxes were running and jumping about), Norton would come downstairs and poke around the kitchen, the den, and the living room. When the dogs were let in, a gate went up, blocking them off from the upstairs part of the house. Norton would lie on the steps just above the gate, secure in the knowledge that they couldn't get to him and enjoying the fact that his presence there nearly drove them mad.

The third problem was a little more delicate.

My father absolutely loathed, hated, and despised cats.

I tried everything I could think of for his first meeting with Norton. "Don't bring him to the house," he said. I went through my explanation that my guy was different from normal cats, that he was incredibly smart, that he wouldn't bother my father, that at some point in my life, I, too, thought that I didn't like cats, but when I met Norton that all changed. This had about as much effect on my dad as it would have had on a slab of marble. He was unmoved and simply repeated his instructions: "Don't bring him to the house."

I have to say a few words about my father here. He was as perfect a dad as he could have been. We were terrific pals, and I don't think I could have had more respect for him. For years he was one of the top television writers in L.A., and then he became, in his late fifties, one of the top television directors as well. He was a bear of a person, dominating a room with both his looks and his personality.

His shtick was to be gruff and cynical, and on the surface he sure was, but in fact he was the most caring and generous man I ever met in my life. He solved problems and gave advice and was usually just strict enough and unbending enough to provide the right kind of fatherly support. He certainly made plenty of mistakes in his life and his career, but his correct choices more than made up for them. Cindy, who for the first two years she knew him was totally intimidated by him, once said he was the first person she ever met who was larger than life. I always thought he was funny and smart and talented and exceedingly moral, and I enjoyed being with him and my mother as much as I enjoyed being with my closest friends. But he was still my dad and I was still his son—and as such we could, without much provocation, drive each other completely crazy.

As I was taking Norton up to the house for the first time, I had a funny feeling he was going to be another one of those crazy-driving provocations.

The only thing I can really add to the picture, as Norton is about to be introduced to the family, is a brief description of my mother, who happens to be the perfect mom. While my dad tended to bluster, my mom would stay quiet and, behind the scenes, make certain everything was really all right. She has always been the quiet strength behind the family, although she always made sure that everyone else always got all the credit.

My mother, by the time she reached the age of fifty-five, had never officially worked a day in her life. One afternoon, she was in a very "in" restaurant—at the time—Ma Maison. She had decided that she wanted to learn how to be an expert French cook, so she asked the owner, Patrick, how

she should go about it. I think she had something dilettant-
ish in mind, such as going to France for a few weeks and
taking cooking classes. Instead, Patrick told her she should
go to work in the restaurant three times a week—without
pay—and that in six months she'd be a great cook. That's
exactly what she did. She started going in three times a
week as an unpaid apprentice, and within a year, not only
was she a terrific chef, she had started and was running a Ma
Maison cooking school. In the twelve or so years since, she's
become a queen of the L.A. cooking mafia, writing several
respected cookbooks, working intimately with people like
Wolfgang Puck, and befriending people like Julia Child and
Maida Heatter. The only drawback to this is that my mother
is now slightly obsessed with food. I can call up and say,
"Mom, I'm a little down—I got fired from my job and my
girlfriend left me and I was just run over by a truck." The
odds are Mom will sympathize for a minute or so and then
say, "Did I tell you about the crème brûlée I made last
night? It was wonderful. I added some lemon and . . ." And
she'll be off giving me instructions on how to make the
perfect custard.

My mom is fairly unflappable. Nothing much seems to
bother her, and especially as she's gotten more secure over
the years, she always seems to take the long view and the
sane view of things. A good way to illustrate the difference
between the two parents is their reaction when they saw my
first New York City apartment.

I suppose everyone who ever had pretentions of being an
artist and who moved to New York has at one time lived
in an apartment similar to mine. But, to be honest, that
seems almost impossible. I think it's safe to assume that my

apartment was the worst apartment ever built in New York City. It was on Perry Street near Seventh Avenue, right in the heart of Greenwich Village. It was a basement. I don't mean a basement apartment—I mean a basement. A good chunk of what was supposed to be the living room had no floor. It was just dirt and, without working too hard, you could poke around in it and peek down to the subway. When I took the place, there was no kitchen, no bathroom, not even a shower. There was also no light. The only two windows faced the street but were blocked by the building's enormous garbage cans. It also wasn't too well constructed. On particularly rainy or snowy nights, there was usually a pretty good chance that the elements would blow through the cracks in the walls. There is no feeling quite like coming home from a Greenwich Village bar at two A.M. on a snowy, icy, winter morn, crawling into bed—and finding that your sheets have been soaked through and through by snow that has been drifting into your apartment all night.

In my apartment's defense, however, it did have a great painted tin ceiling and a brick wall and a great wooden floor (the parts of it that *had* a floor). Also, it was right in the heart of the Village. *And* it was only $105 a month. Even I knew, however, that it wasn't the kind of apartment that parents love to see their child living in.

I had tried, at the time, to prepare my folks for what they were going to see when they visited New York. I found out later that for weeks beforehand, my mother had driven my father nearly mad saying things like, "Now, remember, when you see Pete's apartment, no matter what you think about it, tell him you love it." Nearly every minute of the day, according to my father, was taken up with her lectures

about how important it was to me for them to support my lifestyle and my taste. Finally my father promised he would be on his best behavior and tell me he approved of where I was living—no matter what it was really like.

When it came time for them to actually see it for themselves, my mother spent the entire taxi ride downtown repeating the rules to my dad. "Tell him it's great . . . Tell him you love it . . . Try to remember what it was like when you were young . . ." She'd been psyching herself up for so long that when I finally heard their knock at the door and opened it to let them in, before I could say a word my mother gushed, "Oh my god! It's lovely! It's perfect! Isn't it perfect? What a great apartment!" I had the presence of mind to say, "Mom, don't you want to come in and *see* it first before you decide if you like it?" Embarrassed, she stepped inside. My father followed. After a two-second pause, my father, looking around in wonder, blew his promise to my mother and said, "Holy shit. What a craphouse!"

The best description of my parents—and the difference between them—came from a director named Bill Persky, who, in a toast at one of their anniversary parties, said it was like "Adolf Hitler being married to Julie Andrews."

Adolf, Julie . . . meet Norton.

I came up to the house for dinner, Norton contentedly hanging from my shoulder in his usual bag. I knew my father had told me not to bring him, but I was sure he didn't really mean it.

My mother made an appropriate fuss when she saw him. Not a cat lover herself, she appreciated the two things that were immediately apparent—he was great looking and so sweet natured. She petted him delicately, not used to being around a feline. She relaxed when Norton nuzzled her hand with his nose. As he was nuzzling, my dad called down from upstairs, "Is that *cat* with you?" When I called up that yes, indeed, he was, the next roar was, "Well, make sure I don't see him when I come downstairs!"

After a little bit of confusion and a bit more arguing, we all finally agreed that it was impossible for me to arrange for my father never even to *see* Norton, but I did agree to try to keep him out of the way. First I tried to get my dad to understand how special this particular cat was, but he seemed to be the very first person able to resist Norton's charms.

Norton stared at him with his cutest look. He rolled over on his back, paws up in the air, inviting my father to scratch his belly. He tried rubbing up against my dad's leg. He tried snuggling up to him. Forget it. The man was ice. He truly didn't like cats, and Norton was a cat. There was no way this was ever going to be anything but an uneven truce between man and animal.

I dealt with this as best I could, although I was extremely disappointed. I felt bad that my dad couldn't open himself up to the special pleasures that Norton brought me. But clearly he couldn't.

After dinner, I took Norton back to the hotel, making sure he knew that it wasn't his fault my father didn't appreciate him. The next few days, I made my L.A. rounds, seeing agents, writers, film and TV people—a lot of people who called me "babe," told me they loved me like family, and let me know I was "hot." Luckily, one agent kept me from getting a swelled head by explaining to me that it was "easy to *get* hot. The hard part is *staying* hot."

Sometimes Norton came in the car with me, sometimes he hung out at the hotel. When he was in the car, his new idea of fun, begun on the ride from San Diego, was to perch himself on my shoulder while I was driving and hang his head out my open window. By this time I had no fear that he might jump out. That just wasn't something Norton would do. Even in L.A., where people are used to just about everything, I got a few interesting double takes as we were cruising around.

All in all, I decided that taking Norton from coast to coast was a simple thing to do, bound to get simpler as we both got more experienced. And just as I decided I could see no drawbacks to it, a major drawback occurred.

I got a call from my office. We were publishing a celebrity's autobiography. As is so often the case, the celebrity didn't really write the book; he just talked into a tape recorder and with a writer who was supposed to turn out a book that seemed as if it could only have been written by the celebrity himself. This is fairly common practice, as most celebrities, at least most actors and athletes, have a lot of trouble writing anything other than the words "I," "me," "mine," or "more." I had thought that this particular celebrity's book was under control. The ghost writer had done a terrific job, the book was entertaining, and the timing was right—this lucky celebrity had managed to *stay* hot. But as so often happens, this famous man had gotten cold feet. When he read over his book one last time before we were to go to the printer, he decided that, even though he'd assured us every step of the way that he loved the book that bore his name, he couldn't *really* say all those things for the record. We'd have to cut and rewrite and drastically change things—or he wouldn't let us publish. If we tried to publish anyway, he wouldn't do any publicity, which would effectively kill any chance of selling the damn thing.

This charmer lived in Santa Barbara, just a couple of hours' drive from L.A. Since I was already close by, the powers that be had decided I should get in my car, head immediately up the coast, and get to work. I had five whole days to completely rewrite the book so we could meet our promised publication date.

No problem.

Scratch that . . . one problem.

Since our celebrity was already bordering on hysteria, and since I was going to be staying in his home—another minor problem was that since this guy drank so much, it was thought I should be next to him twenty-four hours a day or we'd *never* get finished—I didn't know what the hell to do with Norton. My author was so deranged he could claim he was allergic to cats and throw me out of his house, killing any chance for my mission to be a success.

I could think of only one thing to do.

My mother gulped but agreed to let Norton stay in their house for the five days I was to be in Santa Barbara.

"Do you want to . . . ummm . . . check with Dad?" I asked weakly. "Just to be sure?"

"No," my courageous mother said. "I think it's better if we surprise him."

I had to agree. So, since my dad was off at a meeting, I drove Norton over to the house as quickly as possible, left even quicker, and went out to spend what I was sure would be the worst five days of my life—but which would *still* be

better than being around my father when he found out he
had to live with Norton for a week.

I was right. When I checked in that night, Mom told me
it hadn't gone as well as she'd hoped. For my mother to
make an admission like that meant that their house on
Hazen Drive must have been something like Nagasaki the
day of the bomb. She assured me, however, that Norton
was still there—and was still welcome to stay.

When I called in the second night, the report was that
Norton had spent some time on the couch in my parents'
bedroom and that my father hadn't thrown him out.

The third night, I had been mentally beaten into a near
stupor by the aggrieved author, so I was sure I hadn't
understood correctly when I heard my mother say the
words "Your father told me he thought Norton was quite
handsome—for a cat."

The fourth night, I figured I must be getting delirious
trying to rewrite fifty pages a day, because I was positive my
mother told me, "Norton slept with us last night."

The fifth night, I was too exhausted to even call home.
I finished my rewrites somewhere around five in the morning, loaded the manuscript into my suitcase, and ran straight
for my car. I arrived back in L.A. at seven A.M.

My mother, who usually is out of bed by six every day,
was already up. I kissed her hello and nervously asked after
my cat. She smiled, motioned for me to be quiet, and led
me up the stairs to her and my father's bedroom. There I
saw one of the greatest sights I had ever been privy to.

On the bed, sound asleep under the covers, was my father. On his chest, on top of the covers, was Norton, also
sound asleep. My father's arm was curled around the top of

the blanket, his hand resting gently on Norton's back.

We tiptoed out of the room, and my mother told me that, during the course of each day, Norton kept trying to get closer and closer to my dad. At first my dad shooed him away. Then, as Norton refused to give up, he began to be intrigued. As soon as the poor guy weakened, Norton went in for the kill. By their fifth night together, he had my dad petting him for hours while he sat directly on his chest. They fell asleep like that. My mom told me that my dad actually kissed Norton good night.

I had a cup of coffee and waited for the two pals to wake up. Norton was glad to see me, although not nearly as glad as he should have been. All my dad talked about was what an amazing thing it was to listen to Norton purr. "He must be happy here," he kept saying. "He purred the whole time."

"I do think he likes it here," my mother acknowledged.

The last words my dad said to me, before I drove to the airport, were, "When are you coming out here again?"

"I guess in a month or so," I told him. "Why?"

He caressed Norton. "Are you sure you don't want to leave him here until you get back?"

# 6. The cat who went on dates

108    Peter Gethers

When I returned from California, two significant—and not
unrelated—events occurred: Norton discovered Pounce.
And I rediscovered the nearly forgotten, rather distasteful
yet undeniably exciting ritual of modern dating.

Pounce, for those of you who are ignorant of this nectar
of the cat gods, is bite-sized morsels, perhaps the size of a
Cheerio. It is serious junk food, the Reeses Peanut Butter
Cup for the discerning feline. Pounce comes in small cardboard cans, each can a different color depending on the
chicken, liver, shrimp, or beef flavor. I saw them sitting on
a supermarket shelf one afternoon and, always on the look-
out for a pleasurable experience for my gray companion,
decided to bring one can home and try it out.

That night, before I went to bed, I gave two Pounce
(Pounces? Pince??) to Norton, then put the can inside a

kitchen cupboard. I got undressed and did some reading for work. After half an hour or so, I was ready to turn out the light. Norton wasn't in his usual position on the pillow next to me, so I called his name. As usual, he came running and jumped onto the bed. But he didn't, as usual, settle right down to go to sleep. Instead he scurried and prowled and nuzzled his nose into my face until I realized he was trying to tell me something. I felt as if I were in the middle of a "Lassie" segment, except when I finally got up and agreed to follow Norton, he wasn't trying to tell me that Timmy was in trouble. He was trying to tell me he wanted another Pounce.

I obligingly opened the cupboard, gave him one, told him that this would not be acceptable behavior on a regular basis, then went back to bed. In the morning, I woke up, stretched, felt for a familiar chin to scratch—but there was nothing there. Somehow—I'm sure I should be a tad nervous about how closely Norton and I are attuned to the same wavelength—I knew where he was. My instinct was confirmed when I got out of bed: Norton was sitting on my kitchen counter, staring hungrily up at the cupboard that held the Pounce, scratching pathetically at the cabinet door. I gave him two more of the biscuits and thus began a daily ritual that goes on to this day. Every morning, before I head off to work, my last deed before I go out the door is to give Norton two or three Pounce. Every night, right before I go to bed, he gets two or three more. I have no idea what makes this stuff so appealing to him, unless it's the scrumptious-sounding pregelatinized wheat feed flour or the equally delicious ferrous sulfate. But I do know that the thought of eating them drives my cat wild with desire. In between his morning and late-night snacks, Norton seems to spend an awful lot of time attempting to tunnel his way through my kitchen cabinet, trying to get to the Pounce on his own. Judging by the scratch marks on the pine, he's just about ready to give the Count of Monte Cristo a run for his money. I expect a major breakthrough in another few months, when he should either reach the cans of Pounce or the apartment on the other side of the hall.

In case you haven't yet come up with the connection between Norton's snacking habits and the title of this chapter, just start thinking of women, during this period of my life, as my Pounce.

For the first time in several years, I was unattached. It was a very strange feeling. As much as Cindy and I had fought against the concept of coupledom, there was no denying that we had been a full-fledged couple—and had been for a long time. As such, we'd fallen into our own routines and been included in the routines of others.

Our deal was that although we were not required to include the other in every little social occasion, there *were* situations that qualified as command performances. If anything particularly good or interesting came up that I knew she would enjoy (or, of course, vice versa), she (or I) had first dibs. The same if anything important, horrendously boring, or terrible popped onto our social calendars, a situation where one of us needed the other's support. On the other hand, if either one of us had a normal, everyday, run-of-the-mill occasion to attend, we were not stuck—either doing the inviting or being the invitee. If I had tickets to the opening of the new Sondheim musical, Cindy *had* to

be my date. If I was invited by an actor friend who was appearing in a summer stock revival of *Six Rms Rv View*, I was free to take anyone I wanted. If Cindy had a dreadful wedding to go to that involved driving two-and-a-half hours into New Jersey, I was there. If she had her semi-boring monthly dinner with her uncle who always insisted—loudly—that people were constantly coming up to him on the street and mistaking him for Rouben Mamoulian, she was appreciative if I went, but I didn't *have* to go. It made sense at the time, and it seemed to work for us, for a while at least. (I actually went to dinner a surprising number of times with Uncle Max, but no one, while I was there anyway, ever came up to him and called him Mr. Mamoulian. He liked me because I was the only person he'd ever met, other than all these alleged strangers on the street, who actually knew what Rouben Mamoulian looked like. In case you're wondering, yes, he was the spitting image.) When it *stopped* working, one of the first things to get used to, if I didn't want to go alone, was finding a partner for special occasions. As much as Norton would have appreciated the opening night of *Cats*, I don't think he could have handled most theatrical events or very many charity dinners.

I think I handled the breakup with Cindy fairly well. The night that it happened, I went back to my apartment and had a decent cry. Norton hung out on the bed and let me pet him and hug him to my heart's content. He kept looking up at me, concerned, trying to figure out what could possibly be wrong. I guess I can't say that he ever truly figured it out, but he did purr particularly loudly for a stretch, an open invitation for me to collapse, put my head on his stomach, and use him for a pillow, which I did gratefully for quite a long while.

When I finally felt like talking to a human, I called my oldest friend, Paul Eagle, in Los Angeles. Paul wasn't there, however, so I had to settle for his phone machine. I left a message, something subtle along the lines of "Hi, it's me. Just checking in. How 'bout those Giants, huh? Rams stink. Oh, by the way, Cindy dumped me and I'm suicidal. Give me a call."

Next on my list was my brother, Eric, also in L.A. The message I left on *his* phone machine was a bit more rational: "Hey. Just calling to say I hate women. Talk to you later."

Between the crying, the soothing purring, and the emotional trauma of the day's events, I was now ready to go to sleep. In fact, I was looking forward to a night of lying in the dark for several hours, gazing ahead with a ghostly stare, contemplating the meaninglessness of life, followed by a fitful period of tortured dreams. That was actually starting to seem like fun. So I turned off the lights, gave Norton one last hug and kiss, and began my suffering.

I had suffered for about a minute and a half when the phone rang. I turned on the light and picked up the receiver. It was Eric, my brother, who had cleverly detected the hysteria in my message and wanted to know what was wrong. I told him. The whole story. Repeating the thing out loud, rather than just inside my head, brought a few more tears. When I was done, Eric began to be supportive.

Now . . . understand this: My brother is a great guy and we've been close all our lives. But he lives in L.A. And he's a screenwriter. *And* he's been through therapy (and, worse, acting classes). Add it all up and you get someone who *loves* to be supportive. He likes to hug and share his feelings and tell people he loves them.

Which is all very nice, I must say, except that I am *not* like this. I don't particularly like to hug anyone unless there's a chance we're going to exchange bodily fluids. I don't actually think my feelings are particularly interesting; sharing them usually is about as appealing to me as the idea of sharing Leon Spinks's dentures. Another reason I'm not wild about all this feeling sharing is that I've found most people don't really want you to share your feelings. They want to share *their* feelings and then have you tell them you feel exactly the same way. In general, when it comes to feelings, I much prefer showing to telling.

Nonetheless, I was in no position to complain about my brother's support. I'd just poured my heart out to him. I could clearly take a little genuine emotional contact in return. So Eric told me he was there for me. He told me he loved me. He told me he was sorry the whole thing with Cindy had happened, but at the same time, he was glad because it gave him the opportunity to tell me he loved me, which he didn't get to do often enough. I, in turn, appreciated all the sentiments, except perhaps the last one, which I thought was going a bit far, and told him I loved him, too, which I certainly did.

After half an hour of such talk, we hung up.

I was now exhausted. All that sharing had taken a lot out of me.

The light went off, my head hit the pillow, my eyes closed. Sleep was very near.

But not near enough. The phone rang again.

It was Eric. He asked if I wanted him to come east. For
support. I was genuinely touched by the offer, but I told
him it wasn't necessary. I had plenty of people to share
feelings with in New York if I really felt the need.

"I love you," he said.

"I know," I said before hanging up. "Thanks again."

I think I actually dozed off for a good thirty or forty
seconds before the phone began ringing. It was now after
two A.M.

"What?" I sighed into the phone.

"Pete," Eric said, "I just hope you understand that I'm
here for you, totally and absolutely."

"I understand," I said. "Totally and absolutely."

"I'm just so concerned. You don't sound good."

"Well, I'm pretty tired right now. I'll sound a lot better
in the morning. After I get some sleep."

"Are you sure?"

"Pretty sure. Sleep is what's important now."

"I love you," Eric said. "I really do."

"Good night," I said.

This time I didn't even bother to try to fake it. I sat up
in bed, lights on, stiff as a board, waiting. I didn't have long
to wait.

"Yup," I said into the phone.

It was Paul this time. He'd just gotten my message. He
was surprised how awful I sounded and wanted to know
exactly what had happened. Well, by this time, I was too
exhausted and too cranky to go into much detail. Also, I'd
already poured my heart out once; twice in one day was
near impossible. So I told him he'd have to settle for the
abbreviated version and then get the full rundown the next

morning. He understood, and I gave him a short take on
the breakup with Cindy: unsuspecting me, trip-to-England
birthday present, evil doctor, crying, crying, purring and
crying, phone call, phone call, phone call, I love you, I'm
there for you, I love you, tired, the end.

Paul sympathized exactly the right amount—about fifteen
seconds' worth—then said good-bye. Before I could hang
up the phone, though, he managed to get in one quick "I
love you."

I sat in bed for a minute, light still on, waiting. I knew
my friend Paul. This would be a hard situation for him to
resist. After all, this was a person who, when I once called
him from New York, long distance, to see if he had the
number of an L.A. florist so I could send some Mother's
Day flowers to my mother, made a big deal out of finding
the right number, keeping me on hold for several minutes,
then gave me the number of a pet store. When I called him
back, demanding the real number and yelling at him for
making me look like an idiot trying to order roses from Phil
of Phil's Pet Parlor, he apologized for his sophomoric sense
of humor, thumbed through the yellow pages, and gave me
another number—which turned out to be a bowling alley.
Running up a huge phone bill now, I called him a third
time, screamed, and he swore he'd do it right—and gave me
the number of a Korean massage parlor. So I was fairly
certain he'd be unable to resist a follow-up call now in my
moment of despair. It was too good an opportunity to
waste.

I was right. In two minutes, the phone rang. Wearily, I
answered it.

"Are you calling to tell me you love me?" I asked.

"How'd you know?" a woman's voice answered.

"Who is this?" I asked.

"Laurie."

Paul's wife. She loved me as much as Eric did, she said.

But not as much as the next person, an old college friend Paul had called the moment he'd hung up on me. And that old friend didn't love me nearly as much as the next three old friends who called. When Paul finally called back to tell me that the more he thought about it, he *liked* me but *loved* Cindy, I decided that my period of mourning for Cindy was pretty much over.

I realize it seems fairly brief—one night of mourning after several years of love—but I have to say that despite the emotional upheaval, there was a certain sense of relief when the relationship ended. It was a little like being reborn, although, granted, it was like being born with an enveloping sense of sadness. To fight off that sadness, I immediately began to indulge all my single-man fantasies: I bought several boxes of Sugar Pops and Cocoa Puffs and ate bowls of the stuff for dinner—with *no* vegetables on the side. I never went *near* the public television channel on my TV dial and watched sports practically every waking minute. (I realized I had gone slightly over the edge when I was starting to care—deeply—about which woman was going to win the Dinah Shore Open golf tournament.) I didn't make my bed. And I left all the little post-shaving hair particles on the sink—for days on end.

Of course, eventually, other fantasies and yearnings came into play. It wasn't too long before I began scratching at the cabinet door for women.

I wasn't really looking for anything serious or substantial at this point. I was much more interested in shallow, superficial, and, preferably, sweaty.

I wasn't much of a dater. People of my generation never really dated. We hung out, we did stuff, we burned banks, we took psychedelic drugs and rolled around on water beds together, but we didn't really date. This was a whole new experience, and I was determined to make the most of it.

The first thing I learned was that attractive women (and here I'm going with the following somewhat limited definition: models, actresses, and any woman who drives her own jeep who isn't named Gutty, Rocky, or Gertie) like to go out with writers. Not all of them, mind you. A lot of them like to go out with investment bankers or very ugly rock stars or photographers who only have first or last names, not both, but on the whole, they think writers are smart and they're attracted to smarts. This works out well because I've also observed that most writers like to go out with attractive women. In fact, going out on a limb, my own theory is that, deep down, male writers, with the possible exception of Vaclav Havel and Oscar Wilde, write *only* so they can impress women. Otherwise, why go through the sheer agony of lonely, torturous days trying to create, not to mention entire lifetimes of poverty and often ridicule? It's all done in the hope of an Ophelia, an Emma, a Daisy coming up to you in a bar and saying, "Excuse me, aren't you Fyodor Dostoyevski? I just *loved The Brothers Karamazov.* That Alyosha was the *sexiest* man. Is it true that writers create characters based on their true selves?"

Models go for smarts, I believe, because they don't respect their own beauty. How could they? They're around women all day who are even *more* beautiful than they are. Where I see perfection, they see hair that's not as thick as Paulina's. I see sculpted grace, they see skin that's not as tight as Christie's. Their beauty has no mystery for them, no allure, because they see it as something they have no control over. It's an external, artificial attribute. Writers, on the other hand, worship beauty above all. This is partly because most of us are ugly little rodents with bad posture and ailing gums whose sole sense of worth comes from what we can produce from within. And it's partly because we spend most of our lives stooped over a word processor trying desperately to *create* beauty—and we know how difficult, how near-impossible and absolutely hellish that is to do.

So . . . it's established that writers go for attractive women and that attractive women go for writers. But there's one other thing that women tend to go for and fuss over and melt at the sight of.

*Riiigghhhtttt.*

Cute gray cats with round heads and folded ears.

Hallelujah.

The first step in restructuring my social life was to decide what to do about a place for the summer. The little blue house in Fair Harbor had never been *my* house as much as it had been *our* house. Cindy and I had found it together

and enjoyed it together. It didn't seem right for Norton and
me to go back without her and Marlowe.

Enter Norm Stiles, a man destined to go down in the Fire
Island Hall of Fame.

A friend for several years, Norm had been out to the
house to visit us a few times over the various summers. Now
he'd decided it was time to take the plunge and begin regular
weekend visits. He asked if I wanted to share a house.

The more I thought about this, the better it seemed. It
would be fun to have a big place instead of the blue doll-
house. It would be great to have a regular tennis partner.
We could have parties—actual people coming over to Pete
and Norm's for fun and recreation. Plus, I liked to cook and
Norm said he liked to clean up.

Done.

We not only took a bigger house, we took over a familiar
one. David, my writing partner, and Diana had decided it
was time to settle in Connecticut, so we moved into their
place. Norton certainly appreciated the convenience of this
resettling, since he already knew how to get to the house
from all points. His only reservation about the spot was one
particular bluejay who lived around there. This bird had a
thing for my cat and would fly around him, mocking him
loudly, occasionally swooping down and pecking at Norton's head. Norton *hated* this bird. I used to try to explain
to him that *he* was the cat, he was supposed to be able to
take a bird one on one, but my pep talks never took hold.
Until the day we left Fire Island, Norton was totally intimidated by the bluejay.

My initial instincts about the move had been correct.
Having a bigger house was a nice luxury. Norm and I played

combative tennis. I learned to make a mean grilled chicken and Norm turned out to be the best dishwasher stacker I ever saw. (I swear, it seemed that he could cram most of the house, including the living room couch, into that thing.) But the one thing I had to get used to was people.

I'd been a summer resident of Fair Harbor for four years. In that time, I hadn't met one single person other than the two guys who ran the market, the Rockette Lady, and my excuse for not writing—the coffee klatch. A good part of this is due, as I'm sure you've realized by now, to the fact that I welcome new, close relationships into my life about as warmly as the eighteenth century welcomed lepers. Norm, on the other hand, had been a weekender for about a minute and a half before he knew every single person who had a home in the community, most of their regular guests, and all of their personal habits. Walking down the street with Norm was an amazing experience. His level of popularity was such that I nicknamed him "the Mayor," as in "the Mayor of Fair Harbor." Thinking of Norm as the Ed Koch of the beach set was not so farfetched.

*"Hey, Norm! How's it hangin'?"*

I couldn't get over the fact that near total strangers would just stop and pat him on the back. Women flocked around him. Norm happens to be the head writer for "Sesame Street," which, in addition to being the best job in the world, means that women automatically think he's intelligent, sensitive, and funny. He actually is all of those things—although if you ever meet him, ask him what he was doing with those binoculars on the porch that night.

*"Norman, you were a wild man last night! Are you discoing tonight?"*

I had to stop at this one and ask him where the hell one discoed in Fair Harbor. Norm told me they turned the restaurant into a club at eleven P.M. Shocked, I wondered when they'd started doing that, a week or two ago? No, Norm told me—four years ago.

Oh, well. So I wasn't big on staying up past ten o'clock during the summer.

One little guy who obviously *had* been out and around, however, was a certain debonair Scottish Fold.

Norton usually tagged along on my strolls with Norm to the tennis court or the market or the bay. It was unbelievable how many Fair Harborites knew him. It seemed that every other person we passed would first say hello to Norm, then give Norton a warm greeting—by name—then look at me and stare quizzically, as if to say, "Hmmm, this guy looks vaguely familiar. Oh, well, maybe not."

Sometimes I'd initiate the conversation and ask how they knew my cat. A common response was "Oh, he comes over and visits with us all the time."

When people would speak to me directly, I'd usually get "Oh, you're the guy Norm told us about. Is it true you refuse to ever leave your porch?" or, my favorite, "Ohhh, you're Norton's dad!" It wasn't until *many* people had greeted Norton on our strolls that it occurred to me he never wore a name tag. Which meant that unless he *spoke* to my neighbors when he went visiting, they couldn't possibly know his name.

I decided not to pursue this line of thinking any further. It didn't seem healthy.

*"Normie, meet you at the sixish* ce soir?"

Now this is something that deserves to be discussed.

There was a strange and eerie Stephen Kingish ritual that took place in Fair Harbor every Friday and Saturday evening. As I'd sit on my porch sipping a beer, shoes off, relaxing, I'd see scores of people, dressed as if for the ballet—or, at worst, a "Miami Vice" audition—parading by, heading toward the dock. Most of the women had on enough makeup to make the National Kabuki Theater of Japan proud. Most of the men had on shirts that revealed enough hair on their chests, shoulders, and backs to re-sod a good-sized minor league baseball stadium. They all had drinks in one hand, and their arms were all cocked at forty-five-degree angles, I suppose the best possible angle to prevent spillage.

It wasn't until Norm was there to explain the mysteries of Fire Island that I truly understood what I was witnessing.

The dock was the best place in town from which to watch the beautiful sunsets. So all the townspeople would gather there under the pretense of enjoying nature's spectacle but, in reality, they would be desperately trying to pick up any member of the opposite sex who didn't have sun poisoning and spend the night with him or her. These gatherings regularly started around six in the evening, thus the endearing word "sixish" was born into our vocabulary.

There were regular sixishes and special sixishes (like July Fourth, when there were not only fireworks but local artisans peddling their photographs, jewelry, T-shirts, and personalized Kadima paddles), and there were theme sixishes. There was something awe-inspiring when, come the annual *Animal House* sixish, fairly successful lawyers, publishers, realtors, what have you, would stand around in togas, sipping their drinks, swiveling their heads in search of amiable companionship, and chanting, "Par-*ty* . . . par-*ty.*"

Norm took me to a sixish, against my better judgment. I didn't really like mingling with people who dressed up in togas (even if they weren't dressed in togas then, it was enough to know that they *would* do so at some point in the summer), but he decided it was something I had to do. This was supposed to be a new life.

I brought Norton along, figuring he'd like to see it. Why not—he already knew most of the people who were there.

I have to say, I didn't quite get it. The whole concept slid right by me. Why would people come from New York City—the stress and dress capital of the world—to the most beautiful, quiet, relaxing beach imaginable and *re-create New York?* Why would anyone wear stockings on an eighty-five-degree Saturday night when they didn't have to? Or silk sport jackets? Why wouldn't people wear shorts and a T-shirt? And what was this fear of spending an evening alone? After five days of pushing and shoving your way through several million people crammed into a few square miles, why would anyone want to cram into a few square feet with several hundred of the same people?

Norton was a big hit at his first sixish—he got many compliments, from old friends as well as new, on his ears as well as his personality. I was less of a hit. No one complimented either my ears or my personality. I think I found it a little too hard to conceal my despair at the amount of exposed cellulite. It was as if I'd been suddenly transported into Jack La Lanne's personal hell. (For those of you who have already been captivated by Norm's charm and think he's a much more sensitive guy than I am, please note that after this first dockside experience of mine and ensuing state of shock, he devised the perfect sixish lure for a member of the opposite sex: First, tie a piece of danish to a string. Any flavor will do, though cherry, prune, or cheese are preferable. Casually drop said danish on the ground. When your unsuspecting prey bends over, thinking he or she can surreptitiously shovel away some free dessert, yank the string, pulling the delectable pastry several feet closer to your house. Your prey will pursue. Repeat as long as necessary, which is until you've got the poor sucker trapped in your living room. This simple trick should be good for up to a solid three blocks. For best results, have lit candles, a batch of frozen daiquiris, and some peanut M&M's all set up, waiting at home.)

Norton, to his credit, seemed to share my lack of interest in the sixish. There were certainly no other cats to befriend. The only other quadruped was a small sheepdog whose idea of fun was barking loudly and chasing Norton into the bushes by the market. We left after I overheard a conversation Norm was having with a woman psychologist. Her specialty was people with ego problems. "Sometimes," she was saying, "I want to shake these people and say, 'Don't you understand? I'm the best damn psychologist in New York! Why don't you just get better?'"

Norton let me carry him after that one. We both wanted to get home as quickly as possible.

Norm, Norton, and I shared a summer house for three years. Norm set new records for popularity on the island and—I like to think that rooming with me was some help here—wrote some of his best sketches for Oscar the

Grouch. Norton had a very happy transition from kitten-hood to adolescence, acquiring all of the traits that go with the teenage and early twenties years. He became an incred-ible know-it-all. It was impossible to tell him anything. If it was raining and he wanted to go out, all my explanations of how he was going to be very wet and miserable if I opened the door went for naught. He insisted on learning everything for himself. He also became much more inde-pendent, taking to staying out all night when we were at the beach (or *almost* all night—he'd usually meow very loudly for me to let him in at five A.M.). I never questioned his whereabouts; I did give him the benefit of the doubt that he was staying away from the all-night disco. Probably the most traumatic event of this period was the removal of Norton's . . . uh . . . manhood. Although I would have loved to have a kitten fathered by him (I'll try to stay away from any grandparent comparison), everyone and anyone who ever had a cat impressed me with their vehemence about avoiding all the things that went with breeding. It was the thought of a cat (and Norton, during this thought process, became *"a* cat," not *"my* cat" or "that cute little guy" or anything like that) spraying all over my apartment, my clothes, my work, my life that finally swayed me. I couldn't face it. So I made an appointment and took him to the vet.

Norton's vet, who has his practice down in the Village, looks exactly like Santa Claus. He's large, jolly, and has long white hair and a white beard. He's a terrific doctor with a great bedside manner. When I took Norton in for this dreaded operation, I was in desperate need of that manner.

"Really," he told me. "It's painless. He won't feel a thing."

"Maybe I should stay," I said. "I could get a cot, set it up in his room . . ."

"He doesn't have to spend the night," Santa told me. "You can pick him up at five."

"Should I do anything special for him? Buy him a soft bed? Should I get the cable guy to disconnect Channel J?"

"He'll be *fine,*" the vet said. "This is not going to be traumatic for him."

The vet was right. Norton handled it like a champ. I, however, was a wreck. I spent most of the day doubled over with cramps in the groin area. I was also sure that Norton would hate me when I came to pick him up. I was positive there'd be lots of resentment. I was already dreading his shrink bills.

At five sharp, I returned to the vet's, and there was Norton, slightly groggy but looking none the worse for wear. Santa showed me the incision, and when the room stopped spinning around, I had to admit that it didn't look bad. He told me to make sure Norton took it easy for one night—and then the whole thing would be forgotten and he'd be completely back to normal.

He was certainly right about that. Norton showed no ill effects from the operation, neither psychological nor physical. It certainly didn't keep him from catting around all night on Fire Island. He didn't even gain weight, which I'm sure was due to his outdoor life climbing trees and prowling the Fair Harbor undergrowth.

As for me, during these house-sharing years, my tennis

game improved tremendously, I progressed from grilled chicken to a superb (if I may say so myself) cold poached salmon with an aioli sauce, and we had an incredible amount of fun. But I never managed to become an habitué of the sixishes. I also never dated any egotistical psychologists; nor did I have to resort to The Mayor of Fair Harbor's Original Danish Lure.

But I did enter the full-fledged world of hemming and hawing, awkward embraces, and tentative intimacy. In fact, I did more than enter. I plunged in headfirst.

My first real post-Cindy involvement was with a woman named Sarah. Sarah and I, it would eventually turn out, had about as much in common as Madonna and the Pope. But for the first three months we went out I thought she was perfect.

To begin with the superficialities, she was absolutely stunning. She had dark hair and skin that tanned a deep, deep brown. She had long, perfectly tapered legs and—remember, I warned you this was during my Shallow Period—she wore the shortest skirts I'd ever seen this side of the Twiggy era. She was sensuous and sensual, and to top it all off, as I got to discover when she decided she could trust me, she didn't mind doing a certain amount of her clothes shopping at Victoria's Secret.

Unfortunately, after beginning with the superficialities, I couldn't come up with anything else. And what kept poking through and causing serious trouble was that there were two areas in which we could never resolve our differences. One was *sense of humor*. Sarah's philosophy—which she happened to mention fairly often—was that "A sense of humor is fine, but there are certain times in life that are inappropriate for humor." She would get rather upset when I would unleash *my* philosophy of life, which was that she was probably right but that "I just haven't ever found any of those times yet."

The other great area for our fights was none other than Norton. Sarah was terribly jealous of him, most specifically because I often used him as an excuse not to spend the night at her apartment. She used to insist that Norton was my means of avoiding commitment. I suppose, if forced to analyze it, she was right, though I prefer to think he was just my means of not having to actually *tell* Sarah I was avoiding commitment. My excuse for not spending the whole night in her apartment was that I didn't like leaving Norton alone.

"He'll survive a night alone," she'd say.

"I know," I'd say back. "But he won't *like* it."

As far as excuses went, this one was mostly true. I *didn't* like leaving him alone. But there were other reasons, too. I also didn't like Sarah's apartment. It was one of those new, white brick buildings that have the same sense of warmth as Stalin's Russia. She had filled the apartment up with little knickknacks and kinetic sculptures and modern art prints. It looked like the kind of place I always figured Andy Warhol would go to die.

We once had a huge fight when, at two in the morning, I slipped out of bed and told her I was going home. She was furious. I told her about my Norton and the Predator Theory. She became even more furious. As I kept trying to explain away my leaving, Sarah finally burst into tears and

told me she absolutely couldn't see me anymore. She was
ending the relationship. A little surprised at the extent of
her reaction, I wanted to know exactly why she felt this way.

"Because Norton is just a cat," she sniffled. "And he only
has cat feelings. I'm a person. I have *people* feelings. But you
don't care about my feelings. You really don't." By this
time she was crying. "I think you like your cat better than
you like me," she said through her tears.

"Sarah, that's just not true," I said.

"What isn't?" she asked hopefully.

"I don't think Norton only has cat feelings."

Needless to say, this turned out to be one of those inappropriate times for humor. Sarah wouldn't see me for two
months after that.

Sarah was constantly refusing to see me for two months or
announcing that our relationship was over. Somehow,
though, we'd always get back together. Our reunions usually came about when we'd run into each other at a restaurant and realize we liked each other better than the person
we were with, or when she'd be depressed about her job
and need someone to talk to, or when I'd get the new
Victoria's Secret catalogue in the mail and happen to be
browsing through it at bedtime. We couldn't seem to stay
together and we couldn't seem to stay apart.

One Valentine's Day, on the spur of the moment, I decided to take her up to Vermont for a weekend of skiing
and romance. Sarah was so appreciative of gestures like this
it was a little scary. We rarely took vacations or trips together. Again, chalk this up to that lack of a commitment.

Once, we almost went to Arizona for a few days at the Phoenix Biltmore, just about my favorite place in America outside of the Liberace Museum in Vegas. But the Biltmore refused to accept cats so, outraged, I canceled the reservation. As soon as I did that, Sarah canceled me for three weeks. Now, with the promise of a long, snowy weekend ahead of us, I don't think I'd ever seen her so pleased and affectionate. Even I felt a little guilty when I realized that all I had to do was, on two days' notice, find a romantic Vermont inn that took cats.

By my twentieth phone call, Sarah was a lot less pleased and substantially less affectionate. As I made my twenty-first call, I was a desperate man. When the innkeeper answered, I went through my by-now rehearsed Norton pitch. I sensed a hesitation on her part—which was far better than the immediate turndowns I'd received already—so I really poured it on. I was almost ready to go the whole route—and tell her about the time Norton rescued my poor lost grandmother in that horrible snowstorm—when the innkeeper cracked.

Which is how my Scottish Fold came to go cross-country skiing.

The day after we arrived at the inn, Sarah told me she was pretty good at downhill but had never gone cross country. We set out to remedy this. First, however, we thought we'd experiment with Norton and snow. He'd never been outside in snow before; most of his outdoor experience up to this point was in the summertime. But in Vermont, summertime was a distant memory. There was a foot-high blanket of soft powder, so we gently tossed Norton out the front door of the inn and waited with bated breath.

The first thing that happened was that he sank without a trace. He was so light and the snow was so high and so soft, Norton was simply enveloped. In the next moment, however, he went flying up into the air, so caked with white flakes he easily could have fit in with Siegfried and Roy's act.

Much to my surprise, he loved the snow. He ran to the nearest tree, raced up halfway, and dove back to the ground. He burrowed, gopherlike, forging a tunnel with his nose and face. He rolled over on his back, now-white paws clawing at the blue sky. I don't think I'd ever seen an animal having so much fun.

After half an hour of this, I think it got too cold for him. He showed up at the inn, snowflakes and tiny icicles dripping off his coat. I wrapped him up in a towel, dried him off, which he seemed to appreciate, and then he lay down in front of the living room fire for a nap. By this time, of course, the owner of the inn was ready to adopt Norton as one of her own.

After lunch, Sarah and I put on cross-country skis and headed out. Norton, as usual when I went for a walk in the country, followed. I tried to talk him out of this one, but he insisted. Snow or no snow, cold or no cold, he was ready to explore.

When we hit the nearby woods, Norton didn't exactly stay on the trail with us. He zigzagged around like a lunatic, jumping onto trees, bounding into snowbanks, then suddenly stopping and meowing like crazy until I'd come and carry him for a while.

All in all, he was happy. And he was even happier when, two hours later, we repeated the toweling and fireplace

routine. Even Sarah was happy and had to admit—over a late-night cognac and backgammon—that Norton was a worthwhile addition to the Valentine's Day weekend. She sighed contentedly and told me she thought she was falling in love.

Two days later, however, when I refused to spend the night at her apartment, she decided she never wanted to see me again.

In between the various romantic interludes with Sarah, there were other romantic (and not so romantic) interludes. Norton managed to involve himself in almost all of them.

For about six weeks, I fell head over heels for a woman sportswriter who lived in Boston. This meant some serious weekend commuting, either to Boston or to some college basketball game in some southern town where lox and bagels were only a disturbing myth.

The first time I went to Boston to see her, I showed up with two steaks, a bottle of red wine, and a cat.

Norton liked Boston (the Pan Am Shuttle stewardesses, er, flight attendants, are *very* nice to small, friendly animals), but the sportswriter couldn't envision interviewing Dean Smith with a cat on her shoulder, so that cooled off fairly quickly.

I went out with an editor at a rival publishing company who used the word "Dickensian" more than anyone I'd ever met. When she was introduced to Norton, she admired his looks but made the mistake of asking if I'd named him after Norton Simon. The idea that someone thought I could actually name my cat after the world's dullest bil-

lionaire was a staggering concept to me. If she'd said Kenny Norton even, she might have stuck around for a reasonable period of time. As it was, we lasted two weeks.

One week was spent in the company of a fashion designer. She probably wouldn't have made it through the whole week except that we met a few days before Halloween and she confessed to me over our first lunch that the previous Halloween she'd gone to a costume party completely naked—except for one coat of body paint. The reason she didn't last longer than a week was that she had a tattoo of a snake on her shoulder, and Norton kept leaping at it in the middle of the night, doing his best to remove it from her skin. For some reason, she felt this a sufficient reason to end our brief fling.

One of the best things about dating was watching Norton's reactions to the women I brought home (or, in the case of the sportswriter, brought him to). Most of them he liked. The normal routine was as follows: I'd come home after dinner, usher the woman into my apartment. Norton would get a late-night Pounce; I'd introduce them. We'd go through the "Oh, what funny ears" exchange, while Norton sized her up. If he liked her, he'd nuzzle up to her with the side of his head, pushing it against her quite seductively. This was a considerable help in encouraging my date to think more seriously about my charms.

As she and I sat on the sofa, listening to music, talking, trying to figure out what the rest of the evening had in store for us, Norton—again, only if he approved—would sit a few feet away, turn over on his back, and peer up at us. This was so startlingly cute that once eye contact was made be-

tween date and cat, almost all female reservations could be overcome.

Of course, if Norton *didn't* like someone, forget it. No cute nuzzling or adorable backward glances. Oh no. In these cases we got a lot of running around, scratching at the legs of the couch (and sometimes of the woman), possibly even a little throwing up. We usually had the same taste in women, Norton and I, so when his behavior turned, it was hard for me to get annoyed. In fact, except for the couch scratching, I often felt like joining him.

Cindy and Norton had adjusted expertly to a mutually agreeable sleeping arrangement. None of her successors was ever able to work things out quite as smoothly (particularly one named Michelle, who would wake up every hour on the hour, sputtering, gasping for breath, and waving her arms wildly because Norton kept putting his tail in her mouth). Norton, unlike his dad, was extremely fussy about whom he'd let scritch him under the chin in the morning.

I tended to trust Norton's judgment when it came to women, and for the most part, he gave me the benefit of the doubt. The only time we ever had a serious disagreement was over Karyn.

Karyn was a Danish model whom we met in Paris (on one of Norton's first trips). She was twenty-two years old, six feet tall, and the most gorgeous woman I'd ever talked to without actually drooling. She also spoke and read many languages, was overwhelmingly sophisticated, had a sharp and nasty sense of humor, and . . . I suppose you're getting the picture that I was smitten upon first meeting. Miraculously, she was smitten, too. Life seemed perfect.

Except for one problem.

A certain member of my family decided that he absolutely couldn't stand this tall blond woman who occasionally took up his side of the bed. Norton hated her.

My cat doesn't hiss—but he hissed at Karyn. My cat doesn't bite—but he bit her. He liked to wait until she was sound asleep, and then he'd jump on her pillow and meow as loudly as he could, scaring her to death. He once urinated in her shoe—just as she was rushing off on a modeling assignment.

I tried to convince him he was wrong. I also tried to convince Karyn that I couldn't leave him in New York when I came over for a brief Parisian stint. I had no luck convincing either one of them.

Happily I never had to choose between them. It is probably a sickness, I know, but in a choice between someone who could have won the Miss Universe contest (and probably performed some sort of simple brain surgery as her talent) and a temperamental Scottish Fold, my little cat would have won hands down. I might have killed him—but he would have won. Before it came to that, however, I learned once and for all to abide by Norton's judgment when it comes to women.

On my first date with Karyn—which lasted a week—we had a spectacular time. We ate at little, out-of-the-way Parisian restaurants, we drank great wine, I sampled my first peach champagne, we danced cheek to cheek, we held hands in underground *caveaus des jazz.* Then I came back to New York. We wrote letters, we ran up phone bills that

rivaled the national debt, we made plans to meet in all kinds of exotic places.

The second stretch of time we spent together was also fantastic. It lasted only five days, which was how long I was able to get away for. That trip, two friends, Nancy and Ziggy Alderman, happened to be in Paris. Nancy, who is extremely attractive but five-feet-four with dark, curly hair, was a little thrown when she strolled into my room at the Tremoille for a glass of champagne, only to find a blond goddess—wearing something not much bigger than Captain Hook's eye patch for an outfit—busy pouring the bubbly for us all. Zig, in one of his suaver moments, panicked completely at the sight of Karyn and told us he just had to step into the bathroom for a moment. His only error was that he stepped into the closet—and was so embarrassed, he *stayed* there for a good five minutes, hoping somehow that we might not notice.

The next trip to Paris, Karyn and I went out to dinner to celebrate my first night back and our love-starved reunion. I hadn't seen her in several months. She looked as lovely and inviting as ever—and Norton hissed just as loudly as ever when she came to the hotel.

When dinner was over, we strolled back along the streets of Les Halles, holding hands, kissing adoringly every few steps. We arrived back at the Tremoille and went upstairs. I prepared for an evening of extraordinary passion. Then she mentioned, "Oh, by the way, my boyfriend is a little bit upset that I've been seeing you."

It's amazing how that kind of line puts a damper on extraordinary passion.

"Wh-what do you mean, your boyfriend?" I asked. "You

told me you'd broken up with him a long time ago."

She looked at me, confused. "Broken up?"

"Yeah. That first time we went out . . . when we spent a week together . . . you told me you'd just ended your relationship and . . ."

"Oh, *that,*" she said. "I just had to wait until he went out of town. He was gone that whole week. I didn't really break it off with him."

"What about the last time I was here?"

"He was gone, too."

"Well, why didn't you *tell* me?!"

"Because I thought you wouldn't see me."

I started pacing around the room. I wouldn't look at Norton because I was sure he'd be smirking.

"What's his name?" I asked. "Your boyfriend."

"Robert."

"What does he do?"

"He's a podiatrist."

If he'd been a race car driver or perhaps an international clothing designer, I probably could have settled for some kind of sophisticated if painful sharing arrangement. At least I could have salvaged some pride. But a podiatrist?!

"How . . . um . . . how does Robert know that we've been seeing each other?" I asked.

"Oh, I had to tell him this time, since he's in town."

"And what did he say?"

"Robert has a very bad temper," Karyn said with a shrug.

"What did he *say?*"

"Something about killing you."

"Does Robert also have a very good sense of humor?" I wanted to know.

"Robert has *no* sense of humor," Karyn told me.

That was the end of Karyn. It turned out that Robert really *didn't* have a sense of humor and really *did* want to kill me. He had some Arab blood in him, and it seemed that killing was an acceptable solution in whatever country that blood came from. Even if he wasn't actually going to murder me, I must say some very unpleasant images—my being strapped in a chair, shoes off, podiatric instruments of torture being put to good use—did flash through my mind. I had no intention of spending my life with no feet, even for a beautiful Danish model.

Norton, to his credit, never gloated. I have deliberately never taken him to Denmark, however, and I doubt I ever will. The last I heard of Karyn, she'd moved to Rome and was living with some count. I can only hope it's Dracula.

One of Norton's regular trips was a yearly jaunt down to baseball's spring training in Florida. I went every year in March with the nine other guys from the Rotisserie League. Originally it was men only and some serious baseball was watched. Gradually, wives and girlfriends were added; then, as we all got a little older, golf somehow became part of the trip. Over the years, as we wrote about our outing in our annual Rotisserie League book, players from other leagues would show up. Now it's turned into something of a big deal—a Rotisserie League convention with a few hundred stat-crazed fans coming from all over the country to watch and talk baseball with us.

The Rotiss weekend isn't for the casual girlfriend. Sarah made it one year (and managed to sell more Rotisserie

League T-shirts than anyone ever imagined possible; she looked a *lot* better in one of them than any of us did), but this weekend usually fell during a period when she wasn't talking to me. So for a couple of years, Norton was my only companion. He loved the hotel we all stayed at, the Belleview Biltmore, an absolutely spectacular turn-of-the-century sprawling monster with all the old Southern charm one could want. Part of that charm was that the people who worked at the hotel loved Norton as well.

The second year that Norton went with me, I also took two married friends, the same ones who met Karyn in Paris, Nancy and Ziggy Alderman. (Ziggy is not his real name. His real name is John, but because he works at a rather straitlaced investment brokerage, he doesn't want them to know that to most people he's something out of a David Bowie album—which makes it somewhat complicated being friends with him. When he's with his officemates, we're supposed to call him John, even though they call him Aldy. As if that's not confusing enough, there's another hotshot named John at the firm, a hotshot with more seniority than Ziggy, so Zig's bosses told him they were going to refer to him as Jack to avoid confusion when people in the office yelled out for John. As a result, some people now know him as Ziggy, some as Aldy, some as John, and some as Jack. It's a lot like being friends with Sybil.)

On the way down to St. Petersburg with the Aldermans (or, if you prefer, Alderpeople), Ziggy/John/Aldy/Jack was giving me a very hard time about my bringing Norton. He couldn't understand how I could lug a cat along to such a macho affair as a spring training trip. I was made an object of ridicule for the entire flight—something my pal Zig is an expert at. Several years ago, the three of us went out to the Arizona Biltmore for five days of tennis and golf (right— Sarah wasn't speaking to me that week). The second day we were there, three friends of mine came down from Tuscon for a meal. We all ate a lot and drank a lot at the fairly expensive hotel dining room. When we were all done, Ziggy insisted on picking up the check. I argued with him— these were my friends after all; he'd never even met them before—but to no avail. He signed the bill with a flourish and basked in our profuse thank-yous the rest of the night. For the next two days, overcome by guilt, I did my best to pay for everything—Nancy and Zig's breakfast before we played golf, the round of golf itself, drinks at the nineteenth hole, you name it. When it came time to check out, as I was handed my bill, Nancy said to her hubby, "Don't you think it's time to tell him?" It was—and Zig broke it to me that he had indeed signed for the big dinner check—only he'd signed *my name.*

Anyway, the expression on his face as we stood in our Florida hotel's lobby didn't make up for the near-millions he'd stuck me with in Arizona, but almost. After hours of tormenting me for bringing my cat, Zig had to stand at the check-in desk and watch every attractive woman who worked in the hotel (no more than ten or fifteen of them) screech, "Norton? Is that *Norton?*" Then he had to watch them come over, play with you-know-who, smile at me, and say, "Remember—if you need anything, just call."

Now that I think about it, it *did* make up for the check. The annual Rotisserie convention was also the site of perhaps Norton's greatest adventure.

A couple of years ago, I went down as usual to do my

Rotisserie scouting. Also as usual, Norton came along. My plane was quite late, so we didn't arrive at the hotel till after eight P.M. After the celebratory greeting of Norton at the desk, I put him in our room on the second floor, set up his food and litter box, then went downstairs for dinner. After a couple of hours of decent food, good beer, and excellent baseball chatter, I was exhausted, so I went back up to the room. The rest of the gang went to the outdoor patio restaurant for more of the big three.

This year, I had a balcony off the bedroom. When I entered, Norton was standing by the balcony door, anxious to be let out. He was used to having the run of the Belleview Biltmore. They have a huge pool area with lots of grass and many bushes for him to skulk around in. His favorite part of the hotel, for some reason, is the basement. He has spent many a day wandering its nooks and crannies. He particularly likes one dusty, concrete corner; it seems to be the perfect napping spot. But he'd never, at least to my knowledge, played up on the various steeples and levels of the roof.

After a moment's deliberation, I figured I'd give it a try. What could go wrong? So I opened the door. Norton scooted onto the balcony, hopped up on the railing, and then went over, exploring the peaked roofs that seemed to stretch for miles. I waited ten or fifteen minutes, called out for him as a test, and sure enough, he came running. That let me know it was safe, so I told him he was free to roam.

Forty-five minutes later, I was ready for sleep. As I stepped over toward the balcony to call Norton in for the night, my phone rang. I picked it up to hear the voice of

Glen Waggoner, an original Rotisserian and one of my best friends.

"I think you'd better come down here."

"What's going on?"

"Norton just fell through the roof of the dining room."

You know the cartoon of the Road Runner, zipping along the road, covering many miles in mere seconds? That was me racing down the stairs to find my cat.

When I got to the patio, the Rotiss group was hysterical with laughter. Glen led me over to the middle of the dining area and pointed up. Ten feet above my head was a gaping hole in the green-and-white striped awning. Apparently, Norton, bored with the roof, had crawled out onto the awning. Midway, he reached a weak spot and the thing gave out. He plummeted sixteen feet down, landing inches from a table where two seventy-year-old women were finishing their dinner. Needless to say, they screamed—you'd scream, too, if you were calmly eating in a restaurant and a cat came flying through the air, landing three inches from your head—and one of them came very close to needing CPR. They were very nice about it, however, as I began apologizing (over the background din of an entire Rotisserie League crying with laughter), and they suggested I find my cat, as doubtless he was far more terrified than they were.

Glen, whom Norton knew well, had tried to catch him after the great fall, but Norton wouldn't be caught. He'd gone racing around in the dark until Glen lost sight of him.

Having no idea where he'd run off to, I stumbled around the giant lawn, calling out his name. No response. I kept

stumbling for fifteen or twenty minutes with no sign of Norton, until I suddenly realized where he had to have disappeared to. I went over to the creaky, wooden basement door, opened it, and stepped inside. My eyes took a few minutes to adjust to the pitch dark; then, when they had, I inched my way toward a familiar, dusty corner. There, sound asleep, was Norton.

"Pssst," I said.

Norton's eyes opened; he *brrrmeowed* and came into my open arms.

For the rest of the weekend, people fussed and clucked over him. But he stayed close to me for the remainder of our stay. He'd had enough adventure. I saw him nuzzling up to only one person who worked at the hotel—a very attractive blond woman who worked at the desk. When I went over to get the little troublemaker, the woman smiled at him, then at me.

"Is he yours?" she asked, practically batting her eyes. "He's so *sweet*."

If I didn't know better, I'd swear that Norton winked at both of us.

# 7. The cat who went to paris

Over the course of Norton's first few years on earth and in my care, he had, for the average cat, led quite an exciting existence. He'd been lugged around the streets of Manhattan in a pocket. He'd taken cab rides and boat rides and train rides. He'd explored the beaches of Fire Island, the snowy peaks of Vermont, and the antique stores of Bucks County, Pennsylvania (a trip that was relatively uneventful, except for the fact that I bought a beautiful eighteenth-century maple cradle that became Norton's favorite and nearly unbearably cute place in which to nap). He'd also become a regular at my office—spending the day with me on the average of once a week—and as soon as that was established as normal behavior, he began coming to company sales conferences. As a corporate guest, he'd been to Phoenix, Arizona; Laguna Beach, California; Bermuda; and

various places in Florida. Basically, if the trip was no more than an hour or two on the plane, he came with me no matter how long or short my stay was going to be, even if it was an overnight trip. If it was a cross-country expedition or something else that could turn out to be grueling for him (e.g., more than five hours without a litter box), then I wouldn't take Norton unless I was going to be away for at least five or six days.

One of my fantasies in my pre-Norton days was to have a dog that I could one day take to France. The French love animals; they treat them a lot better than they treat tourists. Even the fanciest restaurants allow dogs to come and make themselves at home during mealtime. It is not uncommon to see tuxedoed gentlemen and fur-clad society ladies dining in Jamin or Rovuchon or L'Ambroisie with their poodles or their dachshunds lounging under the table. Several years ago, a French publisher put out a restaurant guide rating every restaurant in Paris by how they treated dogs: what kind of scraps they gave them, whether they were allowed in leashless or not, how friendly the waiters were when petting was called for.

It had never actually occurred to me to take Norton overseas. I'm not sure why there was this mental lapse. Perhaps it was simply that in the first few years I had him, I wasn't making a lot of European trips.

That all certainly changed in a hurry.

The change came when I got a phone call from Roman Polanski.

"Peter," he said in his distinctive accent, which combines a bit of Polish rebel, French intellectual, English dandy,

American rogue, and Jewish uncle, "have you ever seen Paris at Christmastime?"

Roman and I first worked together in 1982, on his autobiography, *Roman by Polanski.* We'd worked extremely well together and, for some unknown reason, immediately became fast friends. I know he's been surrounded by controversy for most of his life, but to tell you the truth, I've never seen a particularly controversial side to him. We thought alike on a lot of issues, shared the same sense of curiosity combined with approximately the same amount of cynicism. From a friend's point of view, he happens to be an extraordinarily generous guy—there's nothing he won't do for you if he likes you—and he has a great sense of humor. He tells wonderful stories and likes nothing better than to sit around La Coupole, sipping champagne, slurping raw oysters, and swapping good jokes.

I have met a lot of very, very smart people, but Polanski is probably the only genius I know. He speaks something like twelve languages, has one of the most interesting interpretive minds I've ever encountered, has made some of the finest, most original films of modern times, and, to top it all off, knows somewhere in the vicinity of a million long-legged models named Suzette. All of this is to say he doesn't ask questions like "Have you ever seen Paris at Christmastime?" without having something in mind.

"Uh . . . no," I said, cleverly. "I don't think I have."

"It's very beautiful. Very beautiful. The snow comes down, the lights go up. Ohhh, the lights in Paris, mmmmm, magnificent. It makes you cry. And the women . . . there is a tremendous influx of attractive women at Christmas, Peter."

"Can I ask you one question, Roman?" I asked from my New York City apartment.

"Anything. Anything."

"Why are you telling me all this?"

"How would you like to come to Paris for Christmas and help me write my new movie for Harrison Ford?"

The man has style, *non?*

Of course, I played hard to get. No pushover am I. I told him that it would take me at least four or five seconds to pack and catch a plane out of New York. It actually took me a little longer than that—but not much. Within a week, Norton and I were on our way to Europe.

Many people think that taking an animal overseas is some kind of major deal. A lot of them think there's a quarantine (only in England) or that the travel arrangements are extraordinarily complicated or that hotel accommodations are impossible for pets. The truth is nothing could be easier than lugging one's cat to foreign shores—if you do it right. Naturally, the first time I took Norton I did it all wrong.

Polanski was going to be in Amsterdam to promote his newest film. As I was making my—excuse me, *our*—arrangements, he said, "Peter, why don't you fly to Amsterdam? We'll have a great dinner, do our best to get in some trouble, and then go to work the next day in Paris. Amsterdam is the perfect place to recuperate from jet lag."

Makes sense, doesn't it? It certainly did to me. So as a result, Norton's first European stop—after a one-hour layover at Charles de Gaulle Airport—was Amsterdam.

Before we left, I had to take my pal to the vet so he could

get his cat passport. This procedure was quite simple: the vet gave Norton a shot, swabbed his ears out with a Q-tip, looked down his throat, then filled out a small green card saying that Norton Gethers, an eight-pound Scottish Fold, born in Los Angeles but living in New York, was healthy and able to change continents at his owner's discretion.

The flight was a breeze—with one tiny exception. Norton had been on a number of flights on various American airlines. As a result of their rigidity, I was a strict rule follower. I usually put Norton in his box, kept him under the seat for the whole flight, and only dared to bring him up and out onto my lap if a—okay, I can say it now—flight attendant asked to see him, which didn't happen all that often. But on Air France, Norton was greeted as warmly as if he'd paid full fare. The attendants *loved* having a pet on board and immediately told me to take him out of the confining box and make him comfortable. We were flying first class, thanks to Warner Brothers, and we were both treated in a first-class manner all the way down the line. When I was served champagne and caviar, Norton got a little dish of smoked salmon with a cup of milk. At dessert time, I mentioned that Norton had a weakness for chocolate, and *voilà,* his own personal *mousse au chocolat* arrived *tout de suite.* They were so incredibly nice to my traveling companion that I relaxed. I relaxed so much that about two hours over the Atlantic, with Norton resting contentedly on my lap, I fell sound asleep. I would have slept all the way to Paris except for the fact that, at some point, one of the male attendants gently poked me in the shoulder, waking me up. When I rubbed my eyes and oriented myself, I realized that there was no cat on my lap. When I looked up,

I saw that that was because the attendant was holding him by the scruff of his little gray neck. Horrified, I grabbed Norton, put him back on my knee, and began apologizing to the steward. I was so intimidated by the strictness of American stewardesses, I apologized profusely for a good five minutes before I realized the kindly French steward was saying to me, "Eet's all right. We don't mind. 'E was 'aving a goot walk." Eventually I came to understand that the steward really *didn't* mind. So I got up the nerve to ask the one question I really wanted an answer to: "Where did he go?"

At that, the steward crinkled up his nose disapprovingly. Clearly Norton had done something that this man found repugnant. In fact, by French standards, my cat had committed the ultimate sin.

" 'E was back in toureest," the steward told me with disdain, "talking to a *dog*."

I stayed awake the rest of the trip. Norton spent most of his free time staring out the window, down at the Atlantic. He seemed to find it just as fascinating as the Fire Island bay.

When we landed in Amsterdam, we took a cab to what turned out to be a wonderful hotel, the Amstel. I was all prepared to either hide Norton or lie my head off, claiming that he wasn't actually spending the night there; I was merely dropping him off to some Dutch friend. But there was no need for the cloak-and-dagger routine. The woman who checked us in gave the cat a warm smile, told me to take him out of his bag, and then watched with an amused look as Norton plopped himself down on the counter and made himself at home. The manager of the hotel came over immediately to get in a few friendly pats on Norton's head; so did a couple of bellboys. The check-in woman asked if Norton was indeed staying there for the night, and when I nodded hesitantly, she immediately asked if he would like a small plate of fish. I sensed that Norton's ears, what there were of them, pricked up a bit at the word "fish," so I told her that would be very nice.

Up in the room, I set up Norton's first international cat litter box, waited for his fish to arrive, then called Roman. After a quick nap, I was ready to go.

Norton was content to spend his first night in Europe sleeping on our down bed while I was wined and dined at a spectacular Indonesian restaurant by a few Dutch journalists. (Okay, Roman was the one being wined and dined—but they let me come along, didn't they? That counts!) The next day was a little more eventful, at least for my gray companion.

I didn't really know what our Amsterdam plans were before I arrived. But I soon found out. We were to check out of our hotel at noon, go to a screening of Roman's latest movie for all the top Dutch distributors, go to a taping of some Dutch quiz show that Roman had agreed to appear on to promote the movie, have dinner with the TV people and some of the distributors, and then catch a late plane to Paris.

It all sounded great except for one thing. What in the world was I going to do with Norton from noon till ten o'clock at night?

Since I didn't really have a choice, I simply took him with me.

The first highlight of the day was our introduction to the distributors. We were at a large screening room and were

seated at a podium toward the front of the room. The studio publicity person assigned to Roman gave a little speech, telling everyone how excited they all should be to be distributing another Polanski film. He went through the litany of Roman's successes in Holland—from his *Knife in the Water* days through *Chinatown* and *Tess*. "And now," he said to the crowd, "I would like to introduce some very special guests. To my right is a man who needs no introduction. One of the great directors of our time, Roman Polanski."

There was a great burst of applause.

"To Mr. Polanski's right is the writer of Mr. Polanski's new film, which they are going to Paris to begin work on—Peter Gethers."

I got some polite applause, considering no one had ever heard of me and probably would never hear of me again. And then came the best announcement, as the publicity person realized there was one other introduction he had to make.

"And to Mr. Gethers's right is . . . his *cat???*"

Rarely have I heard anyone sound as confused. And rarely have I been as proud of my cat. Norton didn't exactly take a bow at the mention of his name, but he did sit up as straight as he possibly could when he heard the very puzzled-sounding applause.

We spent the rest of the day at the taping of the quiz show.

The name of the show translated into "Wanna Bet?" It was the most popular TV program in Holland (also in Germany and Belgium). The only way I can possibly describe it is as a cross between "Truth or Consequences," "Laugh-In," and the ever-popular Vegas review, *Nudes on Ice.*

"Wanna Bet" is ninety minutes long and takes about three hours to shoot. Of those three hours, Norton spent two-and-a-half sitting next to me in the audience—the producers were nice enough to give him his own seat—mostly staring at the flashing sign, which, I assume, said "Applause" in Dutch.

The other half hour he spent in the dressing room—where I was not allowed—being petted by the thirty gorgeous and statuesque topless dancers who participate in the show's sketches.

Norton doesn't usually allow strangers to pick him up and carry him off, but when one of the nearly naked women rushed over to him during a break and asked permission to bring him backstage, he didn't even wait for my okay. He hopped onto the ground and followed her, without so much as a backward glance at his envious dad. When he was returned to me at the end of the show—by three of the dancers, none of whom could bear to part with him—it was yet another time in our relationship when I was very sorry Norton didn't speak English. From the look on his face, however, even if he did, I wasn't ever going to get the details of this particular adventure.

When the show was over, we went to dinner with the heads of the TV studio and several of the distributors who'd earlier been introduced to Norton.

We were taken to one of the city's top restaurants. Norton came along as if he were accustomed to dining out every evening. He hadn't been near his litter box in hours and

hours *and* he'd never been out to eat in public, so I was a tad nervous. However, my boy came through with flying colors. He was the hit of the evening.

The first thing that happened was that our waitress practically fainted when she saw how cute Norton was. When she saw how calmly he sat on my lap, she insisted on bringing him his own chair, which she slipped in next to mine. Next, she brought him his own dinner—a nice little plate of herring and potatoes, which Norton gobbled down appreciatively. He was having such a good time that I was almost insulted when she didn't offer him a glass of wine—although he did seem a lot happier with his dish of milk.

This was supposed to be a business dinner, with Roman talking up his movie, but very little business was discussed. Most of the conversation centered around the newest—and smallest—guest of honor. Every few minutes, someone would insist on switching seats with me or Roman, who was on the other side of Norton, so he or she could be near the cat. By the end of the evening, I was on the complete other end of the table, and Norton was in between the head of the Dutch film distribution industry and the woman producer of "Wanna Bet," doing his best Cary Grant impersonation—politely chewing on his herring, sipping his milk, sitting up in his chair, and basically appreciating the restaurant and the attention.

When it was time to leave, several people offered to let Norton stay in their homes if I ever came through the city again, and several asked if they could visit him on their next trip to New York. By the time we boarded the plane for Paris, he was one exhausted cat. In fact, I had to wake him up as we circled over the city, holding him up to the window so he could get his first glimpse of the brightly lit Eiffel Tower.

Norton took to Paris like, well, like a *canard à l'eau.*

We stayed at one of my very favorite hotels in the world, the Tremoille, which is on the corner of Rue de la Tremoille and Rue du Boccador in the eighth arrondissement. It is gorgeous, it is small, it is elegant, friendly, it is *very* Parisian, *and* they *love* my cat.

Last year, when I was writing another movie with Polanski, my agent, Esther—she of Norton's encounter with the stewardess from hell—popped into Paris for a couple of evenings of fun and good food. I was there for three months and, to my regret, wasn't staying at the Tremoille—the studio had decided it was too expensive for such a long stay, so I got an apartment—but I insisted that *she* stay there. After dinner, I walked her back to the hotel and talked about how nice they always were to Norton. As I was elaborating, she stopped me on the street and said, "I don't believe you. You are definitely making this up." Indignant, I insisted I was absolutely telling the 100 percent truth. She refused to accept this. So when we reached the lobby, I went up to the front desk, smirked confidently at Esther, and said to the concierge, "Good evening. Do you remember me?"

"Of course," he responded. "And 'ow is your leetle cat? Is 'e well?"

"Very well," I told him.

"Please send him my best," the man said, to Esther's total

astonishment. "Tell 'im to come visit anytime 'e weeshes."
Esther now believes everything I tell her.

Over the years, Norton has stayed at the Tremoille six or
seven times, usually when I'm working with Roman. Our
writing routine is as follows: start around ten-thirty or
eleven in the morning, break for lunch at one o'clock or so,
a nice leisurely lunch, then work from three until seven or
eight. After an hour- or two-hour break to relax, to have a
glass of icy Polish vodka, or just to get away from each
other, we usually have dinner. I'd always go back to the
hotel to check on and play with Norton, either during our
lunch break or our pre-dinner break. After a while, I realized that playtime was unnecessary. Norton didn't need any
more playing with. Almost every time I returned to the
room, there was at least one maid, usually two, petting him,
scratching him, playing with some new toy they'd just
bought for him. Once he became an accepted member of
the hotel family, they let him hang out in the lobby during
the day (one of the people on the desk or one of the maids
would bring him back to the room if they felt things were
too hectic) and let me bring him down to the formal dining
room for dinner.

One day there was a near catastrophe. I came back at
seven P.M. for my daily check-in, strolled jauntily into the
hotel, and asked for my room key. One of the managers
looked at me very gravely and said, "Oh, Monsieur Gethers, your leetle cat, he is very seek."

Without another word, I grabbed the key and raced up the
two flights of stairs to my room. When I ran inside, a maid
was sitting on the bed, soothingly petting Norton and cooing at him. He was snuggled up on my pillow, curled into a

ball. All in all, he looked pathetic—and was clearly sick.

The maid didn't speak any English, so I didn't catch all of what she said. Basically, I picked up on the fact that she'd come into my room early that morning to clean, began her usual play routine with Norton, only he didn't respond. He wouldn't leave the bed, he wouldn't pick his head up, he wouldn't move at all. She tried to give him some Pounce— I'd brought over a lifetime supply and had shown all the maids where I kept it—and he wouldn't even touch that. This was serious.

Norton had never, ever been sick before. I didn't know what to do. Roman was surprisingly understanding when I told him I was going to skip our usual dinner and carousing because of a sick cat. He was pretty attached to Norton by this time, too.

Norton didn't eat that night. Nor did he move from my pillow (I slept on his side of the bed all night). I did my best to reassure him that everything was going to be all right, but he was not a happy kitten. If you ever hear anyone say that cats don't think or feel, all you have to do is tell them to spend the night in bed with a sick one. If you looked up the word "mournful" in the dictionary, you would have seen a picture of Norton that night. I decided to give him twenty-four hours before calling a French vet.

He seemed to be feeling better the next morning. (I, on the other hand, wasn't doing too well since I'd tossed and turned with worry all night.) He wasn't particularly active—he wouldn't get out of bed to eat his breakfast—but he did munch on a couple of Pounce when I brought them to him, and he did lick my hand appreciatively afterward. When I left to go to work, Norton roused himself slightly,

standing up for a moment on the bed. I came back, told him he'd be fine, and then watched him settle back onto my pillow.

At lunchtime, I came back to see how Norton was feeling. The manager gave me the thumbs-up sign when I picked up my key. Sure enough, in the room were two maids, hovering over Norton, who was now resting playfully on his back, enjoying their gentle scratching and friendly babbling. They had bought him a present—a little catnip tree, which they'd placed on the end table by the bed. They told me that he wasn't quite ready for it, but they thought it would be a good incentive for him to get well.

I went back to work knowing my pal was in good hands. At that night's dinner break, he was back to normal. Not only did he gulp down his dinner and leap at the Pounce when I held it out to him, he munched a few leaves off his new catnip tree. When it was time for bed, he was well enough to sleep on his own pillow. I had no idea what had brought on his one-day illness—perhaps it was all that rich French cat food—but with a sigh of relief, I told him I was glad he was feeling better and kissed him on the top of his head. He gave me a quick lick with his sandpaper tongue and made me feel as if, at the very least, I'd been an understanding and supportive nurse.

We fell into a fun Parisian routine, Norton and I. Since I didn't have to be at work until at least ten-thirty, I got into the habit of going to one particular café, across the Seine from the Eiffel Tower, for my morning café au lait. After a few mornings of this, I didn't see any reason not to take

Norton. So every day he'd hop into his shoulder bag, we'd leisurely stroll the few blocks to my regular haunt, and I'd sit in my straw café chair, sipping coffee and reading the *Herald Tribune* while he sat in his chair, sphinxlike, watching the passersby and, once the waiters got used to his presence, lapping at a small bowl of water or milk.

After breakfast, I'd usually take him back to the hotel. Sometimes I'd take him over to Roman's apartment. That first trip, when I was rewriting the script for what became the film *Frantic*, Harrison Ford came over to spend a couple of weeks working with us. He was the star of the film and, as such, quite properly wanted to have input into character motivation, action, and thought. He and Roman were friends but had never worked together. I'd never met Harrison before. So the first few days were spent feeling each other out, seeing how we'd all get along, all of us trying to be firm with our convictions for the movie yet flexible and sensitive to the other two's egos and desires. Harrison has a reputation—which my experience certainly bears out—for being a remarkably intelligent actor. It's remarkable because actors, in general, are not considered much higher on the intelligence scale than your basic, everyday dining room table. They are also known for screwing up scripts in order to make their characters look better. Not only is Harrison smart, he's more concerned with the *movie* than whether or not his character is braver, brighter, and cleverer than all the other characters. I liked him and respected him a lot right from the beginning. However, my guess is that Harrison wasn't overly impressed with me the first day he showed up. We shook hands, started discussing the first draft of the script, which was written by Roman with his longtime collaborator, Gerard Brach—what was wrong with it and what was right with it—and then, just as we were really getting into it, just as some passion was coming out in the conversation, Roman started sniffing the air.

"What smells so terrible?" he asked.

"Wait. Hold it," Harrison said, getting excited. "I think I'm on to something here. I think this guy, this doctor, has to really love his wife, has to be *incredibly* jealous of her—"

"Whoooo, what could smell so bad?" Roman was clearly distracted. His face was scrunched up as if breathing were a painful matter.

"Roman, Roman, listen to me! I think we need a scene between me and my wife, something tender, right at the beginning . . . Jesus, what *is* that smell?"

Eventually, all discussion of the script stopped. The entire apartment was starting to smell as if someone had died—about three weeks ago. Both heads turned to me when I muttered quietly under my breath, "Uh . . . I think I know what it is."

I marched them into Roman's bathroom. There in the tub sat my cat. There next to him sat a very large pile of . . . well . . . what can only be described as cat shit.

"I forgot to bring his litter box today," I explained meekly. "He usually goes in the tub when there's no litter box."

"That's pretty smart," Roman noted.

"This is *your* cat?" Harrison asked.

I nodded.

"You brought him from New York??"

I nodded again.

"I'm working with a writer who brings his cat to Paris so he can shit in the bathtub?"

"I know it looks bad," I said, "but give him a second chance."

"It's not *him* I'm worried about," Harrison said to me.

This was my introduction to a lifetime's fantasy—writing a movie in Paris with a brilliant director and a superstar actor: the brilliant director and the superstar actor on their knees in the bathroom trying to scrub away the smell of cat shit while I held the cat, trying to assure him that he hadn't done anything wrong.

Over the years, I believe Norton has come to prefer Paris to New York, much like his dad. He likes his morning alfresco breakfasts; he enjoys his occasional restaurant dinners. (By coincidence, Norton and I were in Paris when I signed the contract to do this book. He *definitely* enjoyed the celebratory dinner I took him to that night. We went to my very favorite joint, L'Ami Louis, where Norton received his own giant plate of Louis's specialty, the best foie gras one could ever hope to eat.) This cat has even been to a nightclub or two. I will go out on a limb and say, absolutely, that he is the only cat ever to have danced the night away at Bains Douches, one of Paris's very coolest clubs. A lot of people get turned away by the doorman at Bains Douches—but Norton has guaranteed entry when he shows up.

One of my little cat's favorite pastimes was exploring the famous rooftops of Paris. He had access from our room at the Tremoille. The hotel has those old-fashioned, very heavy windows that swing open. (Wait a second—perhaps, at last, I understand why they're called *French* windows!) Norton used to sit with his nose pressed up against the bedroom window, just waiting for me to get the hint that he was desperate to go outside. At first I was hesitant, but once again logic lost out to a cat's desire and the window was thrown open. I held Norton in my arms for a few moments, explaining to him that he was in a strange city and that he shouldn't go too far away—then up over the balcony he went, scrambling out onto the red tile rooftops of the city.

I don't know how far he actually traveled. I once saw him three peaks away—perhaps half a block. He always came back when called, so he couldn't have been out of hearing distance. Eventually, I relaxed with his outdoor prowling, and as soon as I could get the maids to understand that if he wasn't in the room, they shouldn't ever shut the windows, I even began leaving them open during the day so he could strut his stuff when I wasn't there.

The other thing Norton enjoyed for a while was our unusual Paris–New York commute. Although it's usually a safe rule of thumb for a writer to assume that everything he does is either going to fail or never come to fruition, there was a stretch of about a month where everything I was working on happened at the same time—the Polanski movie, a novel I'd written, a TV pilot—and Norton and I spent this particular February practically living on the Concorde. Once a week I'd go to Paris for a few days to work on the screenplay. Then I'd hop back on the speedy plane, zip back to New York, do whatever I was doing there—I could barely tell one activity from the other by this point—and then head to the airport and jump back on the Concorde. I would spend the quick flight either reading, writing, or rewriting. Norton would spend the few hours wandering around the small cabin, making friends with the attendants and fellow passengers.

This was definitely the height of luxury for a cat and the highlight of his European travels. The Concorde attendants got to know him so well they didn't even make me bring his box. After a while, all I needed was his cloth shoulder bag. He was so much at home on the plane that I half expected, on one of the flights, to hear the following message over the loudspeaker: "Ladeez and gentlemen, we have ze guest pilot for zis flight today. Monsieur, please say hello to ze passengers." Then the pilot would come on the loudspeaker and I'd hear: "Meow."

Things never went that far, of course, but it wasn't for lack of trying on Norton's part.

In fact, if you're thinking of flying to Paris anytime in the near future, I wouldn't rule out the possibility. If you want to make sure your plane lands on time, I suggest you bring a good supply of Pounce.

# 8. The cat who fell in love

My cat was getting older, and with age was coming a certain complacency, a slightly existential, lackadaisical attitude. Plus, he was starting to get fat.

So I did what any normal person would do for his cat. I bought a house.

During the summers at Fire Island, Norton would run everywhere, all the time, having a ball, and every season he would lose a pound between Memorial Day and Labor Day. By the time the leaves started to change colors, that Scottish Fold was one lean, mean fighting machine. Over the autumn and winter, however, he never left the confines of my apartment (except for the occasional cross-country ski trip), which meant he did a lot of sitting, sleeping, and begging for Pounce. I knew that wasn't good for him. Since I tended to do the same thing—the lazing around part, not the beg-

ging—I suspected it probably wasn't good for me either. So I decided to go house hunting.

Well, I didn't actually house *hunt*. As usual, I house *stumbled*.

Nancy and Ziggy had a place in Sag Harbor, and I went out to visit them one weekend. Norton was supposed to be left at home because Zig is highly allergic to cats. At the last second, however, my trusty cat-sitter wimped out. (I haven't really discussed what happens when my traveling cat occasionally has to be left behind. Luckily, a friend named Lynn Waggoner has decided that sitting for Norton is comparable to chauffeuring Tom Cruise around the city. Well, perhaps I'm exaggerating, but Lynn takes awfully good care of Norton—buying him toys, taking him for walks, all those good things he's come to enjoy and expect. Once, when Lynn was unavailable, my assistant took him for a weekend. She brought him to her in-laws' house in Montauk. Norton had been in the house for all of two minutes when someone left the front door open—and Norton took off. Laura, the by-now terrified assistant, and her husband spent the night in the woods searching high and low for him. They gave up somewhere around two A.M. and came home—to find Norton waiting patiently by the front door. Laura later told me the story—*much* later—and also revealed her strategy on how to break it to me that she'd lost my cat. It was going to be in the form of a suicide note.) Anyway . . . since no cat-sitter was available, I surprised my weekend hosts and brought Norton after all.

My surprise was greeted with all the enthusiasm of an earthquake. He'd be no problem, I assured them. He'd stay outside the whole day. He'd come in only at bedtime, and

then he'd sleep with me. I wouldn't let him out of my bed. Zig would never know there was a cat in the house.

That was true. He didn't know there was a cat in the house—until the middle of the night, when Norton, slipping away while I was asleep, went upstairs and decided he'd sleep on Ziggy's head.

That night at the Aldermans was not dissimilar from what I imagine Krakatoa must have been like. At three A.M. I went upstairs, grabbed Norton off the sputtering master of the house, and took him back into my bed. At three-thirty A.M. he was back on Ziggy's head. We repeated the procedure. At four A.M. Norton had returned to his new favorite spot, covering most of Zig's face with his entire body. At four-thirty A.M. Zig gave up. At five A.M. he realized he wasn't sneezing anymore. By morning, he'd decided Norton was the first cat he'd ever met that he wasn't allergic to. Fury and despair turned to delight and triumph. I was not a favorite house guest (in fact, I won the poll for Most Annoying Weekender)—but somehow Norton had wormed his way into their hearts.

The next day, we went to check out the real estate. My search was only a halfhearted one. I can't say I *really* wanted a house. For one thing, I'm not the handiest guy in the world. I still wake up screaming in the middle of the night at the thought of my high school wood shop. The idea of using a drill or repairing some electrical wiring can quickly bring on my best Curly Howard impersonation, with all the face smacking, high-pitched blubbering, and floor whirling trimmings. For another, I loathed the idea of any kind of commute, even if it was just on weekends. I had no desire ever to do any gardening or to rake up leaves or to shovel snow off the driveway. In fact, I didn't even want a drive-way, since I didn't own a car.

But Norton needed a year-round playpen, so . . .

The first four houses we looked at were all nice, all spacious, and all wrong. They didn't have any personality or charm. The realtor, a woman named Peggy Meves, to whom I am forever indebted, asked me to describe my ideal house—my *affordable* ideal house. I did so: at least a hundred years old, in such good shape it needed no work, original wood floors and beams, a fireplace or two, eccentric rooms, two stories, an office that was so nice I'd *want* to go sit at the typewriter, a manageable size—perhaps two or three bedrooms but not cramped and not so spacious that I couldn't take care of it. In other words, something that was so perfect I'd never find it.

When I finished my description, Peggy said, "You know, I think you should take a look at this one place. But the people have received an offer on it. I think they've accepted, so I don't think you can have it—but it sounds like what you're looking for. At least it'll give me an idea of what your taste is like."

I agreed to go look at the house, knowing that I couldn't buy it. That was all right with me. Again, I didn't really want to buy anything. I mostly just liked looking at nice houses.

I didn't even make it upstairs. One look at the living room—with its original 120-year-old wood floors, its antique potbellied stove, its *personality*—and I heard myself saying, "I'll take it."

Peggy, being that rarest of breeds, a completely honest person, tried to tell me again that I couldn't have this house.

She was just showing it to me for taste purposes.

"This is my dream house," I said. "I think I *have* to have it."

"At least look upstairs before you decide it's your dream house," she advised.

Upstairs made it even worse. There was a tiny, heart-breakingly charming guest bedroom, a large master bedroom (the bathroom had an old claw tub in it!), and to round out my fantasy, there was a small office that hung over the driveway, with French windows that looked out onto the beautifully landscaped garden. I haven't even mentioned the outside of this place, which looked as if Hänsel and Gretel could have comfortably settled in and been right at home.

I ran down the steps, outside to my rented car, and opened the door. Norton came bounding onto the front lawn. He stepped cautiously inside the house, looked around the living room, then plopped himself down in the middle of the floor, directly catching a ray of sunlight streaming in through the window. He looked up at me and meowed happily.

The next day, I bought the house.

All of a sudden I had a country house, I had a cat, I had good friends for neighbors. I was just missing one little thing.

Despite a rather flip exterior (hiding, many people would say, an amazingly shallow interior), I was becoming a bit concerned that Cindy's parting words—"you don't know what love is"—had more than just the hollow ring of truth to them. I was beginning to think that too many years of going for the gag, hanging out with Danish models, and working round the clock had possibly limited my capacity for "something more." Of course, every time I began to think this, I tried to imagine what could be "something more" than laughs, Danish models, and satisfying work. I have quite an active imagination, but in this area, my imagination had run totally dry.

And yet . . .

There was Janis.

This was an unusual affair because Janis was not at all my type. Physically she was quite lovely but not the kind of looks I usually go for. She was short and slightly round rather than long and lean. She was extremely classy looking, elegant, and sophisticated, where my taste usually ran to the slightly trashy. She was Deborah Kerr in *An Affair to Remember* as compared to my usual leaning—the soap-covered girl who washed the car in front of the prisoners in *Cool Hand Luke*. Even her personality was off-kilter alongside any past infatuations. I wasn't wild about confrontations. To say Janis was combative would be like saying Lawrence Taylor has an aggressive streak. She had the independence and confidence of British royalty and was as stubborn and opinionated as anyone this side of Saddam Hussein. Yet, despite all our differences—or perhaps because of them—she was the most intelligent, most stimulating, least boring person I'd met in a long, long time.

There was a slight hitch, however, to my having a long-lasting, perfect, satisfying relationship with Janis. She didn't *want* a long-lasting, perfect, satisfying relationship. At least, she didn't want one with me.

The closer we became, the more she'd pull back. Eventually, she pulled back so far I needed a telescope to find her. Which was a good sign the romance was over.

The relationship didn't end, however. What happened was that Janis and I became best friends. Without the threat of a romance, we became as close as two people could be. We even wound up working together. We saw each other during the day, we had dinner several times a week, we even went away on weekends together a few times—strictly platonically. She saw me through a couple of tough romances, through several professional crises. I did the same for her. Despite the Sarahs and the Karyns and the sportswriters and the Dickensian editors, it was Janis who always seemed to be there, whether the "there" was for fun, for support, or for anything that struck either one of us as interesting. We became so inseparable that most people thought we were still a couple. But she didn't want that. She didn't want a relationship because, in her experience, relationships only pointed toward the *end* of relationships. With ending came pain (and the better the relationship, the more painful the ending). With pain came bitterness. With bitterness came sorrow. You can take it from there.

Over time, I accepted that there was never going to be any kind of real relationship with this woman. It took some doing—a lot of teeth gnashing, a good bit of stomach hurting, and way too much head banging—but I did eventually accept it.

Only one person didn't accept it.

And I suppose I have to use the word "person" loosely. Norton liked Janis.

It was particularly noticeable because she didn't much

care for him. Animals were something else she didn't want
to get attached to. She didn't see the pleasure in such an
attachment. She didn't see the point. But Norton didn't let
up. Usually, when someone ignored him, my cat was happy
to be ignored. Janis was the only person other than my
father that I ever saw him pursue. When she came over, she
wouldn't pet him—but within moments he'd be by her side,
rubbing his body up against her leg or trying to burrow his
face into the palm of her hand. Rarely did she so much as
respond—but over the course of several years Norton
never gave up. Whenever he saw her, he rolled over on his
back in his best impersonation of the world's cutest cat. If
she refused to look at him, he'd move to her, rubbing,
cuddling, purring. Janis was tough—she knew the dangers
of getting involved. But Norton was tough, too—he knew
the *pleasures* of getting involved.

For a lot of this period—Norton vs. Janis—I was content
to remain neutral. Then came Sag Harbor.

When I bought the house out there on Long Island, I had
already rented a house on Fire Island with Norm for the
summer. The thought of one last season avoiding the sixishes appealed to me (especially since I'd already paid for
it), so I came up with the perfect solution. I arranged for
Janis to live in my new house for the summer, rent-free, on
the condition that she fix it up—furnish the kitchen with
utensils, buy and put up drapes, start to get the garden in
shape. All the things that I would never have either the
time, taste, or inclination to do. It was a fair deal and she
accepted happily. At the end of the summer, Norm and I
drove out to Sag Harbor to check up on the house and to

have dinner with Janis. She insisted on cooking; dinner was served amidst delicate candlelight on the front porch. When I stepped inside—this was my first time there since I'd signed the papers three months earlier—I was amazed. The place was no longer just charming—it was beautiful. It no longer just had its own personality—it had Janis's. It was clear to me that she loved the house as much as I did. It was clear to anyone who bothered to look inside and see what she'd done with it.

That night we had a wonderful time. The food was delicious, we drank a lot of wine, everyone laughed until we were too tired to laugh anymore, and—for the first time in several years—it didn't feel right leaving Janis. It felt as if there was unfinished business.

Driving back to the city with Norm, we discussed it. He noticed that Janis had seemed softer than usual, that her guard was down, or at least lowered (she usually had barbed wire and German shepherds surrounding and protecting her vulnerability). We discussed the question of the homing instinct—was it actually enough to push two people into a relationship?

Norm thought that it was—if the two people were finally ready for a relationship. He also thought it was interesting that Janis had gone out of her way to do one thing she'd never done before. Right before we got in the car to head back to New York, she'd bent over the couch and petted Norton. Stroked him once, gently.

It had started to rain during our drive, and I remember looking at Norton through the rearview mirror. He was sitting comfortably in the backseat, relaxed, dozing. I wondered if I could really use a cat as a gauge for a relationship. Norton didn't open his eyes to peer back. He wasn't going to make it easy for me.

Janis's birthday comes in the middle of September. It was on her birthday that we decided to bring our relationship to a new level. Or just bring it back to what it had once been. Or bring it back but make it different. As you may gather, we weren't exactly sure *what* we were doing.

What I *am* sure of is that whatever we were doing or becoming, we wouldn't have done it or become it without Norton.

*My* house became *our* house—mine, Janis's, and Norton's. Norton was fun to be with on the weekends in Sag Harbor, and he made us both laugh. Janis couldn't get over the fact that he'd walk with me to Sean's Murray Hill Market, three blocks away from the house. Unlike Fire Island, Sag Harbor had traffic, so it was difficult to get him to take mid-afternoon strolls. But early in the morning, before cars started clogging up the streets, Norton would leisurely walk along behind us, meowing forcefully as usual. He'd wait patiently outside the market while we shopped, then hike back with us. Initially, Janis would get impatient if Norton decided to duck into the bushes for a two-minute (or ten-minute, depending on his mood) time-out from the walk. She'd try to convince me to leave him behind when it was time to buy groceries. Soon, however, she was coaxing him into taking the walk with us. And once he was along for the journey, if I started walking too fast for the cat, she'd urge me to slow down. "Don't be so impatient," she'd lecture me.

She stopped complaining when he got sidetracked and welcomed him back happily when he rejoined us.

She also liked to watch Norton prowl the garden. There were no bluejays to torment him in Sag Harbor, but there was a mockingbird, and he quickly became my kitten's new nemesis. Once the mockingbird had sized up the situation—the macho-level of the gray, furry animal in the backyard—he started zooming out of his tree, landing on the ground a few feet from Norton, and then would stand there screaming at the poor cat. Norton was totally intimidated. Janis would urge him on, try to get him to beat up on the puny bird, of course to no avail. She began to take it as a personal insult, and I would often find her explaining to Norton—as I had years before on Fire Island—about the law of the jungle and the concept of the food chain.

She grew catnip in the garden for him. It never got high enough for us to cut it and let it dry. As soon as she'd plant it, Norton would make a beeline for the spot, dig up the ground around it, and spend a happy few hours rolling around in the dirt while Janis would mock-scold him.

It was fun to watch a relationship develop between the two of them, both so independent. I'd gotten used to Norton's near-magical powers over the years, so it was rejuvenating to see his effect on her and to watch her witness his effect on others.

Janis was with us one day as we were driving along the L.I.E. out to Sag Harbor. I was driving, Janis was passengering, and Norton was in his usual position, lying down in the back, staring out the rear windshield. (When just the two of us drive, Norton will sit on the front seat, but Janis doesn't like him up there. For one thing, she thinks it's dangerous. For another—the real reason—Norton's claws will occasionally come out, to help him balance himself if the car lurches, and he will ruin her stockings or rip a small hole in her blouse. So Norton will lie patiently in the back, content to watch the countryside zip by, until Janis falls asleep. Then he'll sneak up cautiously to the front and make himself comfortable.) It was a beautiful day; I was lost in thought and, apparently, also speeding like a lunatic. When the motorcycle cop pulled us over, he already had his ticket pad in hand as he broke it to me that I'd been going seventy-five miles an hour. Before he could write up the ticket, though, he glanced at the backseat.

"Is that a Scottish Fold?" he asked.

I nodded. I'm much better nodding than I am talking to policemen.

"He's beautiful," this leather-jacketed cop said. "I have a Fold, too."

I won't bore you with the sappy details. Suffice it to say that Norton let himself be held and petted by the arresting officer—and the arrest was never made. My record remained unblemished and the ticket was torn up.

Janis was around for another car confrontation with Norton, this one without quite the happy ending of the earlier one. I had driven to the office that day and had decided to take the cat. He was a perfect corporate companion, spending the whole day either lying on my desk or resting on the couch in the corner. Periodically, he'd wander out of my office and stroll along the hallways, stopping to visit the people he liked. It was no longer a surprise to anyone at the publishing company—even the Chairman

of the Board—when a cat would wander in to say hello.

It was a brutally hot summer day, and naturally enough, the air conditioner in my car was broken. Driving home— Janis in front, Norton in the back hoping she'd doze off—all the windows were wide open. Downtown, in the Village, on the way to the garage, we stopped at a red light. On the street corner was a bag lady, filthy, kind of crazy seeming, clearly homeless. It had been a hard day at work, it was too hot, whatever the reason, but when the woman came up to our car and asked for money, both Janis and I looked right through her. It was as if she weren't a real person, as if she didn't exist. Perhaps we'd been in New York too long, where homelessness is a way of life, something too easy to inure yourself against.

As the car idled, the woman asked me a question.

"Is that a special breed of cat?" she said, pointing to Norton, who was looking out at her, his paws up on the back door, his head sticking through the open window.

Without really thinking about it—except snobbily to decide I didn't want to explain Norton's pedigree to a homeless woman—I simply said, "No. He's a regular cat."

"Oh," she said. "He looks like a Scottish Fold."

The light turned green. Before I could drive on, she added with a wistful sigh, "I used to have seven Siamese."

She stuck her hand through the window, gave Norton a pat on the head, and with astonishing dignity, walked on.

Much to Norton's delight, Janis allowed him onto the front seat for the few-block drive to our garage. She even hugged him. I'm sure also to his delight, neither one of us has ever looked at a homeless person in quite the same

way. It was a good cure for our haughty superiority.

Janis was also present for Norton's one and only cat fight, a sorry affair by any standards.

I had long suspected that Norton was no Rocky Marciano. In the garden, he liked to hunker down and stalk the occasional and ever-dangerous butterfly, but that was the extent of his aggressive tendencies. Unfortunately, when one rears an outdoor cat, one must face up to the fact that other outdoor cats will come a-calling.

We had noticed a large orange, furry guy who seemed to enjoy strolling around our backyard in Sag Harbor in the late afternoons. If Norton was outside for these appearances, he would either meow immediately to be let in or he'd quickly disappear around the front of the house to one of his secret hiding spots. If this bully was visiting while Norton was safely inside the house, Norton would bravely stand at the back door, protected by a screen, and hiss loudly. He'd arch his back and release his claws, then he'd look over to us for approval. Either Janis or I would tell him what a tough guy he was and how proud we were of him. Perhaps that's what made Norton cocky.

One afternoon, while sitting upstairs in my office working away, I heard the most god-awful noise. It was a wail of pain and fear, and it seemed to stretch on forever. That was followed by Janis's scream. She screamed my name and then yelled for me to come downstairs.

I made it as quickly as I could, but in the few seconds it took me, I heard violent hisses and howls, high-pitched growls and what sounded like two sumo wrestlers thudding into each other. By the time I got outside, the orange monster was walking triumphantly across the lawn. I

screamed at him and waved my arms. That didn't seem to scare him—he gave me a look that made it clear he felt he could take me, too—but he did get the message that he wasn't welcome. Once he had hurdled the fence and landed in my neighbor's yard, I went looking for Norton.

Now, my cat *always* comes when I call him. *Always*. But not this time. Janis and I spent twenty minutes searching for him high and low. No Norton. I really began to be afraid when I finally heard a very soft and rather pathetic meow. I stopped and listened, heard it again. So did Janis. It seemed to be coming from under my car, which was parked in the driveway.

I got down on my hands and knees to look, and sure enough, Norton was cowering there. It took several more minutes of coaxing, but I finally got him to come out. When he slunk out between the rear tires, Janis gasped. Norton was bleeding above the nose and on his right shoulder. His fur was matted and sticky, and he was so frightened, he seemed to have curled up to half his normal size, which wasn't very big to begin with. When I picked him up in my arms, I realized he had been so terrified, he had also defecated, somehow all over himself.

I calmed him down as best I could, then carried him upstairs to the bathroom. Putting him down in the bathtub, I turned on the water, just a gentle stream from the tap, and did my best to clean him up. He made no effort to resist. Once he was clean, I could see that his scratches and scrapes were minor. The physical wounds were surface, but the emotional scars seemed to run deep. After I dried him off, talking to him and cooing at him the whole time, he timidly went into my bedroom, hopped onto the bed, and crawled under the covers. He burrowed his way to the foot of the bed and stayed there for the rest of the afternoon. Every so often, I'd try to get him to come out, but, ashamed, he wouldn't even look at me. By dinnertime, he still hadn't poked his head out from under the quilt.

At that point, Janis decided the situation called for a woman's touch. I watched as she sat on the bed and gently pulled the covers back. Norton curled up into a ball, his face hidden. But where he had refused to look at me when I'd tried to cheer him up, he slowly began to uncurl as Janis stroked him and whispered to him. Within a few minutes, his little tongue was out, licking her fingers. When she told him it was now time to come downstairs and eat dinner, he rose, jumped off the bed, and followed her down the steps.

It took Norton a couple of days before he was up to snuff. He didn't look me in the eye for quite a while. It was more humiliating for him to face his dad than his new mom after his run-in with the orange Chuck Norris. I did notice a new bond between Norton and Janis after that. Somehow, he trusted her more than he had before. And somehow, she knew it and responded in kind.

Because Janis was so resistant to a relationship, it was easy to chart her ups and downs by her responses to the cat. When she would be overcome by fear or the claustrophobia of a relationship, she would push Norton away. When she was feeling affectionate toward me, it was easier to show it to the cat. It was safer.

Our biggest arguments at the beginning were over Norton's sleeping arrangements. She *hated* that he slept with us. I had reached the point where I couldn't sleep well if he wasn't in the bed with me. She felt smothered by him—

especially because he insisted on sleeping directly to her left, by her head. Since I was directly to her right, she was caught smack dab in the middle of us—for eight hours a night.

Norton would get in bed before either of us, usually settling down on Janis's pillow (he still slept like a person—head on the pillow, body under the covers). She'd crawl into bed before I would, pick Norton up, and unceremoniously toss him onto the floor. I'd finally come in, ready for lights-out, call for my pal, and he'd come running. He'd start out sleeping by my side, but as soon as it was feasible—which meant as soon as Janis was asleep and couldn't protest—he'd move to her side. She'd start out distant and comfortable, only to wake up in the middle of the night surrounded again.

The First Stage of softening came when she stopped dumping Norton off the bed. She started moving him over to my pillow instead. Then she'd go crazy watching me try to get into bed without disturbing him.

"He's just a cat!" Janis would say. "Throw him off!"

"No, he's too comfortable," I'd say while I was trying to squeeze my tired body into two feet of available space.

"Get rid of him!" she'd say scornfully—but we were both aware that *she* hadn't gotten rid of him.

This stage lasted a long time. Over a year. It was the period in the relationship when neither person knows whether what they have together is permanent, but each is starting to think it *might* be, if such a thing as permanency is humanly possible. She wasn't throwing anything away—not me or my cat—but she wasn't exactly embracing anything either.

During this period, our relationship grew and strengthened—we both relaxed; we both stopped trying so hard and

just accepted what was—and so did Janis's relationship with Norton.

Stage Two arrived when I came upstairs one night to find Janis asleep and Norton curled up against her—on *her* side of the bed. He was taking up half her pillow. She hadn't moved to accommodate him, but she hadn't moved him away from her. It was about that time that she first told me she loved me.

Stage Three came months after that, soon after the infamous cat fight. Exhausted, I had fallen asleep early, long before Janis was ready for bed. Norton, overjoyed that he had me all to himself, plopped himself down directly in the middle of her pillow and got into our old sleeping position, me with half the bed, him with half the bed.

I didn't really fall into a deep sleep, so I was half awake when Janis finally crawled under the covers. I was conscious enough to watch her carefully climb over the sleeping Norton—*very* carefully, so as not to disturb him. Exactly as I had done so many times over the years, she scrunched herself into two feet of sleeping space, wedging herself between me and the cat. I fell asleep soon after I felt her gently kiss my forehead—and saw her put her ear against Norton to listen to his purring, then softly kiss him good night.

It was around this time that we began to realize we might be spending a good chunk of our lives together.

Stage Four came about in a complicated and roundabout way. One thing I can say about it is that it was certainly a good test of the relationship. It all happened because I agreed to take my cat *back* to Paris.

It started with another phone call from Roman Polanski, who called to say he thought we should write something

together. Not a rewrite—this time he wanted to do it from scratch.

We decided we would adapt a book. Neither one of us was brimming over with wonderful, original story lines, and we thought an adaptation would be fun, easy, and, from a technical standpoint, interesting. Within moments of this decision, I thought of a book I wanted to adapt. It was brilliant, it was dramatic, it was wonderfully funny and tragically sad. I pulled it down from my bookshelf, stared at it for several seconds, and then stuck it right back where it came from. Too weird, I decided. They'll think I'm crazy. The book was *The Master and Margarita* by Mikhail Bulgakov. I never mentioned it to anyone. Not to Roman, not to the studio.

I didn't find another book. Neither did Polanski. The studio kept sending us thrillers. The director kept rejecting them. Then, a full year after we'd decided to work together, Roman called me. "I know what I want to do," he said. "Have you ever heard of a book called *The Master and Margarita?*"

I thought it had to be a joke. He assured me it wasn't. My heart soared, and two weeks later Norton and I were in Paris adapting one of the greatest literary works of the twentieth century. I do not know if our screenplay will ever get made. Probably not is my guess. Too expensive and too weird. No chance for a sequel. Those are the vagaries and frustrations of working in the movie biz. But I do know one thing about that job:

It was not easy.

The work was torturous. (Or at least as torturous as writing can be. I don't ever like to confuse writing clever dia-

logue with fighting oil fires or harvesting the rice paddies.)
Roman is obsessive about research and meticulously faithful
to whatever material he's working from. He read the novel
in English. Then he read it in American (they are two
different translations). Then in Polish, French, and finally
Russian. Every time he read a different version, it would
spark a different idea or direction. With every new idea,
there was a new night I spent working—and working alone;
nighttime for Roman was definitely not for working—until
two or three A.M.

Thank god for Norton. Never had I appreciated having
him around quite so much. Most evenings, I'd come back
from a day at Polanski's spent and exhausted, intellectually
and emotionally drained. I'd collapse on the bed for an hour
or two, Norton cuddled up against my side; then I'd order
room service or take Norton out to a café for a quick
bite—then back to the apartment for several hours huddled
over the typewriter, trying to make sense of the day's notes
and decisions. Norton would sit on the desk, directly to my
left, watching me struggle trying to whip this book into
shape. By ten in the morning I was supposed to have new
scenes, new ideas, new dialogue for Roman to see.

As I worked, trying to make sense of this twisting, turning novel, as I talked it over with Roman—and over and
over—something started to click. The morass of political
and intellectual theories that abound in the book started to
come into a very definite focus. As we wrote and discussed
and argued and yelled and struggled, this great and dense
fantasy of a novel began to make sense to me in a way it
never had before. Oddly enough—*very* oddly, since my life
could not be farther from the lives depicted in the book—

the sense of the book and the meaning of the screenplay came from the relationship that had developed with Janis. And, yes, with Norton.

*The Master and Margarita* was written during the 1930s, finished in 1939, and it was considered finished only because the author died, blind and destitute, a victim of Stalin's repression. It is easy to tell what happens in this novel. It is not easy to tell what it's about. The main characters are the Devil, a suicidal writer, a bad poet, a six-foot cat in a top hat and waistcoat, Jesus Christ, Pontius Pilate, and the most beautiful woman in the world. There are brutal murders, public humiliations, crucifixions, and a confrontation with the ultimate evil. There is also sharp satire, laugh-out-loud slapstick, political parody, religious revisionism, and devastating philosophical insight. There are ghosts and people flying through the air and magical transformations. Oh—it also happens to be one of the greatest love stories ever written. All in all, I suppose it's understandable that so far it's been difficult to get a Hollywood studio to give this movie a financial green light: we're not exactly talking sequel to *Home Alone.*

Anyway, after much sifting, sorting, researching, cutting, and stalling, I ultimately made a decision about what *The Master and Margarita* is all about. It all came back to Cindy and her parting words of years before.

*You don't know what love is.*

Thanks to that trip to Paris, thanks to Janis and our developing relationship, mostly thanks to a little gray cat with a round head and folded ears, I *do* know what love is. I not only know what it is, I've found it. I've seen it work and seen what it can do.

Days before I wrote the ending to the script, I got a call from Janis. She was out in Sag Harbor. It was early in the morning her time, early afternoon for me.

"What are you doing up so early?" I asked.

"I couldn't sleep," she told me. "I haven't been sleeping well lately."

"Why not?" I wanted to know.

"I miss you," she said.

As perhaps you've noticed, I'm a sucker for this kind of stuff. "Awww," I said. "That's so nice."

"But it's not *just* that," she added.

"What else?"

"I don't sleep well anymore unless Norton sleeps by my side."

So it was Janis reaching Stage Four that gave me the nerve to decide that our screenplay for *The Master and Margarita* should be, above all, about love. Love in its most real sense. Love between two people. Two real people. Love surviving politics and oppression and art and history and cruelty and even death. The script for the movie ends the way Bulgakov ends his book. The Master and Margarita ascend, not to heaven but to a world of two, where they can escape the often vicious and always absurd world into which we are born.

My interpretation of this great novel was that the most important thing any of us can do is to live in a world where love is a greater priority than pain. Only in my case, as now in Janis's, it is not just a world of two. As I am reminded by Norton, who this very moment sits on my desk, six inches to my left, watching me write these words, it is very definitely a world of three.

# 9. The Cat who went to Los Angeles

All of our lives, those of us who live in Western civilization, are not really so very different. We all suffer the same constraints—of time, of strength, of laws, of expectations. Within each life there are purely individual peaks and valleys, wild swings of ecstasy and despair, great triumphs, noble failures, yet, taken as a whole, there is a definite commonality of experience. The thrills we experience, which we feel no one can ever appreciate the same way, are thrills experienced by everyone—love, sex, success. The sadness that envelops us, in such a life-changing way that we are sure we are unique in the power of our feeling, envelops us all—illness, separation, poverty, death. There are two ways to go after experiencing one of these highs or lows—one can either withdraw into isolation, or one can accept the commonal-

ity and use it as a way of learning more about ourselves
and others.

Last year I experienced my first of these sadnesses. Last
year my father died.

My mother called, a few days before Thanksgiving. His
lung cancer, which had once spread to the hip but had been
dormant for several years, had returned and had spread
even further. It had recently crushed his hip like an eggshell
and was now riddling his back. My father had returned to
the hospital, the pain was unbearable, and the feeling was
he didn't have long to live.

Norton and I were on a plane the next day. The stewardesses, perhaps sensing my sadness, never said anything
when I let the cat out of his box and onto my lap. He spent
the whole flight sitting there, letting me pet him, occasionally licking my fingers with his rough little tongue.

I remembered when my dad had had his first operation.
He'd had a lung removed. We were all terrified of what
would happen, and Norton and I had flown out then, too.
When my dad got out of the hospital, he was in tremendous
pain. Every breath was agony, and the only way he could
get comfortable was to sit back in a giant, ugly, cushiony
Barcalounger that my mother bought just for this purpose.
He would sit back, practicing breathing with one lung,
trying to cope with the agony of broken ribs (that's how the
surgeons get to the lung, through the ribs). What I remember most was how afraid my father was. Afraid of death,
sure, but even more afraid of the pain.

The Barcalounger was set up in my parents' bedroom, at
the foot of their bed. My dad would lie there for most of

the day, watching television, the pain spoiling the concen-
tration required even to read.

He'd been set up in the chair like this for two, maybe
three days, spending most of those days just being afraid.
I was in my room, maybe forty feet away, when I heard my
dad call my name. It wasn't a friendly call, or even a weak
one, at least not as weak as he'd been sounding. It was a
fearful call and I came running.

When I got to his room, I saw what my father was afraid
of. Norton was crouched below his chair, ready to leap,
eyeing the blanket on my father's lap. It looked like an
inviting spot to sit and be petted—especially since these two
had long ago befriended each other. But my father's face
was not a friendly one. He was afraid that Norton would
jump on him, would jostle him, would possibly even land
right on the long, jagged scar, and hurt him even more. My
father was too afraid even to move.

I didn't get to Norton in time to stop him. When I came
into the room, he somehow took my presence as further
encouragement. And so he jumped.

I distinctly recall feeling frozen in time, as if everything
were moving in slow motion. The cat was floating through
the air, aimed at my father's chest. My father was staring
aghast, perhaps as afraid as he'd ever been in his whole life.

Of course it was over in a split second. Norton landed on
the cushioned arm of the chair, not even touching my father. My dad sagged back, exhausted from the effort of
being so afraid, and Norton, ever so gently, as if he
weighed not a pound, settled onto my father's lap and
began to lick his hand. My dad, trembling, used his other

hand to pet my cat. The blood came back into his face and
finally he looked at me. He smiled—not much of a smile but
a smile—and nodded weakly.

I came back an hour later to check up on him. My father
was asleep now, his head back in the chair, his body relaxed.
His hand was still resting on Norton's body, and Norton
was still curled up on the blanket in his lap. My dad woke
up when I came into the room, and he smiled again. This
time a real smile. Somehow he didn't look as afraid. I think
he felt a little foolish that he'd been so terrified of Norton.
At the same time I think he was relieved. The possibility of
pain had been very real, yet the pain hadn't materialized.
I actually think that moment was the first time my father
thought he might get better, the first time he realized he
wasn't going to die.

Three years later, as I saw him in the hospital room, he
*was* going to die and this time he knew it.

My brother, Eric, and my mother had been under an
incredible strain, living with this pressure day to day, so I
was, by reason of being the newest and freshest face on the
scene, elected designated strong person. The decisions
weren't pleasant ones—levels of medication, when to stop
the therapy, when to stop fighting and give in to the inevitable. Within a few days there weren't many more decisions
to make, however. There was very little to be done. My
father was in and out of lucidity, usually out. In a ghoulish
way, we actually got some laughs out of the situation—final
proof that I was right and Sarah was wrong: there don't
seem to be any inappropriate times to find humor.

At one point, my dad, totally under the influence of
pain-killing drugs, mostly morphine, was convinced Pete

Maravich was playing basketball in the hall. (My dad had never met Pete Maravich to any of our knowledge; however, as Eric pointed out, since Maravich had died several months before this, it probably wasn't a good omen.) In one coherent moment, my dad was confused by the hallucinations he'd been seeing on the wall—confused because they'd suddenly disappeared. "But they were so beautiful," he said.

"At last," I told him, "you can understand why Eric and I took all those drugs back in the sixties and seventies."

"So *this* is why," he said. And then he said, "Now what I don't understand is why you *stopped.*"

My dad did not want to die in the hospital. So when we knew there was nothing else the doctors could do, we brought him home.

A round-the-clock nurse had set up a hospital bed in his bedroom, and that's where he settled. The bed was near his old Barcalounger. For the several days he stayed alive at home, Norton never left that Barcalounger. He stayed there all day; he slept there at night, keeping my dad company.

One night I wanted him in my bed. It was late, maybe two A.M., and I wanted the company. I slipped into my dad's room. He was asleep—rather, by this time he'd slipped into a semi-coma—and the nurse was reading. Norton sat in the chair, awake, staring at my father as if waiting for word that he was allowed to jump onto his bed and comfort him. The word didn't come, at least not while I stood watching. I didn't bring Norton back into my room. I left him there in the chair and went back to sleep on my own. Just in case the word did come, I figured he might as well be prepared.

The next day my father died. It was in the late afternoon. I wasn't there. I'd gone out shopping for groceries. Somehow, pulling into the driveway, I knew. When I stopped the car, my brother and my mother came out of the house. They were crying. I'd missed it by just a few minutes. Eric had been by his side. One minute he was breathing deeply, asleep, the next minute the breaths stopped. That's all there was to it.

I'd said my good-byes a couple of days before. My dad had been slipping in and out of consciousness. When conscious, sometimes he would call for one of us, or all of us. Sometimes when the nurse told us he was awake, we'd just come in, never knowing if it was our last opportunity to speak or listen.

At some point, the nurse told me that he was awake and I should say whatever it was I wanted to say to him. She said I might not have another chance. So she left the room, and I stood next to my dying father, holding his cold, clammy hand. I knew he knew who I was. He couldn't talk by this point, but he was shaking his head, rolling his eyes as if to say, "What a bitch, huh?"

I didn't have anything to say to him. We'd been very close when he was alive—I mean *really* alive, not barely alive—and I'd said a lot to him when it meant something. I didn't have to tell him I loved him. He knew that. I didn't have to tell him I'd miss him. He knew that too. Anything I could say to him now would somehow seem fake or overly dramatic or ultimately meaningless. So I didn't say anything. I just held his hand and waited until he fell back asleep. My dad was never one to tolerate the bullshit. I think he preferred the silence.

That afternoon, Janis had arrived from New York. My dad had been crazy about her and vice versa. They had a great relationship, a lot of banter back and forth. He gave her a very hard time and she returned it with gusto. He appreciated anyone who could give him a hard time.

When she came up the stairs, the whole family was sitting around my dad's bed. He'd been unconscious, but when she walked in he seemed to stir. He was always a bit of a ladies' man.

"Dad," I said, "it's Janis. Janis came here to see you."

He lifted his head, saw us all, then saw her. She smiled at him. He looked back at my mother, at my brother, at me—and rolled his eyes. A big, exaggerated roll, done for Janis's benefit. The roll said, "Jesus—as if things weren't bad enough, *now* look who shows up!"

We all got hysterical; even my dad did his best to laugh. Then he fell back asleep and never woke up.

There's something comforting in the fact that his last act in life was to make people laugh. He kept his sense of humor right up to the end, and it made everything a lot easier on all of us.

We didn't have a standard funeral. We had a party instead. That's the way he would have wanted it—my dad loved parties. He loved being a host.

My dad was in a wine group, and the members of the group brought exquisite wine to toast him. We had one of the best restaurants in L.A. cater the event. Three of Dad's closest friends gave speeches, talking about him. Their talks were wonderfully funny. I would say that, through the tears, there were as many laughs at the funeral as at any party my dad had ever thrown.

That night, after everyone was gone, after Janis was asleep, I went into my bathroom, the bathroom I'd had as a little kid, and I broke down and cried. I cried for perhaps fifteen minutes, real wracking sobs. I cried until I was exhausted, until I not only didn't have any tears in me, I didn't have any emotions left at all.

When I was done, I looked up to find Norton staring at me. He'd pushed the bathroom door open with his nose and had come in to seek me out.

I picked him up, kissed him on top of the head, and held him while I sat in the bathroom, staring out the window at our backyard. Norton didn't meow; he didn't even lick me. He just let me hold him as long as I wanted. I appreciated the silence, too. I wasn't in the mood for bullshit either.

I don't know how long I was in there. I do know it was almost light when I got back into bed.

I lay down, my head on the pillow, closed my eyes, and went to sleep. Norton put his head on my pillow and snuggled in against my chest.

When I woke up, it was a new day. Many things had changed, but not Norton. He was still asleep, still by my side, still content to let me hold him.

# Afterword

*Sometimes I worry that perhaps it's just me, that perhaps I make up all this stuff about Norton being so great, being so special. But every so often I'm reminded that that's not the case.*

*Not long ago, my friends Nancy and Ziggy had a baby, a truly marvelous little boy named Charlie Elroy Alderman. (Yes, if any of you are wondering, it is indeed Elroy as in "The Jetsons.")*

*Soon after Charlie was born, Nancy walked him down, in his stroller, from their house in Sag Harbor to mine. It was a Sunday morning and it was early. Ziggy was still asleep and so was Janis. This was Charlie's first trip down the block to visit his neighbors.*

*Nancy wheeled him up to the back door, picked him out of the buggy, and carried him inside.*

*Norton, who'd been napping on a kitchen chair, raised his head to check out the newcomer in his life. Nancy took her tiny little baby and held him down toward Norton.*

*"Look, Norton," she said. "This is a baby."*

*Norton looked up at Charlie, took him in, and sort of nodded as if assimilating the information.*

*There was a very long pause, and then I heard Nancy gulp.*

*"You've finally done it," she said to me.*

*"What?" I wanted to know.*

*"Most mothers would have said, 'Look, Charlie, this is a cat.'"*

*I started to laugh.*

*"Not with Norton," I said.*

*Nancy started to laugh, too.*

*"No, not with Norton," she agreed.*

# About the Author

Peter Gethers lives in New York City and Sag Harbor, New York. He has written television shows, films, newspaper and magazine articles, way too many memos, and is now hard at work on his third novel. He is the proud owner and general manager of Peter's Famous Smoked Fish and the Gethers YeRosebuds.